MW00620424

Gleanings
Reflections on Ruth

Michael Scharf Publication Trust
Yeshiva University Press

MAGGID

GLEANINGS
Reflections on Ruth

Edited by
Rabbi Dr. Stuart W. Halpern

Yeshiva University Press
Maggid Books

Gleanings: Reflections on Ruth

First Edition, 2019

Maggid Books
An imprint of Koren Publishers Jerusalem Ltd.

POB 8531, New Milford, CT 06776-8531, USA
& POB 4044, Jerusalem 9104001, Israel
www.maggidbooks.com

Cover art based on a detail from the painting
Ruth in Boaz's Field, by Julius Schnorr von Carolsfeld
(1794–1872), located at The National Gallery, London

ISBN 978-1-59264-518-3, *hardcover*

A CIP catalogue record for this title is
available from the British Library

Printed and bound in the United States

Contents

Editor's Introduction

As the world's premier Jewish institution for higher education, Yeshiva University consists of students, faculty, and community members who are passionate believers in the power of the texts and values of the Jewish tradition to positively impact both contemporary Jewish society and the world at large. While the Book of Ruth, on its surface, may appear to be a simple story of one family's struggle for survival, a deeper look reveals a paradigmatic example of how an ancient Jewish text can enlighten, educate, and inspire.

In this volume, rabbis, professors, scholars, educational innovators, and community leaders offer their readings of Ruth, and insights into its themes, through the prism of their respective academic interests and professional fields. These essays, replete with sophisticated observations, theoretical and practical frameworks, and keen social analyses, demonstrate how our perspectives on the challenges and opportunities of our era, and on the Book of Ruth itself, can be enhanced through the synthesis of *Torah Umadda* (Torah and general wisdom). As illustrated in chapters on immigration in the Bible and Jewish law (Berman), David's origins (Carmy), American history (Eleff), pedagogies of empathy (Fleischmann), psychology (Grossman), family and friendship (Halpern), poetry (Kurshan), nineteenth-century rabbinic interpretation (Lerner), comparative ancient literature (Maged), American immigration law (Nash), the concept of peoplehood in Ireland (O'Malley),

Sephardic studies (Perelis), Midrash (Peters), American and Israeli literature (Rindner), contemporary conversion (Romm), rabbinic tradition (Simkovich), elder care (Tweel), social work (Wozniak), and biblical intertextuality (Ziegler), we have much to glean by looking at the world through the prism of Jewish wisdom.

This book emerged from the fertile environment of YU's classrooms and academic dialogue. In the spring of 2017, I was fortunate to teach a class in YU's Isaac Breuer College on the Book of Ruth. Through the generous support of YU's Zahava and Moshael Straus Center for Torah and Western Thought, directed by Rabbi Dr. Meir Soloveichik, our class benefited from the wisdom of multiple distinguished guest lecturers, some of whose presentations are found in this volume. Additionally, in the spring of 2018, under the leadership of YU's president, Rabbi Dr. Ari Berman, and its provost, Dr. Selma Botman, I, along with Prof. Paul Glassman, the dean of YU Libraries, was privileged to convene an interdisciplinary faculty symposium on the topic of "Immigration and Identity." Some of the presentations from that program also appear in this volume in modified form. I thank Dr. Berman, Dr. Botman, and Dr. Soloveichik for their constant support, wisdom, and leadership, and Prof. Glassman and my wonderful colleagues in the Office of the Provost for their partnership and friendship. My gratitude is also extended to my colleague and cousin, Rabbi Ari Lamm, for his input in the early planning stages of this project; the Michael Scharf Publication Trust of Yeshiva University Press; and the Maggid Books team, led by the visionary Matthew Miller and Rabbi Reuven Ziegler, alongside the talented copy editor Nechama Unterman, managing editor Ita Olesker, and translator Rabbi Daniel Tabak. This book is dedicated in appreciation to Ahuva Warburg Halpern and our wonderful children, Erez, Ayal, and Mayim.

In Maccabees II (10:1–8), we read that the victorious Hasmoneans, on the 25th of the month of Kislev, celebrated a delayed holiday of Sukkot, since the military struggle against the Seleucid Greeks had prevented them from observing that holiday on time. The holiday commemorating the wanderings of the Israelites through the desert had been delayed due to further Jewish wanderings through mountains and caves. We, however, are blessed to live in an era in which the nation of Israel no longer has to wander. Though the Messiah, the ultimate descendant of

Ruth who wandered with Naomi from the plains of Moab to the Land of Israel, is still delayed, we thank God that we as a nation have arrived and dwell securely in our homeland once more. The Jewish people have the opportunity, like never before, to be a "light unto the nations" (Is. 49:6). May our learning of the Book of Ruth, and all of our efforts to light the way to the ultimate redemption, allow us to celebrate the arrival of the Messiah speedily in our day.

Rabbi Dr. Stuart W. Halpern
Hanukka 5779

Communities of Care

It's in the Gene(alogy): Family, Storytelling, and Salvation

Rabbi Dr. Stuart W. Halpern

In 1924, the State of Virginia passed the Racial Integrity Act, criminalizing interracial marriages. There was a special dispensation built into the law, however. Through the so-called "Pocahontas exception," Virginians proud of being descendants of Pocahontas who still wanted to be classified as "white" were able to do so instead of being classified as "Native American."[1] Similarly politically weighted claims of ancestry have received extensive coverage in recent years, including the question of why former president Barack Obama is widely considered a black man with a white mother, rather than a white man with a black

---

1. For an extensive discussion of the science, politics, and history of genetics, see Carl Zimmer, *She Has Her Mother's Laugh: The Powers, Perversions, and Potential of Heredity* (New York: Penguin Random House, 2018). For a review of recent studies on Jewish genetics specifically, see Cynthia M. Baker, *Jew* (New Brunswick: Rutgers University Press, 2016).

father; President Trump's questioning of Democratic Senator Elizabeth Warren's claimed Native American heritage (Trump has, on numerous occasions, referred to her as "Pocahontas");[2] and the extensive doubts recently raised about the Jewish identity of socialist New York State Senator Julia Salazar.[3] As Rutgers professor Eviatar Zerubavel discusses in his *Ancestors and Relatives: Genealogy, Identity, and Community*,[4] how we define or frame our ancestry, and how others define it, is of tremendous importance.

Questions of genealogy are so crucial because our ancestry is often a key element in our social structure, the axis on which many of our social interactions, obligations, loyalties, and emotional sentiments turn. Though we like to believe in meritocracy, that individuals are self-made, our identities can be deeply tied to those we descend from. As Zerubavel writes, "[o]ur psychological integrity depends very much upon…the extent to which we feel linked to our genealogical roots… striking a person's name from his or her family's genealogical records used to be one of the most dreaded punishments in China."[5] And of course, biologically, heredity has a tremendous impact on our traits, personality, and self-perceptions. As Columbia University professor Robert Pollack has noted, our "genomes are a form of literature…a library of the most ancient, precious, and deeply important books."[6] Through studying where we come from, we learn how to tell our own story.

ARE OUR RELATIVES "RELATIVE"?

In *It's All Relative: Adventures Up and Down the World's Family Tree*,[7] humorist and author A. J. Jacobs recounts his attempt to assemble his

---

2. Maggie Astor, "Why Many Native Americans Are Angry with Elizabeth Warren," *The New York Times*, October 17, 2018. https://www.nytimes.com/2018/10/17/us/politics/elizabeth-warren-dna-test.html.

3. See, for example, Mijal Bitton, "Julia Salazar's Defenders Reveal the Limits of Identity Politics," *The Forward*, August 31, 2018. https://forward.com/opinion/409391/julia-salazars-defenders-reveal-the-limits-of-identity-politics/.

4. Oxford: Oxford University Press, 2011. For his discussion of the Obama question, see the discussion beginning on p. 3.

5. Ibid., 5, 7.

6. *Signs of Life: The Language and Meanings of DNA* (Boston: Houghton Mifflin, 1994), 117.

7. New York: Simon & Schuster, 2017.

extended, and by that I mean *very* extended, family in the largest family reunion ever. After receiving an e-mail from a man in Israel claiming to be his twelfth cousin, part of an 80,000-person family tree which included Karl Marx and some European aristocrats, Jacobs set out to bring as many of his living relatives together as he could, figuring "people [who spend countless hours tracing their family roots] want to feel connected and anchored. They want to visit what has been called the 'Museum of Me.'"[8] Utilizing online genealogical tools, he connected to countless celebrities, as well as former president George H. W. Bush. Through this project, Jacobs sought to make the case for people to be kinder to one another because of our shared "cousin-hood."[9]

Finding out about 79,999 relatives raised for Jacobs questions about the nature of family and the hierarchy of closeness we feel toward certain individuals. He argues that if all of humanity is one, very large, extended family, it is less important who our immediate relatives are. Maybe,

> ...we can sometimes make room in our hearts to love others without diminishing what we feel for those already dearest to us. Love is not a zero-sum game.... They tell of a seventeenth-century French missionary in Canada who tried to explain traditional monogamous marriage to a tribesman. The tribesman replied, "Thou hast no sense. You French people love only your own children, but we love all the children of our tribe." Ignorance of their kids' paternity apparently [can make] for a more compassionate society.[10]

---

8. Ibid., 22.
9. Jacobs even had a column in *People* magazine in which he interviewed the "cousins" he found by tracing his extended family roots. Here's a representative exchange from an interview he conducted with *Hot in Cleveland* actress Valerie Bertinelli, available at https://people.com/celebrity/author-a-j-jacobs-interviews-his-very-distant-cousin-valerie-bertinelli/:
    Jacobs: You are, officially, my aunt's 6th great uncle's wife's mother's husband's brother's wife's 8th great-granddaughter.
    Bertinelli: So I'm practically your sister.
10. Jacobs, 180, 57. As Rabbi Dr. Ira Bedzow noted to me in private correspondence, Plato, in *The Republic*, suggests abolishing nuclear families and advocates for the communal raising of children.

Taking this line of reasoning a step further, maybe our conception of family shouldn't even be limited to biological relatives, or even people in our local community or tribe. One modern writer has even offered calling those who share your passion or worldview your "horizontal family" as opposed to your "vertical," biological family.[11] Though we would assume those with common interest are friends rather than family, Zerubavel gives some credence and sociological substance to this counterintuitive idea:

> The family... is an inherently boundless community. Since there is no natural boundary separating recent ancestors from remote ones, there is also no such boundary separating close relatives from distant ones, or even relatives from nonrelatives. Any such boundary is therefore a product of social convention alone. Thus, although it is probably nature that determines that our obligations to others be proportional to our genealogical proximity to them, it is nevertheless unmistakably social norms that specify whose blood or honor we ought to avenge and determine the genealogical reach of family reunification policies. It is likewise social conventions that specify who can claim the share of blood money paid to relatives of homicide victims and determine who we invite to family reunions. Thus, whereas the range of other animals' kin recognition is determined by nature, it is social norms, conventions, and traditions of classification that determine how widely humans' range of kin recognition actually extends, and societies indeed often vary in where they draw the line between relatives and nonrelatives.[12]

And as the renowned astrophysicist Neil deGrassi Tyson put it in a letter to Jacobs:

---

11. Jacobs, 96, citing Andrew Solomon, *Far From the Tree: Parents, Children and the Search for Identity*.
12. Zerubavel, 72.

My philosophy of root-finding may be unorthodox. I just don't care. And that's not a passive, but active sense of caring. In the tree of life, any two people in the world share a common ancestor – depending only on how far you look. So the line we draw to establish family and heritage is entirely arbitrary. When I wonder what I am capable of achieving, I don't look to family lineage, I look to all human beings. That's the genetic relationship that matters to me. The genius of Isaac Newton, the courage of Gandhi and MLK, the bravery of Joan of Arc, the athletic feats of Michael Jordan, the oratorical skills of Sir Winston Churchill, the compassion of Mother Teresa. I look to the entire human race for inspiration for what I can be – because I am human. Couldn't care less if I were a descendant of kings or paupers, saints or sinners, the valorous or cowardly. My life is what I make of it.[13]

ARE YOU MY MOTHER?

The challenge to the idea above, however, is that while it might make for a sound philosophical argument, it doesn't seem to hold water empirically. There have been many experiments and contexts, including Israeli kibbutzim, in which children have been raised communally, as opposed to in a nuclear family model, only to discover it made parents and children less happy. There is social, psychological, and moral value provided by what we intuitively classify as our family, which, assuming it contains a generally positive dynamic, serves to aid in both general health and even survival, and inculcate values that an individual applies to his or her colleagues, neighbors, and friends. As the saying goes, "Men may change their clothes, their politics, their wives, their religions, their philosophies, [but] they cannot change their grandfathers."[14]

---

13. Jacobs, 163.
14. Ibid., 58, 54. See also Diane Swanbrow, "Raising a Child Doesn't Take a Village, Research Shows," Phys.org, September 9, 2011, https://phys.org/news/2011-09-child-doesnt-village.html; Lars-Toralf-Storstrand, "Utopian Ideals Don't Mix Well with Child Welfare Policies," *The Sunday Guardian*, March 31, 2018, https://www.sundayguardianlive.com/culture/utopian-ideals-dont-mix-well-child-welfare-policies; and Rachel Epstein,

THE JEWISH FAMILY

Judaism, of course, is based upon the story of a family. The Book of Genesis is the story of chosen children, with the tales of those who were not chosen relegated to the periphery.[15] Like many families, the Jewish family's "dynastic mental structure" is conceived of as a "single identity" with "particular norms of remembrance."[16] Thus, while one might refer to one's country of origin as "motherland" or refer to the "founding fathers" of the United States, to the Jewish people, Israel is the land of our *actual* mothers and fathers, and our norms of family remembrance are found in the Torah. We are *Benei Yisrael*, the children of our forefather Israel.

Following the completion of the Bible, the advent of the monarchy, and the sweep of subsequent Jewish history, what has emerged within the story of the Children of Israel is the anticipated restoration of one particular line within our family. We hope and pray multiple times throughout our liturgy for the resumed authority of the Davidic line through the coming of the *Mashiaḥ*, the ultimate redeemer.[17]

With this background in mind, let us examine the Book of Ruth, which ends with a genealogy culminating with the birth of David, the ancestor of the eventual Messiah. Let us examine how the ancestral story of David's family is told and how it might inform our understanding of family in our own lives.

Paula Rerer, Orna Tzischinsky, and Peretz Lavie, "Changing from Communal to Familial Sleep Arrangement in the Kibbutz: Effects on Sleep Quality," *Sleep* 20 (5): 334–339.

15. This phenomenon has been examined extensively by many. See, for recent examples, Cynthia R. Chapman, *The House of the Mother: The Social Roles of Maternal Kin in Biblical Hebrew Narrative and Poetry* (New Haven: Yale University Press, 2016); and Jonathan Sacks, *Not in God's Name: Confronting Religious Violence* (New York: Schocken Books, 2015).

16. Zerubavel, 19, 67.

17. *In God's Shadow: Politics in the Hebrew Bible* (New Haven: Yale University Press, 2012), 66. See also Michael Wyschogrod, *The Body of Faith: God in the People Israel* (London: Roman & Littlefield, 2000), 252–254.

TEN GENERATIONS

The Book of Ruth ends with a list of ten generations:

> Now these are the generations of Perez: Perez begot Hezron; and
> Hezron begot Ram, and Ram begot Amminadab; and Ammi-
> nadab begot Nahshon, and Nahshon begot Salmon; and Salmon
> begot Boaz, and Boaz begot Obed; and Obed begot Jesse, and
> Jesse begot David. (Ruth 4:18–22)

A story that began with an Israelite family leaving Bethlehem
and dwelling in Moab for around ten years (1:4), during which time a
father and two sons died, now lists ten generations of progeny, a healthy
and vibrant family line. The birthing of sons has replaced the death of
sons.[18] Beyond this portrayal of restoration, the list has a structure that
serves a political function as well. The list could have started with Judah,
father of Perez, or even Jacob, Judah's father, but starting with Perez puts
David tenth in line, matching an earlier biblical pattern. Just as there
were ten generations from Adam to Noah, and another ten from Noah
to Abraham, David is listed as the culmination of ten generations. This
structure suggests that the book is situating David in the pantheon of
foundational biblical figures.[19]

The "surprise ending" of David's birth also reshapes our perception of the entire preceding narrative. Through the realization that this
tale of a bereft Naomi and her former daughter-in-law, the Moabite Ruth,
ends up producing the ultimate Israelite king, the reader sees how a sav-
ior is born through the acts of loyalty and kindness demonstrated by its
characters. In the words of Professor André LaCocque:

---

18. Todd Linafelt, *Ruth: Berit Olam – Studies in Hebrew Narrative and Poetry* (Colleg-
eville: The Liturgical Press, 1999), 80.

19. See Zvi Ron, "The Genealogical List in the Book of Ruth: A Symbolic Approach," *Jewish
Bible Quarterly* 38:2 (2010): 85–92. As Ron notes, this is the only occurrence of the word
"toldot" outside of the Torah. As he also points out, starting the list with Perez also places
Boaz in the seventh spot on the list, another common favorable biblical number. Note,
as well, that despite Boaz stating that he is marrying Ruth to preserve the name of her
dead husband, it is Boaz's family memorialized in the genealogy, not Mahlon's.

The genealogy is their announcement of victory...in the West, individualism has become so excessive, so egocentric, that all devotedness to a future generation appears obsolete and even ridiculous in the eyes of some...but the facts of history do teach us that we cannot take the survival of the group for granted. After Auschwitz, the people of Naomi – who are also Ruth's people – know that they are vulnerable. It was already so in ancient Israel. The discontinuation of the name – that is, of the family, the clan – meant annihilation...what has to be assured is not the number but history, the promise, the hope. The typical modern individual does not have any history, only episodes, like the soap operas on television. But Israel has a history, a history oriented toward the coming of the kingdom of God and its regent, the Messiah...put simply, the story of Ruth is pulled from the episodic and placed, from the perspective of Israel's history, into salvation history.[20]

Living during the troublesome era of the Book of Judges, in which each man did what was right in his own eyes because there was no ruler to unify the nation, Ruth's selfless acts bore the nation's salvific figure, the conqueror of Jerusalem and the singer of Psalms. As Tamara Cohn Eskenazi and Tikva Frymer-Kensky suggest, "For an ancient audience this final genealogy would have been an exhilarating conclusion; good people have been rewarded with the high honor of illustrious progeny."[21]

THE FEMALE GENEALOGY

Like all such biblical lists, the final verses of Ruth list male progenitors.[22] However, prior to those last few verses, the narratives offer what

---

20. *Ruth: A Continental Commentary*, trans. K. C. Hanson, Continental Commentaries Series (Minneapolis: Fortress Press, 2004), 122.
21. *The JPS Bible Commentary: Ruth* (Philadelphia: JPS, 2011), 92–93.
22. Jacobs notes that this phenomenon is not exclusive to the Bible: "Even if we find the names of women from our past on various government documents, we often know little beyond that. Women are frequently ciphers, lacking stories, feelings, opinions" (p. 232). Along similar lines, in *Leveling the Playing Field: Advancing Women in Jewish Organizational Life* (St. Paul: Cambridge Leadership Associates, 2008), editors

some have suggested is a female genealogy as well, one whose allusions offer even greater insight into the story of David's birth. In this scene, in which Ruth is married to Boaz, the names of certain female biblical heroines are evoked:

> And all the people that were in the gate, and the elders, said: "We are witnesses. May God make the woman that is coming into your house like *Rachel* and like *Leah*, those two who built the house of Israel; and be worthy in Ephrat, and be famous in Bethlehem; and may your house be like the house of Perez, whom *Tamar* bore to Judah, of the seed which God shall give you of this young woman." So Boaz took Ruth, and she became his wife; and he was intimate with her, and God gave her conception, and she bore a son. And the women said unto Naomi: "Blessed be God, who has not left you this day without a redeemer, and let his name be famous in Israel. And he shall be for you a restorer of life, and a nourisher for you in your old age; for your daughter-in-law who loves you, who is better to you than seven sons, has borne him." And Naomi took the child, and embraced him, and became his nurse. And the women her neighbors gave it a name, saying: "There is a son born to Naomi"; and they called his name Obed; he is the father of Jesse, the father of David. (4:11–17)

This is the only time in the entire Bible where characters are blessed through the invoking of female characters. Ruth is mentioned as an analogue to none other than Rachel and Leah, two foundational women, mothers and wives. In this radical acceptance of a stranger, a Moabite widow becomes an honorary biblical matriarch.[23]

In the coda of Ruth, the invocation of Rachel and Leah, as well as Tamar, is more than a simple reference to memorable female biblical

---

Shifra Bronznick, Didi Goldenhar, and Marty Linsky suggest we "listen carefully at meetings and public events. Extract the stories and folklore from the organizational history. Are the triumphs and inspirational moments tethered only to male 'heroes'? Where have women played important roles?" (p. 88).

23. See Chapman, 220; and Rachel E. Adelman, *The Female Ruse: Women's Deception & Divine Sanction in the Hebrew Bible* (Sheffield: Sheffield Phoenix Press, 2015), 91.

characters. All three of these earlier women, along with the daughters of Lot, have been subtly alluded to over the course of Ruth's tale. All of them, like Ruth, ensured the viability of their family line through personal sacrifice in the form of "bedtricks" of varying degrees of deception and morality.[24] After fleeing the destruction of Sodom, the daughters of Lot made their father drunk and slept with him, thereby producing Ammon and Moab, the latter of which is Ruth's ancestor (Gen. 19). Leah was switched for Rachel on Jacob's wedding night (Gen. 29:25) and the two sisters often fought over their husband, once trading a night with Jacob for mandrakes (30:16). And Tamar dressed as a veiled harlot and slept with Judah (ch. 38).[25] However, as contemporary scholar Ruth Kara-Ivanov Kaniel emphasizes, Ruth and Boaz's story stands both among and beyond those earlier narratives.

---

24. See Adelman, 94. Noticing the usage of the masculine *"shteihem"* – "the two of them" in the invocation, writers Shera Tuchman and Sandra Rapoport suggest:

    > It was their passionate desire for bearing and raising children that formed the dominant theme of Rachel and Leah's lives, and this driving force is the basis for the millennia-old blessing of Ruth. The elders, *invoking the names of Rachel and Leah*, were intoning the benediction of family, generational continuity, and covenantal inheritance upon Ruth … the Bible uses the masculine form with reference to these biblical women when they take equivalent action to that of their male counterparts. The elders blessed Ruth to be like Rachel and Leah because *both* these matriarchs built the "house of Israel" as partners with the patriarchs [emphasis in the original]. (*The Passion of the Matriarchs* [Jersey City: KTAV, 2004], 346)

    See also Prof. Ezra Sivan, "Team of Rivals: Building Israel Like Rachel and Leah," *The Lehrhaus*, November 15, 2018, https://www.thelehrhaus.com/scholarship/team-of-rivals-building-israel-like-rachel-and-leah/, who similarly suggests that *"shteihem"* is meant to emphasize that, like Ruth, who also transcended family challenges, "Rachel and Leah were more effective and powerful agents in 'building of the house of Israel' than we might have imagined."

25. Numerous scholars have pointed out the thematic and literary parallels between the episodes of Lot's daughters, Tamar, and Ruth, including the death of two husbands, departure from a place of residence, a father figure and daughter figure, and the root words for "knowledge" (*yada*) and "destruction" (*shaḥat*) appearing in each context, among others. Sivan, "Team of Rivals," lists numerous parallels between Ruth and Rachel and Leah, including displacement, leaving foreign gods, the presence of witnesses reinforcing rites, and the crucial role played by Bethlehem.

In contrast to the masculine list, which is summarily *"his*torical," the feminine list is portrayed as *"her*story" and as part of…Boaz and Ruth's wedding scene. This list functions as a connecting link for the formal closing of the book and a disposition to recast forbidden actions into "an expression of blessing" is prominent in it. Absent here is the unforgiving terminology found in the original story: the figure of the *qedeisha* or the prostitute at the entrance of Enaim, the problematic revelation at Boaz's feet, and the hesitation of the redeemer to corrupt his inheritance, the threat of the world's annihilation in the story of Lot's daughters and their abandonment to be raped in the beginning of the story of Sodom, the poverty, calamity, and death that accompany Ruth and Tamar, the clashing of the sisters Rachel and Leah. All of these are transformed into unified harmony in the mouths of the congratulators at the city's gate.[26]

Through their mention in this story, these earlier women are woven into the fabric of Israel's royal history, and their sacrifices reach an apex in Ruth's actions. Whereas those earlier stories were tales of deceit, lack of knowledge, seduction, and trickery, Ruth's "bedtrick" at the threshing floor was a call to action that necessitated recognition and awareness on the part of the individual actors, and that resulted in "fully legitimate, legally certified" marriage. From Lot's daughters' incest, to Rachel and Leah's wedding night switch, to Tamar's disguised harlotry, we have progressed, finally, to a public marriage ceremony at the city gates of Bethlehem.[27] Through Ruth, those earlier episodes are thus redeemed, affirmed, and celebrated.[28] Maybe this is why the male

---

26. *Holiness and Transgression: Mothers of the Messiah in the Jewish Myth* (Boston: Academic Studies Press, 2017), 14.

27. Kaniel, 35.

28. See Harold Fisch, "Ruth and the Structure of the Covenant History," *Vetus Testamentum* 32 (1982): 425–437. He notes the episodes reflect a social development in the ancient world with Lot's daughters representing a cave-dweller society, Tamar (and one could add Rachel and Leah) a pastoral society, and Ruth an agrarian society. See also Adelman, 95, 119–121 and Eskenazi and Frymer-Kensky, 93.

genealogical list begins with the name Perez, which means "breach."[29] Daring to breach propriety for the sake of family, these women not only ensured the continuation of their family line, they provided national salvation.

STRUGGLES, STORYTELLING, AND SALVATION

By telling the story of King David's genealogy through the Book of Ruth, the text is offering a nuanced framework for thinking about our own history, both national and familial. As psychologist Dr. Lisa Miller has demonstrated, the ability for families to articulate their struggles and challenges builds resilience among their members.[30] Through the tale of a foreign, marginalized widow, whose personal risk mirrors that of other biblical mothers, we are reminded of the sacrifices that sustain the continuity of the Jewish people. We are reminded of the ability of kindness to heal. And we are reminded of the power of family, both biological and beyond. Ruth's story inspires us to meet the challenges of our own circumstances. Through the tale of communal openness to a disconnected stranger, we are given the keys to redemption [31] After all, it is the eventual offspring of Lot's daughter, Rachel and Leah, Tamar, and Ruth, with a family bloodline of struggle, alienation, and foreignness, coupled with selfless dedication to continuity, who is uniquely suited to lead the Children of Israel and bring the nations of the world closer to God.[32] Like Moses, whose virtues and leadership abilities were

---

29. See Adelman, 121–122.
30. See *The Spiritual Child: The New Science on Parenting for Health and Lifelong Thriving* (New York: Picador, 2015), 291.
31. Orit Avnery, "Who is in and who is out? The two voices of Ruth," *Havruta Magazine* (The Pardes Institute of Jewish Studies, 2010): 77.
32. See Ruth Rabba 8:1 and Rabbi Elie Munk, *The Call of the Torah: An Anthology of Interpretation and Commentary on the Five Books of Moses – Bereishis* (Brooklyn: Mesorah Publications, 1994), 256–257; See also, Kaniel, 20:

    These women, going to the threshing floor, to the cave, and the entrance of Enaim, disguised and hidden, are figures whose essence is flexible and their "unstable" identities are a source of power, allowing them to enlarge circles and create a life outside of strict tribal boundaries. By not belonging to any place, they belong to every place. In accordance with their identification with "untamed nature," they are depicted as running wild and crafting "culture" anew.

developed through his fractured, foreign experiences in both Egypt and Midian, Ruth too embodies the marginal figure's messianic capabilities.[33]

It is through our own striving to survive and flourish alongside our imperfections, struggles, and feelings of disconnectedness that we will eventually repair a fractured world. To quote Rabbi Tzadok HaKohen in his discussion of the Messiah in *Tzidkat HaTzadik* (#111), "the lowest will become the highest."

> This is why Ruth is the progenitor of the Messiah, because the Messiah is the ultimate *meishiv nefesh* (Ruth 4:15), restorer of life and dignity when hope seems lost...to restore the name (Ruth 4:5) is to reach across the generations, and across interpersonal divide, and at times across the divide between aspects or periods within one's own self, in active recognition, provoking true transformation. That is what compassionate redemption means...in the end, Ruth reminds us that nothing is more beautiful than friendship, that grace begets grace, that blessing flourishes in the place between memory and hope, that light shines most from broken vessels. What else is the Messiah about?[34]

> This is the way Tamar, Ruth, and Lot's daughters are integrated into the people of Israel, and the messianic heroes are born. From an ethnic perspective, they represent the power of the weak, and their seductive manner reflects...a vital survival practice against oppressive or life denying forces.

33. See Bonnie Honig, *Democracy and the Foreigner* (Princeton: Princeton University Press, 2003), 3:

> The figure of the foreigner serves as a device that allows regimes to import from outside (and then, often, to export back to outside) some specific and much-needed but also potentially dangerous virtue, talent, perspective, practice, gift, or quality that they cannot provide for themselves (or that they cannot admit they have)...sometimes foreignness operates as an agent of (re-)founding.... Moses appears as an Egyptian prince to lead the Israelites out of Egypt and bring to them the law from the mountain. The biblical Ruth's migration from Moab to Bethlehem reanimates the alienated Israelites' affective identification with their God while also beginning the line that will lead to King David.

34. Nehemiah Polen, "Dark Ladies and Redemptive Compassion: Ruth and the Messianic Lineage in Judaism," in *Scrolls of Love: Ruth and the Song of Songs*, ed. Peter S. Hawkins and Lesleigh Cushing Stahlberg (New York: Fordham University Press, 2006), 69, 74.

In our striving to embody the values inspired by Ruth, may we merit the writing of the next chapter of the Jewish story. May we, as individuals, as members of our family, and as members of the Children of Israel, bring the world compassionate redemption.

To Sit with Another, to Resurrect a Floundering Faith

Malka Fleischmann

There is a great difference between still believing something and believing it again.
Georg Christoph Lichtenberg

Two are better off than one, in that they have greater benefit from their earnings. For, should they fall, one can raise the other: but woe to him who is alone and falls with no companion to raise him! (Eccl. 4:9–10)

There is something about Ruth's staying – about the posture of clinging to her mother-in-law, Naomi – that has forever endeared her to the Jewish people. Instinctively, we fall deeply in love with her character for remaining when and where Orpah chose to leave. But, still, she and her choice are shrouded in mystery, and this widely venerated inclination to cleave begs our curiosity.

We might wonder, is deep attachment selfless and mature or fearful and childlike? Is it future-oriented or born out of loyalty to the past? Is it faithful and brave or apprehensive? Deliberately chosen or based in addiction?

In Ruth's case, in particular, what did she imagine would come of staying? Why does the loss of her husband not plainly unveil a path of return to her former home and family? And why does Ruth – or must Ruth – so aggressively implore her mother-in-law to permit her enduring as a companion?

* * *

In the first chapter of the Megillah, Ruth and Orpah are faced with the deaths of their husbands and, subsequently, their mother-in-law's urging them to return to their families of origin and secure new unions. While, after initial resistance, Orpah ultimately heeds Naomi's counsel, Ruth is steadfast, with the text's remarking, "But Ruth cleaved unto her" (Ruth 1:14).

This pregnant term makes its biblical debut in the second chapter of Genesis, poignantly describing or prescribing *dveikut*, clinging, as the antidote to man's solitude. After God observes that "it is not good for man to be alone" (Gen. 2:18), resolves to form a "fitting helpmate" (ibid.), unsuccessfully attempts to partner Adam with one of the animals, and, finally, produces the first woman, Adam says, "This is now bone of my bones, and flesh of my flesh" (Gen. 2:23). Immediately thereafter, the Bible states, "Therefore shall a man leave his father and his mother, and shall cleave unto his wife, and they shall be one flesh" (Gen. 2:24). For man, the cleaving inherent in partnership is life's answer to some amorphously, but assuredly, deficient or painful alternative.

And while the parallel clinging as a response to the threat of loneliness is evident between the Books of Genesis and Ruth, there is yet a deeper conceptual and linguistic symmetry between the two stories, an echoing too resonant and stunning to ignore.

What elicits the *dveikut* of Genesis is Adam's recognition that his female counterpart was "bone of my bones, and flesh of my flesh."

Somehow, the kindred nature of this creature demands of man that he leave his parents and cling to his partner, forming a merger resulting in some newborn whole. It would seem that *dveikut* is warranted when a man's soul recognizes its harmony in another; when the opportunity for marriage emerges.

It would make sense, then, having lost such a union in the death of her husband, for Ruth to depart. She, it would seem, has lost the "bone of her bones" and "flesh of her flesh," making her abiding *dveikut* to Naomi confounding. Without the possibility for the partnership of man and wife, is there a place and call for *dveikut*? If not to her marital *ezer*, her helpmate, to whom or what – and, above all, why – is Ruth clinging?

* * *

In response to Orpah's and Ruth's initial commitment to return with their mother-in-law to her people, Naomi says, "No, my daughters. My lot is far more bitter than yours, for the hand of the Lord has struck out against me" (Ruth 1:13). Soon thereafter, when she and Ruth arrive to Bethlehem and the townspeople greet her as Naomi, she says, "Call me not Naomi, call me Marah; for the Almighty has dealt very bitterly with me. I went away full, and the Lord has brought me back home empty; How can you call me Naomi, when the Lord has dealt harshly with me, and the Almighty has brought misfortune upon me?" (Ruth 1:20–21).

So, we see, in the unfolding of her new life as a widowed and child-less woman, Naomi stands at the center of a spiritual crisis. While still present in her life, God has altered in her mind's eye and is revealed to be a severe and grim force against her. It stands to reason, then, that her adamance in pushing Orpah and Ruth to leave may be owing to more than just their heightened chances for second marriages elsewhere. Perhaps, the utterly bereft Naomi sees the lot comprised of her home, community, faith, and God as one that, in all respects, will disappoint. After all, in response to Ruth's lingering, she says, "See, your sister-in-law (Orpah) has returned to her people and her gods. Go follow your sister-in-law" (Ruth 1:15), as if to suggest that another spiritual community and foreign gods would better serve Ruth. Naomi's urging emanates from more than mere rationality or motherly concern about Ruth's marital status. It is the mark of a hopeless woman, of a woman who believes that both she and the God for which she stands have become worthless: a source of souring inside her own heart, a valueless offering to the wider world.

* * *

In one of the most memorable and touching scenes in *Mr. Rogers' Neighborhood*, Fred Rogers interviews Jeff Erlanger, a young, wheelchair-bound boy with a host of physical discomforts and dysfunctions. Mr. Rogers makes two notable decisions that, together, demonstrate a pedagogy of empathy.

First, Rogers lowers himself to a nearby stoop, erasing the distance between his able-bodied stature and his young guest's own diminished build. Then, after intently listening to Jeff's account of his paralysis, Rogers says, "Do you know that song that I sometimes sing called, 'It's You I Like'? I'd like to sing that *to* you and *with* you." With both his choice of position and words, Rogers signals appreciation for Jeff and recognition of his worth. The demonstration of feeling is clear, as if to say – *Where you are, my friend, there I want to be.* You are valuable. You possess something that begs proximity.

Years later, when Rogers was inducted into the Television Hall of Fame, an adult Erlanger made a surprise appearance in tribute to the man who had sat beside him eighteen years prior. Taking the podium, Rogers asks the audience, "Who in your life has been such a servant to you? Who has helped you love the good that grows within you?" – the interrogative embodiment of his empathic posture.

To love that good that grows within another is to awaken him to the good with which he is endowed, to the good that courses within him, to the good he should cherish inside himself.

* * *

In turning to Naomi as she does, Ruth more than offers companionship. She models the very faith that Naomi seems to have lost, reminding her mother-in-law of the spiritual abundance of which she is yet in possession.

Pleading with Naomi to let her remain, Ruth says, "For wherever you go, I will go; wherever you lodge, I will lodge; your people shall be my people, and your God my God" (Ruth 1:16). And here, in the sing-song and doubled language of her pledge, Ruth hearkens back to Genesis with her stunning echo of Adam's "the bone of my bones, and the flesh of my flesh," with her soul's recognition of a likeness or kinship warranting marriage.

No, there is no traditional wedding immediately available to Ruth in Naomi's grieving company. But, there *is* another kind of marriage implied by her clinging – the marriage of a nation to its God. In remaining by her mother-in-law's side and claiming her people and Lord as her own, Ruth reminds Naomi that there is still a union – a family, a home, and a promise – at the center of her existence. That, despite the deaths of their loved ones, there is reason yet, another sort of marriage calling for *dveikut*.

By forgoing a world of foreign possibilities and choosing the fate of the Israelites as her own, Ruth is signaling to her mother-in-law that her existence and wider world are worthy, rich, and still fertile. More than merely standing beside Naomi, Ruth begs to join her. She begs for a spiritual home among Naomi's people, upholding the meekly glowing embers of her mother-in-law's life and breathing upon them to reignite her faith.

Evidencing the effects of Ruth's staying, Naomi's first reference to God after her embittered speech about Him in the first chapter of the Megillah is one of blessing. Even more significant, it is one of faith. Overcome by Boaz's benevolence toward Ruth, Naomi says, "Blessed be he of the Lord, who has not failed in His kindness to the living or to the dead!" (Ruth 2:20).

The Malbim explains that Naomi's reference to God's kindness with the dead reveals her understanding that Boaz would perform *yibum*, thereby "doing good for the soul of the deceased." But, perhaps, Naomi's statement is even more meaningful, deepened, and enriched by a later allusion to the biblical character of Hannah, one of the tradition's greatest female paradigms of faith.

In the final chapter of the Megillah, after Ruth bears a child, the townswomen remark to Naomi that "He will renew your life and sustain your old age; for he is born of your daughter-in-law, who loves you and is better to you than seven sons" (Ruth 4:15).

The comparison of Ruth's worth to that of seven sons is strange, and the commentators do little to illuminate it. However,

Hannah's devout prayer of passion in the Book of Samuel bears an eerie reflection to the reference. Amid a much longer statement of praise for and faith in God, she says, "While the barren woman bears seven, the mother of many is forlorn. The Lord deals death and gives life" (I Sam. 2:5–6), a parallel mentioning of seven sons and the renewal of life.

Thus, like Hannah after the birth of her own child, at the closing of the Megillah, Naomi stands before us renewed of faith, thanks to Ruth's wisdom in remaining, thanks to her knowing that to cling to Naomi was more than the moderation of loneliness but an expression of profound and unwavering commitment to the nation and God of Israel.

* * *

In our society, we're often told not to grow "too attached," whether to people, places, ideas, or things. If we develop emotional ties to fleeting experiences and fickle or mortal beings, we doom ourselves to the pain that accompanies inevitable loss. But to live in God's image – to design wee worlds of experience within the vast world He created – is to know that there can be no light without darkness, no day without night, no love without pain.

Musing about these very dichotomies in *Seek My Face: A Jewish Mystical Theology*, Arthur Green writes:

> Ours has always been a strongly nonmonastic tradition. We view human love and true attachment to others in an entirely positive light. Our ability to love and to live in familial relationships and in close friendship is testimony to the image of God in which we are made. But that very ability to love is also a great source of human suffering…. Caring and hurting go together in the human experience. There is no allowing ourselves to love that does not also entail making ourselves vulnerable.[1]

---

1.   Arthur Green, *Seek My Face: A Jewish Mystical Theology* (Woodstock: Jewish Lights Publishing, 2012), 89.

Among other critical cultural differences between the Israelite and Moabite nations was the latter's regular practice of human sacrifice (II Kings 3:27). To relinquish one's own child, as the Moabite leader in the second Book of Kings does, is to demonstrate a profound lack of attachment.

Perhaps, then, Ruth's *dveikut* signaled something more than compassionate lingering. Perhaps it was a moment of vaulting across the Israelite-Moabite cultural divide, a girl's demonstration to her mother-in-law of the desirability of *dveikut* as a religious and cultural principle and of the spiritual bounty within her reach; a valuing of attachment to this world in the image of God, to attachment in the way of the Jew; abandoning the fear of suffering in recognition of its inextricability from love. No light, without darkness; no day, without night.

* * *

The Book of Ruth is more than the story of a foreigner who gleans in the fields of an Israelite. It is more than the story of a compassionate young woman who undertakes the responsibility of elder-care, and it is more than the story of Ruth's marriage to Boaz. This is the story of *dveikut*, the story of the compulsion within us to bind ourselves to God and of the capacity of an empathic clinging to resuscitate the faith of a hollowed friend.

The holiday of Shavuot, during which time we retell Ruth's story, is our wedding. It is the anniversary of the eternal *dveikut* implied by our acceptance of the Torah. And, every year, whether to heighten or resurrect our belief, we must face God and recognize that He and we are the bone of each other's bones and that, where this tradition and faith go, there, too, we shall go.

Reading Ruth with Winnicott: Boaz and Naomi as "Transitional Objects"

Dr. Jonathan Grossman

The Book of Ruth is a story of people in motion. First and foremost, the protagonists physically relocate from the territory of one nation to that of another, and this concomitantly entails the psychological and social transition of Ruth the Moabite into the Israelite society of Bethlehem. In this chapter, I seek to interpret this movement through the notion of the "transitional object" coined by the famous psychoanalyst Donald Winnicott (1896–1971). Winnicott assigned great significance to the object a baby adopts at the cessation of breastfeeding, which he called the "transitional object." By this he intended the class of items a child becomes attached to, lavishes great affection on, and is unwilling to part with. In most cases, this piece of cloth cannot be washed by the parents without dire consequences, and under no circumstances can it be replaced with a newly purchased imitator. According to Winnicott, this transitional object is part of the process by which a baby becomes separated from his or her mother. So long as a baby nurses, it perceives the mother's bosom as part of its subjective existence and cannot yet conceive of its mother (especially her breast) as having an objective, independent existence. By the end of the process, the baby (now a child) accepts that things external to it have an objective, independent reality. It is in the transitional period between these two bookends of the child's development that the child becomes attached to some object that reminds it of its mother (absent now for extended periods) and drags it around everywhere – it has become an inseparable part of him. The child does not experience it, however, as he did his mother's breast, as part of his own subjective reality, but as an object external to him that he keeps close, as a transitional object that represents and eases him into accepting external reality. Winnicott's idea that a single object can simultaneously represent something and the absence of that thing is a brilliant insight with literary implications and applications. If we may permit ourselves to replace the psychoanalytic terminology with literary terminology, we will find that even within biblical narratives there are elements intended to represent something while at the very same time marking that thing's absence.

The Book of Ruth is, as we have said, Ruth's tale of transition. At the very beginning of the story, Ruth is forced to say goodbye to her husband (to the love of her life? to her hopes and dreams?) due to circumstances out of her control, but when she actively chooses to join Naomi the act of severance is of much greater consequence; she has chosen to cut herself off from her culture, her family, her people, and her mother tongue. Even if chapter 1 mentions "returning" (s-w-b) to Bethlehem a number of times,[1] and the reader senses the sympathy and solidarity of the two figures of Naomi and Ruth through their dialogue,

---

1. See, e.g., Edward F. Campbell, Jr., *Ruth: A New Translation with Introduction, Notes, and Commentary*, Anchor Bible Series 7 (New York: Doubleday, 1975), 79–80; Werner Dommershausen, "Leitwortstil in der Ruthrolle," in *Theologie im Wandel*, ed. J. Neumann and J. Ratzinger (Munich and Freiberg: Wewel, 1967), 394–407; Frederic W. Bush, *Ruth/Esther*, Word Biblical Commentary 9 (Waco, Tex.: Word Books, 1996), 84–86; Jonathan Grossman, *Ruth: Bridges and Boundaries*, Das Alte Testament im Dialog 9 (Bern: Peter Lang, 2015), 60–64.

chapter 2 presents the reader with the other side of the coin in the following statement by Boaz: "how you left your father, your mother, and
your birthplace to go to a people you had not previously known" (2:11).
Elsewhere, I propose considering Boaz's words as the central axis of the
scene, around which revolves a complex concentric structure.[2] His statement gives us a different perspective on the story, one that received less
emphasis in chapter 1: Ruth's choice to join Naomi is not only a decision to attach herself to something new, but a decision to cut old ties
loose. Boaz's words teach us that the story of Ruth is also about a vol-
untarily displaced young woman who has left her family and homeland.
As many have noted, Boaz's description of Ruth having left her father,
mother, and birthplace echoes God's instruction to Abraham to leave
behind his own family and birthplace: "Go from your land, your birthplace, and your father's house to the land I shall show you" (Gen. 12:1).[3]
But Abraham was promised substantial rewards for heeding God's call;
Ruth was promised nothing. In fact, Naomi spelled out quite clearly that
the only thing she could expect in Bethlehem, with neither husband nor
child, was loneliness. The intensity of Ruth's separation from her natural
environment is further underscored by Boaz's inclusion of her mother
on the list of those left behind, a figure who goes unmentioned in God's
command to Abraham.[4] Ruth is cut off from her natural habitat, from
the home in which she was born and raised, from her mother in Moab
who would take her back and have her back.

---

2. See Jonathan Grossman, "'Gleaning among the Ears' – 'Gathering among the
   Sheaves': Characterizing the Image of the Supervising Boy (Ruth 2)," *Journal of
   Biblical Literature* 126 (2007): 703–716.
3. See, e.g., Gillis Gerleman, *Ruth: Das Hohelied*, Biblischer Kommentar Altes Testa-
   ment 18 (Neukirchen-Vluyn: Neukirchener Verlag des Erziehungsvereins, 1965), 26;
   Robert L. Hubbard Jr., *The Book of Ruth*, New International Commentary on the
   Old Testament (Grand Rapids, Mich.: Eerdmans, 1988), 165; Yair Zakovitch, *Ruth*,
   Mikra LeYisrael (Jerusalem: Magnes Press, Hebrew University, 1999), 76 (Hebrew);
   Kirsten Nielsen, *Ruth: A Commentary*, trans. E. Broadbridge, Old Testament Library
   (Louisville, Ky.: Westminster John Knox Press, 1997), 59; Yael Ziegler, *Ruth: From
   Alienation to Monarchy*, Maggid Studies in Tanakh (Jerusalem: Maggid, 2015), 224.
4. André LaCocque, *Ruth: A Continental Commentary*, trans. K. C. Hanson, Continental
   Commentaries Series (Minneapolis: Fortress Press, 2004), 71.

By the story's end, Ruth has a new husband and is a full-fledged Bethlehemite: she enters the city gate and her son is recognized as part of the dynasty of the Perez family. The last vestiges and labels of her old way of life are gone. The tortuous process she has undergone to get to this point is aptly marked throughout the book by her epithet "the Moabite." Its use indicates how those around her (especially the youth supervising the reapers [2:6])[5] viewed her with ambivalence, but it also reflects her own complicated self-identity throughout the story (2:21). Consequently, tracing Ruth's experiences reveals a "tale of transition": how Ruth gradually detaches herself from "her mother's house" (1:8), her "birthplace" (2:11), and her old Moabite identity in order to build a new life as an Israelite, and how Ruth the widow finds *menuḥa*, that is to say, how she finds comfort and settles down, once more.

The narrative space in the story also contributes to our understanding of it as Ruth's "tale of transition" from foreigner to recognized resident of Bethlehem. The space of the story grows increasingly narrow as it moves further toward the city and farther away from Moab. Chapter 1 is set on the road from Moab to Bethlehem, in essentially a no-man's-land; Ruth has left home but has yet to arrive at her destination. As mentioned above, in this chapter returning to "her mother's house" (1:8) is still a live option for Ruth. This is followed by Ruth's declaration that Naomi's people and God will become hers, which led Katrina Larkin to argue that from this point on Ruth's otherness is increasingly muted. If she has joined Naomi's people, she can no longer be eyed warily as the ultimate foreigner.[6] Judith McKinlay is correct, however, in pointing out that the motif of otherness continues to hover around Ruth even after she professes her allegiance to a new people and God,[7] as emerges sharply from the scene in which the two women reach the outlying fields of Bethlehem. There is no real contradiction between the two readings because it boils down to a matter of perspective. On the one

---

5. See further Grossman, "Gleaning."
6. Katrina J. A. Larkin, *Ruth and Esther*, Old Testament Guides (Sheffield, England: Sheffield Academic Press, 1996), 53.
7. Judith E. McKinlay, "A Son Is Born to Naomi: A Harvest for Israel," in *A Feminist Companion to Ruth and Esther*, ed. A. Brenner, Feminist Companion to the Bible (Second) Series (Sheffield: Sheffield Academic Press, 1999), 152.

hand, Ruth no longer considers herself a Moabite, and out of devotion to her mother-in-law she is prepared to endure the cultural transition required of her. On the other hand, the Bethlehemites do not accept her without reservations and with open arms, and continue to regard her as the Other. In chapter 2, the action takes place in an open field outside the city itself. The field is a semi-public space populated by young men and women gleaning after the reapers, by Boaz and his workers, and by Ruth. In this chapter, the youth explicitly mentions her Moabite origins, and the narrator also refers to her as "Ruth the Moabite" (2:2, 21). Her old identity is conspicuous in the field, as Boaz has to warn his young men not to harass her. In chapter 3, the encounter still happens outside the city at the threshing floor, but unlike the field it is not in full view of the public and has a touch of intimacy about it. The reader senses a contraction of the narrative space such that Ruth can meet Boaz in a private setting, where prying eyes cannot profile her based on the Moabite label affixed to her. At the threshing floor, the natural field undergoes an agricultural transformation at human hands, thus representing a suitable space for the transformation of Ruth herself. The epithet "Moabite" is not appended to Ruth's name at all in this chapter; instead, we read for the first time that the upstanding citizens of Bethlehem, whom Boaz refers to as "the gate of my people" (3:11), hold Ruth in high esteem. At the end of the book, in chapter 4, Ruth is lawfully wedded to Boaz through an act that takes place at the gate, the official entrance to the city. The narrative space, then, shrinks as the chapters go on (the road to Bethlehem – the field – the threshing floor – the gate), until we arrive at the city gate, which represents the boundary between the city and outsiders, making it the place where one can be formally admitted into the city and become one of its sons or daughters.[8]

Before investigating Ruth's transition, I would like to dwell for a moment on the moral justification, as it emerges from the story, for her acceptance into the Israelite society of Bethlehem. The outstanding quality of Ruth's character is her generosity, her altruism. Simply put,

---

8. See further Orit Avnery, *Liminal Women: Belonging and Otherness in the Books of Ruth and Esther* (Jerusalem: Shalom Hartman Institute, 2015), 36–37 (Hebrew); Grossman, *Ruth*, 58–64.

she puts others first. This comes across clearly throughout the book: in chapter 1, by joining Naomi she gives up a possible future in Moab; in chapter 2, when gleaning she collects more than she needs so she can give Naomi "what she left over after eating her fill" (2:18); even in chapter 3, she is portrayed as acting at Naomi's behest, which is why her request from Boaz is not a petition for mercy but an appeal to his obligation to the family ("you are a redeeming kinsman" [3:9]). Naomi seems to be the formal protagonist of the story,[9] and it is out of a desire to help her mother-in-law that Ruth makes certain decisions and takes certain actions that lead to the acquisition of her new identity.

Therein lies the story's internal logic for Ruth's acceptance into this new society. Ruth has the capacity for meeting the Other and making room for them in her heart and life. As an act of reciprocity, which is a constitutive motif of the entire story, society treats those who open themselves up in this way by opening itself up to and accepting them, in spite of their foreign origins and otherness.

Reciprocity is especially prominent in the dialogue between Boaz and Ruth in the open field. Ruth's otherness is out in the open, as Ruth says to Boaz: "Why have I found favor in your eyes that you acknowledge me, when I am a foreigner?" (2:10). Here, one can hear the reciprocity mentioned above: "I was told everything you have done for your mother-in-law after the death of your husband, how you left your father, your mother, and your birthplace to go to a people you had not previously known" (2:11). Boaz does not commend Ruth for her desire to join the ranks of the Jewish people; to the contrary, he only mentions her new national allegiance as a corollary of her devotion to Naomi. Ruth is meritorious for "everything you have done for your mother-in-law after the death of your husband," for leaving her parents for parts unknown. This kindness of hers is what justifies special treatment, why

---

9. So argues, for example, LaCocque, p. 6. Naomi's definition as the literary protagonist does not contradict her presentation as a passive figure who needs others to act in order to bring about her salvation. It is possible that we should adopt the more complex formulation of Eissfeldt, who argued that we should view Naomi and Ruth as two figures who together constitute the protagonist (Otto Eissfeldt, *Einleitung in das Alte Testament* [Tübingen: Mohr Siebeck, 1964], 481–482).

Boaz does not treat her as a "foreigner" and instead showers her with kindness of his own.

How does this "tale of transition" occur? Does the narrative contain elements that facilitate Ruth's detachment from her past and her newfound attachment? Does she have transitional objects?

Two figures around her seem to fit the definition of the transitional object. As remarked above, the uniqueness of the transitional object – which I would like to implement as a literary symbol – is its duality: it represents the mother and stands in for her, but it also makes her absence felt by its very act of substitution. This is exactly why the transitional object is a crucial part of the child's separation from her mother.

NAOMI

The obvious substitute for Ruth's father, mother, and homeland is, of course, Naomi. In the story, she represents both aspects of the transitional object for Ruth.

First, she replaces the mother Ruth left behind in Moab. Ruth lives under Naomi's roof and Naomi routinely calls her "my daughter." Ruth goes out to the field and threshing floor only with Naomi's express permission, and comes back to her to report what has happened. This maternal bond really stands out at the beginning of chapter 3, where Naomi tells Ruth: "My daughter, shall I not seek *mano'aḥ* for you so that you may be well?" (3:1). The use of the word "*mano'aḥ*" as an allusion to a husband is not coincidental here, and it echoes the earlier exchange between the two upon departing Moab. There, Naomi implored Ruth to return to Moab where she could find comfort and put down roots with a new husband: "May the Lord grant you to find *menuḥa*, each in her husband's house" (1:9). But the chiastic structure of Naomi's words to Ruth and Orpah reveals that, in Naomi's thinking, finding *menuḥa* in the house of a new husband requires returning to their mothers' homes (1:8–9):

> A. "Let each of you go and return to her mother's house.
> > B. May the Lord deal kindly with you,
> > B1. As you have dealt with the dead and with me.
> A1. May the Lord grant you to find *menuḥa*, each in her husband's house."

The connection between the middle lines (B–B1) is self-evident. Naomi formulates her words in the form of reciprocity – just as you have done kindness with your deceased husbands and with me, so may God do kindness with you.

More important for us is the connection between the two framing statements. In the beginning (A), she encourages her daughters-in-law to return to their "mother's house," and in the end (A1) she prays that they find *menuḥa* in their "husband's house." The two "house" references reflect the order of events Naomi's daughters-in-law could expect upon their return to Moab: first they would reenter their mothers' homes, and then God would grant them to build new homes with new husbands. Aside from the typical practice reflected by Naomi's words, they also give us a glimpse of Naomi's mindset, in which the mother is the one who leads her daughter to the marriage canopy.

This insight may also explain Naomi's unexpected reference to the "mother's house" of her daughters-in-law in place of the more commonly found "father's house" in such contexts (see, e.g., Gen. 38:11, Lev. 22:13, Judges 19:2). Wilhelm Rudolph surmised that this surprising phrase indicates that the fathers of Ruth and Orpah were already dead, so their mothers were their only resort.[10] Daniel Block and Orit Avnery suggested that this phrase is part of feminine language unique to

---

10. Wilhelm Rudolph, *Das Buch Ruth – Das Hohe Lied – Die Klagelieder*, Kommentar zum Alten Testament 17/1–3 (Gütersloh: Gerd Mohn, 1962), 41. While Boaz tells Ruth that he has heard how she left her father and mother (2:11), suggesting that her father is still alive (Hubbard, 102–103), this may be an idiomatic expression which deviates from its classic meaning. Some have claimed that this expression, rather than being unusual, reflects the deep bond between mothers and daughters in biblical times, which is also evident from the aforementioned Genesis 24:28. See Carol L. Meyers, "Returning Home: Ruth 1.8 and the Gendering of the Book of Ruth," in *A Feminist Companion to Ruth*, ed. A. Brenner, Feminist Companion to the Bible Series (Sheffield: Sheffield Academic Press, 1993,) 85–114; Nielsen, 46. Compare also to John Gray: "this may be an anachronism, alluding originally to the part of the tent reserved for the women and presided over by the mother" (*Joshua, Judges, and Ruth*, New Century Bible Commentary [London: Nelson, 1967], 386). On the social and literary function of "house of the mother" and "house of the father" in the Bible, see Cynthia R. Chapman, *The House of the Mother: The Social Roles of Maternal Kin in Biblical Hebrew Narrative and Poetry* (New Haven: Yale University Press, 2016). See also Ziegler, 139n3.

the Book of Ruth.[11] Robert Hubbard seems to have the right explanation in claiming that the "mother's house" connotes love, sexuality, and intimacy (in light of Song. 3:4, 8:2).[12] By using a phrase at the outset (A) that evokes intimacy and marriage, Naomi is already hinting at the closer (A1) – from this house her daughters-in-law will transition to the houses of their husbands.

Therefore, when Naomi tells Ruth in chapter 3 that she seeks her *menuḥa*, she is taking over the job of matchmaking traditionally performed by the mother. Naomi's house substitutes for Ruth's "mother's house" mentioned at the beginning of the story.

In actuality, the reader is already meant to sense this substitution in chapter 1, when Ruth chooses to follow Naomi instead of the clear alternative of returning to "her mother's house," and in so doing defines Naomi as her surrogate mother.[13] Since Naomi is already Ruth's "mother-in-law," having her represent the absent mother is an easy literary feat.

While taking on this new maternal role, Naomi also signifies the absence of Ruth's biological mother, for Naomi does not see to Ruth's needs. She does not provide for her "daughter"; it is Ruth who provides for her. Presumably, Naomi does not have the wherewithal to find a husband willing to marry Ruth, a Moabite, as she instructs Ruth to go to the threshing floor and seduce Boaz in order to secure his hand in marriage.

Naomi's inability to fully replace Ruth's mother is fittingly captured by the youth overseeing the reapers. Although this character and his contribution to the development of the story deserve their own study, for the purposes of this discussion I will focus the reader's attention only on his characterization of Ruth, or, more precisely, on what he omits from it. After Boaz asks him who the young woman is gathering among the sheaves in the field, he replies: "She is a Moabite girl who returned with Naomi from the field of Moab" (2:6).

---

11. Daniel I. Block, *Judges, Ruth*, The New American Commentary (Nashville: Broadman & Holman Publishing, 1999), 633n47; Avnery, 31–32.

12. Hubbard, 102–3.

13. In Ruth's responses to Naomi in chapter 1, one can sense how she conceives of her as a surrogate for her biological mother and absent husband. The sentences spoken by Ruth are laden with evocations of intimacy.

Scholars disagree over how the youth views Ruth. Many believe he is sympathetic.[14] Others claim he has not formed his own view and is being intentionally vague, waiting to see what his master thinks.[15] But I believe that the correct approach belongs to a third group of scholars, who claim that the youth has reservations about Ruth.[16] There are various indications of this, but his characterization of Ruth betrays this most. He calls her "Ruth the Moabite," a young woman who decided to latch onto Naomi when the latter was on her way back from Moab. For whatever reason, the young man omits their familial connection, so that anyone unfamiliar with the details of the story would get the impression that she joined Naomi on her journey for her own reasons and that no familial bond united them.

Whatever his reasons, the youth apparently reflects the widespread opinion in Bethlehem that Naomi and her accompanying Moabite daughter-in-law are not related. His words voice the popular view that unravels their family ties and casts doubt on Naomi's role as Ruth's surrogate mother.[17]

Naomi, therefore, represents the classic transitional object: she represents the absent mother but does not become her. She asks Ruth, "Who are you, my daughter?" (3:16), which simultaneously expresses her maternity ("daughter") and the perpetual perplexity inherent to their bond, for they are not bound by blood and the marriage linking them has long ago dissolved. The absence of her real parents hits Ruth every evening when she comes home to Naomi.

---

14. Zakovitch, 71.
15. Avi Hurvitz, "Ruth 2:7 – A Midrashic Gloss?" *Zeitschrift für die Alttestamentliche Wissenschaft* 95, 1 (1983): 121–123; Gary A. Rendsburg, "Confused Language as a Deliberate Literary Device in Biblical Hebrew Narrative," *JHS* 2 (1999): 3–4.
16. Moshe Garsiel, "The Literary Structure, Plot Development, and Narrator's Intentions in the Scroll of Ruth," *Hagut BaMikra* 3 (1979): 71 (Hebrew); Danna Nolan Fewell and David M. Gunn, "Boaz, Pillar of Society: Measures of Worth in the Book of Ruth," *Journal for the Study of the Old Testament* 45 (1989): 49; Grossman, "Gleaning."
17. Precisely because this rumor is bandied about in Bethlehem, the narrative considers it important to conclude with Naomi's connection to Ruth's son – "A son is born to Naomi," the neighbors exclaim, and so the connection between mother- and daughter-in-law is reaffirmed.

BOAZ

Beside Naomi, Boaz also functions as a transitional object for Ruth, not with respect to her mother but with respect to the husband who predeceased her in Moab. In his literary role as transitional object, Boaz fills the gaping hole left by her dead spouse, but at the very same time makes his absence tangible. Boaz steps into this role in the first part of the story, when he makes sure that Ruth and Naomi's needs are met. The two widows have no breadwinner or guardian, so Boaz provides Ruth with enough sustenance for both and ensures Ruth goes unmolested on his turf. Since Boaz's special treatment of Ruth was not a one-time result of a chance meeting but extended throughout the entire period of reaping, Boaz can be viewed rightfully as the family's provider, a responsibility borne by the husband in the biblical period.

Although Boaz takes on the financial responsibility of a husband, his actions are a reminder of the absence of Mahlon, Ruth's source of *menuḥa*. The manner in which he provides for Ruth (and Naomi) is a bit baffling. After Boaz's meeting with Ruth in the field, one might have expected him to go the extra mile and send food straight to her and Naomi's house, unburdening Ruth of the need to glean and of its associated discomfort. Boaz is portrayed as exceptionally magnanimous, but he does not take the extra step and arrange delivery of produce straight to their house. In chapter 2, Ruth receives protection and support, but this is also the chapter of the book in which her poverty and solitude are most on display.

There is more. In chapter 2, the prospect of intimacy is hinted at but then rejected and unrealized. When Boaz says, "how you left your father, your mother" (2:11), he calls to mind the first act of intimacy, as described in the creation of woman: "Therefore a man leaves his father and his mother" (Gen. 2:24).[18] If the reader of the book expected to hear an echo of the verse's continuation, "and clings (*vedavak*) to his wife so that they become one flesh," he or she is disappointed to hear Boaz offering Ruth a different kind of connection: "stay close (*tidbakin*) to my maidens" (2:8). This dashed hope is crucial for understanding Boaz's

---

18. Ellen van Wolde, *Ruth and Naomi*, trans. J. Bowden (London: SCM Press, 1997), 33–35; Hubbard, 164; LaCocque, 73.

role at this point in the book. His character heightens the expectation of intimacy, but it is swiftly cut down; his introduction gestures toward marriage, but nothing comes of it. Boaz is thus the classic transitional object, filling a void while accentuating it. For all the time that Ruth gleans in the field she does not find any pillar of support in Bethlehem; Boaz's support is but a pale reflection of what is to come when he will grant her refuge under his wing.

The overtones of intimacy in Boaz and Ruth's campestral encounter lend some credence to the claim made by a number of scholars that it should be viewed as a kind of betrothal scene. Robert Alter reads it this way, noting that its details are an inversion of the classic betrothal narrative:

> The betrothal type-scene, then, must take place with the future bridegroom, or his surrogate, having journeyed to a foreign land. There he encounters a girl – the term נערה invariably occurs unless the maiden is identified as so-and-so's daughter – or girls at a well. Someone, either the man or the girl, then draws water from the well; afterward, the girl or girls rush to bring home the news of the stranger's arrival … finally, a betrothal is concluded between the stranger and the girl – in the majority of instances, only after he has been invited to a meal.[19]

According to Alter's reading, which others have adopted,[20] the meeting of Ruth and Boaz presents a complete gender inversion of such a scene: "The protagonist is a heroine, not a hero, and her homeland is Moab, so the 'foreign soil' on which she meets her future mate near a well is Judah."[21]

Nevertheless, even if we choose to adopt Alter's proposal of a "betrothal scene," the obvious disparity between a typical betrothal scene and the scene in Boaz's field is that chapter 2 does not end in marriage. The meeting of Abraham's servant and Rebecca at the well ends with Rebecca's journey to Canaan to meet her betrothed (Gen. 24); Jacob

---

19. Robert Alter, *The Art of Biblical Narrative* (New York: Basic Books, 1981), 52.
20. E.g. Hubbard, 187–88.
21. Alter, 58.

and Rachel's meeting at the well culminates in a double wedding, first Leah's and then Rachel's (Gen. 29); Moses' protection of Reuel's daughters at the well is followed by his marriage to Zipporah (Ex. 2). However, Boaz's encounter with Ruth in the field eased her economic suffering but did not – at this stage – result in offspring. From this perspective, the meeting of Boaz and Ruth recalls Alter's description of Saul's meeting with the girls in I Samuel 9:11–13: "The type-scene has been aborted."[22] Ruth and Boaz do eventually marry two scenes later, but after their meeting in the field, the two part ways, and if not for Naomi's dramatic intervention in the following chapter, their budding relationship would never have a chance to mature and bear fruit.[23]

THE STORY'S CONCLUSION – FROM TRANSITIONAL OBJECT TO REPLACEMENT

In one crucial way, the characters in Ruth's story diverge from Winnicott's transitional object. According to Winnicott, the transitional object is merely an object of signification and has no essence of its own. It has no inherent identity; its identity is solely the product of the child who invents it, which is why its referentiality can be imparted and removed at will. By comparison, Naomi and Boaz are not unidentified living objects whose roles are dictated by Ruth. This essential divergence especially comes to the fore at story's end.

Boaz and Naomi were both there for Ruth as transitional objects throughout her long journey, filling in for absent family. Now, they become that family. At the conclusion – or, rather, starting at the threshing floor and continuing until the marriage – Boaz becomes a real husband and not merely an effective substitute. In our story, the transitional object comes to fully replace what it previously had only signified. Ruth left "her mother's house" a widow and ended up being "the woman who is coming into the house" (4:11) of Boaz.

The narrative bears out this conception of Boaz as Mahlon's replacement when his marriage to Ruth is not portrayed as the consummation of romance but as the preservation of the deceased's name. From

---

22. Ibid., 60.
23. Cf. Garsiel.

this angle, Boaz is a transitional object who facilitates Ruth's integration into Israelite society, but at the end of the story he brings the name of her deceased husband back to life. According to the symbolic logic of levirate marriage, Mahlon is the father of the son Ruth conceived from Boaz. Even if Ruth has abandoned her Moabite past, she has not forgotten her first husband Mahlon, whose place Boaz fully takes.

The arc of Ruth and Naomi's relationship is not as easy to follow at the end of the book. When the new boy is born the narrative emphasizes Naomi's special relationship with it, despite their lack of shared blood. In the final scene of the story, Naomi takes the baby boy into her bosom and dandles it as if she were its mother, and the neighbors who name the baby exclaim: "A son is born to Naomi!" (4:17). This is an unexpected turn of events, but it appears to be the purpose of the finale: to make Naomi the child's legitimate grandmother. Although Naomi and the boy are not blood relations, from the perspective of levirate marriage this child is the progeny of her deceased sons, and so in some sense she is his grandmother.

And so the bonds between Naomi and Ruth are publicly recognized. By the end of the story, doubters of Naomi's familial connection to her Moabite daughter-in-law have been turned into believers, who affirm that Ruth is the "daughter-in-law who loves" Naomi (4:15). Naomi previously represented Ruth's absent mother, and now she becomes a grandmother to Ruth's son; she is a mother once more.

Such is the difference between our story and the classic transitional object of Winnicott. All grown up, the child leaves behind her security blanket, the object that represented her mother's separation, and she becomes an autonomous individual. In the Book of Ruth, however, the transitional objects fulfill the implicit promise they hold: in the end, Ruth acquires a husband and a mother.

The Exquisite Challenge of Care

Dr. Tamara Mann Tweel

The fear is not for what is lost.
What is lost is already in the wall.
What is lost is already behind the locked doors.
The fear is what is still to be lost.

Joan Didion, *Blue Nights*

Imagine, for a moment, that your mother-in-law confronts you on a desolate road. She is depressed and overwrought, needy and withdrawn, desperate for help and emotionally unreachable. Now imagine you are alone with the responsibility. Your husband, her son, has died, and there is no one else left to care for her. What do you do? What are the limits of your responsibility?

Most of us, living in the twenty-first century, in a world of medical technology, material comforts, and institutional options, jump to the logistics. We ask ourselves, what do I need to do to make sure she stays healthy? We run through the length of a day and map out countless scenarios: who will purchase the food, do the baths, fill out the paperwork, count the pills, and be there at night? Our minds fill up with the anxiety-ridden questions of maintaining the status quo. How will she get to the bathroom? What happens if she falls? How will I get her to all the appointments? Responsibility becomes a mental occupation, full of depleting details devoid of spiritual grandeur and meaning.

In *Being Mortal*, the physician and author Atul Gawande encapsulates this experience of care in the age of the medical possibility as an "overwhelming combination of the technological and the custodial."[1] He describes the daily tasks of Shelley, the daughter caregiver of Lou, a man devoted to his independence whose health begins to deteriorate after his wife dies. Gawande writes: "Lou was on numerous medications, which had to be tracked and sorted and refilled. He had a small platoon of specialists he had to visit – at times, nearly weekly – and they were forever scheduling laboratory tests, imaging studies, and visits to other specialists.... And there was almost no help for Shelley.... Shelley had become a round-the-clock concierge/chauffeur/schedule manager/medication-and-technology troubleshooter, in addition to cook/maid/attendant, not to mention income earner.... She felt her sanity slipping."[2] This is the crisis of care in the medical age, primed to overwhelm the mind and deplete the soul. Megillat Ruth offers another way to care, a way centered on the gravity of the task and the moral sustenance of the response.

When Ruth faces her mother-in-law in the desert she hears the agony of old age and responds with an affirmation of life. She turns to Naomi and utters these timeless words:

> Do not entreat me to forsake you, to turn back from you. For wherever you go, I will go. And wherever you lodge, I will lodge. Your people is my people, and your God is my God. (Ruth 1:16)[3]

---

1. *Being Mortal: Medicine and What Matters in the End* (New York: Metropolitan Books, Henry Holt and Company, 2014), 85.
2. Ibid.
3. Translations slightly modified from Robert Alter, *Strong as Death Is Love: The Song of Songs, Ruth, Esther, Jonah, and Daniel – A Translation with Commentary* (New York: W. W. Norton & Company).

To better understand how these words unlock the sanctity of eldercare, we must first go back and investigate the challenges that often mark the experience of aging.

In the twentieth century, old age came to be defined chronologically, at the age of sixty-five. But for many experts in the field, chronology has never been a perfect marker of health, of wisdom, or of a stage of life. "Old age," Ollie Randall, one of the pioneers of eldercare, wrote in 1947, "is a period of losses – loss of family, of friends, of job, of health, of income, and most important of all, of personal status."[4] It does not begin at the same time for everyone. It begins when the losses trigger unexpected needs.

For Naomi, as with so many elders, the losses came in stages. First, there was famine and the loss of economic security. Then there was the loss of home and land, familial intimacy, and the self-worth that comes from being known.

> And it happened in the days when the judges ruled that there was a famine in the land, and a man went from Bethlehem to sojourn in the plains of Moab, he and his wife and his two sons. (Ruth 1:1)

In retrospect, these losses seem tame. There is more to come. Naomi loses her husband, Elimelech, and "she, together with her two sons, is left." The text alerts the reader to the way in which the loss is not yet eviscerating. Naomi has her sons; she is needed, respected, and cared for. And yet, she is left without a partner, without someone who knew her in her youth, who understood her history and her home, who connects her past to her present. And then comes the truly destabilizing loss, the deaths of her sons, Mahlon and then Chilion.

> And the two of them, Mahlon and Chilion, died as well, and the woman was left of her two children and of her husband. (Ruth 1:5)

The additional phrase, redundant in fact but necessary in emotion, "and the woman was left of her two children and of her husband,"

---

4. "The Psychological Aspects of Aging," May 28, 1947, folder 403, box 34, Ollie Randall Papers, 1.

accentuates the agony. Naomi has no spouse, no children, and no grandchildren; she has no hope for continuity or a future for her family. It has all perished.

This is the loss that Joan Didion describes in *Blue Nights*, her wrenching memoir about the loss of her husband, her daughter, and her own connection to the purpose of life. She explains, "When we lose that sense of the possible we lose it fast.... One day we are absorbed by dressing well, following the news, keeping up, coping, what we might call staying alive; the next day we are not."[5] The *not* does not hit Naomi right away. She is busy surviving. She has to leave Moab, she has to keep the last of her loved ones, her two daughters-in-law, alive.

We can imagine the scene: valuables packed away, food purchased, and yet another round of painful goodbyes. Naomi has done this before; her daughters-in-law, Orpah and Ruth have not.

> And she went out from the place where she had been, with her two daughters-in-law, and they went on the way to go back to the land of Judah. (Ruth 1:7)

It seems that the minute they set out, Naomi changes her mind and tells them to return. Perhaps this was her plan all along. She waited until they had to face the emptiness of the road, the deep sadness of a life without anchors, and encountered the fear of the unknown. Or perhaps she only now realizes the folly of continuing their bond, of assuming that she is the only one who can protect them, that she is the one who is needed. The audacity of her self-importance hits her, and then the eviscerating, suffocating, reality of her own limits, her own inability to provide, her own mortality.

> May the Lord grant that you find a settled place, each of you in the house of her husband. And she kissed them, and they raised their voice and wept. And they said to her, "But with you we will go back to your people." And Naomi said, "Go back, my daughters, why should you go with me? Do I still have sons in my womb who could be husbands to you? Go back, my daughters, go, for

---

5. *Blue Nights* (New York: Vintage Books, 2011), 183.

I am too old to have a husband. Even had I thought 'I have hope. This very night I shall have a husband and bear sons,' would you wait for them till they grew up? For them would you be deprived of husbands? No, my daughters, for it is far more bitter for me than for you because the Lord's hand has come out against me." (Ruth 1:9–13)

Ruth listens to Naomi, not just to the content but to the call. Naomi describes a body that can no longer attract physical love, a body that can no longer carry life, a body that no longer feels useful. It is that final line Ruth hears, not just the words but the full meaning for Naomi. There is nothing for her to live for, no love, no intimacy, no life. It feels as if even God has left her. This is also how we age. Understanding this truth is how we learn to care for the aged.

For years, elderly patients with dementia were drugged. Doctors and nurses gave them medications to make them sleep, to make them go to the bathroom, and to reduce constant agitation. At Beatitudes, a retirement community in Phoenix, Arizona, Tina Alonso, the director of education and research, has a different approach. "When you have dementia, we can't change the way you think," explains Alonzo, "but we can change the way you feel." Dementia is an experience of such acute loss for the patients and their families that it is often challenging to see what remains. Research, however, demonstrates that even with dementia, human beings retain emotional lives and that endorphins released during moments of pleasure last past the intellectual memory of the experience.[6] For this reason, caregivers at Beatitudes have the gift of being explicitly tasked with providing moments of joy. There are teacarts and chocolate, hand rubs and enjoyable fabrics, objects designed just for comfort, and practice in making repetitive conversations fun. Gawande supports this approach to eldercare in *Being Mortal*, when he writes: "We've been wrong about what our job is in medicine. We think our job is to ensure health and survival. But really it is larger than that. It is to enable well-being. And well-being is about the reasons one wishes to be alive."[7]

---

6. Rebecca Mead, "The Sense of an Ending," *The New Yorker*, May 20, 2013, https://www.newyorker.com/magazine/2013/05/20/the-sense-of-an-ending-2.
7. Gawande, 259.

But how do we help loved ones embrace life in the years of loss? This is the question at the center of Ruth's majestic response to Naomi. Ruth sees Naomi, she sees her as a widow and as a grieving mother and while Orpah turns to kiss her mother-in-law goodbye, Ruth responds with a dramatic act – she clings to her.

> And they raised their voice and wept once more, and Orpah kissed her mother-in-law, but Ruth clung (*davka*) to her. (Ruth 1:14)

The word *davka*, to cling or cleave, connects Ruth's act to the deliberate joining of man and wife. It is a word deployed to explain a grasping of one to another for the sake of creating life.

> Therefore, a man shall leave his father and his mother and cleave (*vedavak*) to his wife, and they shall become one flesh. (Gen. 2:24)

The Sforno explains that "the expression *divuk*, 'cleaving,' being in a state of true union, is not possible between two people who are not alike in their common purpose in life."[8] Ruth draws on the metaphors of marriage to establish not just a common purpose but a common future with Naomi. Ruth gives Naomi a reason to be alive, but what does this form of care give to Ruth? How does clinging transform the caregiver?

In Marilynne Robinson's Pulitzer Prize-winning novel *Gilead*, the Reverend John Ames explains to his young son that having someone to honor is a "great kindness" bestowed by God.

> Every human being is worthy of honor, but the conscious discipline of honor is learned from this setting apart of the mother and father…. Believe me, I know this can be a hard Commandment to keep. But I believe also that the rewards of obedience are great, because at the root of real honor is always the sense of the sacredness of the person who is its object.[9]

---

8. Translation taken from https://www.sefaria.org/.
9. *Gilead* (New York: Picador, reprint edition, 2006), 139.

What is the sense of sacredness and how does one begin to see it in another?

Ames, in an almost inversion of the rabbinic tradition, explores this idea by describing the kind of love a parent feels for a child and that a child feels for a parent: "When you love someone as much as you love your mother," he tells his son, "you see her as God sees her, and that is an instruction in the nature of God and humankind and of Being itself."[10] The act of honoring and loving elders can be the act of seeing them as God sees them.

It is a joy to see divine beauty in an infant; it is a discipline to see it in the elderly and frail. Ruth's magisterial act is twofold: she sees the existential pain at the center of Naomi's words and she expresses a form of divine sight when she sees the sacred beauty of her mother-in-law. We must remember that Naomi feels as if God has forsaken her. By clinging to her, Ruth pulls her back into a world of holiness and establishes holiness at the center of their relationship. Ruth proclaims, "Do not entreat me to forsake you, to turn back from you. For wherever you go, I will go. And wherever you lodge, I will lodge. Your people is my people, and your God is my God." But that is not the end of Ruth's proclamation. She continues,

> Wherever you die, I will die, and there will I be buried. So may the Lord do to me or even more, for only death will part you and me. (Ruth 1:17)

You will not be alone Ruth proclaims. You will not be alone where you walk and where you sleep. Your tradition and peoplehood will still gain another life, even if you can have no more children. God will not forsake you because your God is now my God and – I am here.

Now, imagine again that your mother-in-law confronts you on a desolate road. She is depressed and overwrought, needy and withdrawn, desperate for help and emotionally unreachable. Now imagine you are alone with the responsibility. Your husband, her son, has died, and there is no one else left to care for her. What do you do? From Ruth we learn to pause before the logistics, to face our elders, to see them as God sees them, and to proclaim that they are not alone.

---

10. Ibid., 139.

Love, Literature, and Interpretation

You've Got a Friend in Me: Ruth and the Dynamics of Friendship

Rabbi Dr. Stuart W. Halpern

You got troubles, I've got 'em too
There isn't anything I wouldn't do for you
We stick together and see it through
Cause you've got a friend in me.
Randy Newman, "You've Got a
Friend in Me," *Toy Story* (1995)

When you pick up the Tanakh and read the Book
of Ruth, it is a shock how little it resembles memory.
It's concerned with inheritance, lands, men's names,
how women must wiggle and wobble to live. Yet
women have kept it dear for the beloved elder who
cherished Ruth, more friend than daughter.
Marge Piercy, "The Book
of Naomi and Ruth"

Is your coworker your friend? Can your child be your friend? Can your cousin be your friend? Can men and women just be friends?

Of course, one's perspective on these questions would begin with the very definition of friendship itself. Most North Americans and Europeans would probably agree that friendship is "a voluntary association between people who enjoy one another's company and care, at least to some degree, about one another's welfare."[1] However, this basic definition still leaves many questions unanswered. What about people whose ages differ by decades? Or whose wealth, power, or social status are diametrically opposed? Do friends have to be on par with each other in every respect? Is a certain level of emotional intimacy required for a friendship? The answers to all of these are debatable even within contemporary Western society, and are likely to vary based on the cultural, gender, and class background of the respondent. Of course, non-Western and ancient cultures, due to their linguistic, cultural, or historical distance from our context, offer approaches that might differ widely from our own.

AN ANCIENT FRAMEWORK

The classical theoretical framework for thinking about friendship is offered by Aristotle (384–322 BCE) in his *Nicomachean Ethics*. As summarized by Princeton philosophy professor Alexander Nehamas in his volume that will serve as a crucial guide in our study,[2] Aristotle suggests that:

> some of us…are attracted to one another because we have something to gain from our relationship, some because of the pleasure we provide for one another, and some are drawn to one another's…"excellence" or "virtue."… When I bear you good will, I do so either because of the practical benefits I derive from our relationship, or because of the pleasure our interaction gives me, or finally because I am drawn to your virtues – courage, justice,

---

1. Saul Olyan, *Friendship in the Hebrew Bible* (New Haven: Yale University Press, 2017), 1.
2. *On Friendship* (New York: Basic Books, 2016).

temperance, magnificence, wisdom, and the features that are necessary to make a life a good and happy one.[3]

For Aristotle, there are three categories of friendship: 1) *Friendship of utility*, in which we stand to gain something from the relationship – for example, business partners or classmates; 2) *Friendship of pleasure*, which, as Aristotle writes, we engage in with others "not because of what they are in themselves, but because they are agreeable to us" – for example, lovers, fellow poker players, or fellow sports fans; and 3) *Friendship of the good*, which, unlike the other two, is not fleeting:

> The perfect form of friendship is that between the good, and those who resemble each other in virtue. For these friends wish each alike the other's good in respect of their goodness, and they are good in themselves; but it is those who wish the good of their friends for their friends' sake who are friends in the fullest sense, since they love each other for themselves and not accidentally. Hence the friendship of these lasts as long as they continue to be good; and virtue is a permanent quality.[4]

THE MODERN ERA

Contrast the simplicity of Aristotle's categories with how friendships are conceived of today. As British author Tim Lott's award-winning novel *White City Blue* puts it in the following representative exchange:

> How many varieties of friends are there? She replies.... Oh, loads. For a start there are friends you don't like. I've got plenty of those. Then there are friends you do like, but never bother to see. Then there are the ones you really like a lot, but can't stand their partners. There are those you just have out of habit and can't shake off. Then there's the ones you're friends with not because you like

---

3. Ibid., 13, 16. Nehamas does not address friendship in the Bible, though, as I hope to convey in this chapter, his work can inform our understanding of the dynamics of biblical friendship.
4. *Nicomachean Ethics* VIII 3.

them, but because they're very good-looking or popular and it's kind of cool to be their friends. There are friends of convenience – they're usually work friends. There are pity friends who you stay with because you feel sorry for them. There are acquaintances who are on probation as friends. There are – "Enough!" he finally interrupts her.[5]

Nehamas expands with some additional categories, noting that "there are fair-weather, heart-sink, dangerous, fossil friends, and 'frenemies' – not to mention friends who know each other only through the virtual spaces of social media."[6]

BIBLICAL PERSPECTIVES

What Does the Bible Say About Friendship?

While there is no biblical word that directly translates into "friendship," there are many words that connote "friend" which have been translated to reflect various senses of the word. Most well-known is from the root word *"rei'a"* as it occurs in Leviticus 19:18, *"ve'ahavta lerei'akha kamokha"* – "love your fellow as yourself." It also appears in Exodus 33:11 in the context of the relationship between Moses and God,[7] and in the context of the laws of those who would entice an Israelite to idol worship, where the concept of a "closest friend" is referred to.[8] Similarly, Psalms 38:12 laments the Psalmist being abandoned by those he expected to stand by

---

5. Penguin Books, 2000, pp. 45–46.
6. Nehamas, 102. For an extensive discussion of online friendships, see Mark Vernon, *The Meaning of Friendship* (New York: Palgrave Macmillan, 2010), 104–121.
7. "The Lord would speak to Moses face to face, as one man speaks to another (*el rei'eihu*)."
8. "If your brother, your own mother's son, or your son or daughter, or the wife of your bosom, or your closest friend (*rei'akha asher kenafshekha*) entices you in secret, saying, 'Come let us worship other gods'" (Deut. 13:7).

his side – "*ohavai verei'ai.*"[9] Less well-known Hebrew words connoting "friend" include "*aluf,*"[10] "*ish shalom,*"[11] and "*meyudaav.*"[12]

The expectations the Bible conveys in these and other verses is that a proper friend should display love, trust, and support in times of trouble. These biblical expectations for friendship are very much in line with Nehamas' assessment of friendship generally:

> The love friendship provokes gives depth and color to life; the loyalty it inspires erodes the barriers of selfishness. It provides companionship and a safety net when we are in various kinds of trouble; it offers sympathy for our misfortunes, discretion for our secrets, encouragement for our efforts.[13]

Does "Friend" Always Mean "Friend"?

Several times throughout Tanakh, a word that could otherwise be translated as "friend" seems to refer to someone less intimate than a friend, such as a neighbor or peer. In such cases, the exact meaning of the word is dependent upon its contextual usage. In Deuteronomy 19:4, for example, the Israelites are told "You shall not move your neighbor's (*rei'akha*) landmarks, set up by previous generations," and I Kings 20:35 refers to a peer who belongs to the same group with the same word.[14] In the building of the Tower of Babel, the word seems to connote simply "another person."[15] Even more starkly, when Samuel tells Saul that God

---

9. "*Ohavai verei'ai mineged nigi yaamodu*" – "my friends and companions stand back from my affliction."
10. As in Proverbs 17:9, "he who seeks love overlooks faults, but he who harps on a matter alienates his friend (*aluf*)," and Micah 7:5, "trust no friend, rely on no intimate (*be'aluf*); be guarded in speech with her who lies in your bosom."
11. As in Jeremiah 20:10, "I heard the whispers of the crowd – Terror all around: 'Inform! Let us inform against him!' All my friends (*anshei shelomi*) are waiting for me to stumble."
12. As in II Kings 10:11, "And Jehu struck down all that were left of the House of Ahab in Jezreel – and all his notables, intimates (*umeyudaav*), and priests – till he left him no survivor."
13. Nehamas, 187.
14. "A certain man, a disciple of the prophets, said to another (*rei'eihu*)."
15. Genesis 11:3: "They said to one another (*rei'eihu*), 'Come, let us make bricks and burn them hard.'"

has decided to take away his kingdom and give it to a rival, he says, "The Lord has this day torn the kingship over Israel away from you and has given it to another (*rei'akha*) who is worthier than you" (I Sam. 15:28). Lamentations 1:2 similarly uses the same form to refer to former political allies who have now turned their backs on Jerusalem.

Family vs. Friend

Besides "friend" not always meaning "friend" in the conventional sense, there is the complex relationship between "friend" and "family." There is significant overlap in Tanakh between expectations of family members and expectations of friends. Like friends, family members display love,[16] have their own internal hierarchies,[17] are expected to behave honestly and be supportive,[18] and manifest kindness toward each other.[19] Family and friends seem to be part of the same spectrum of emotional and practical ties.[20] As Proverbs 18:24 notes, "there are companions to keep one company, and there is a friend more devoted than a brother." Even the word "brother" itself can connote a biological brother or an unrelated friend.[21]

---

16. Genesis 25:28: "Isaac loved Esau because he had a taste for game."
17. The laws of inheritance within the family, as well as other family-related regulations, are reflective of an internal hierarchy of obligation. With regard to hierarchy within friendships, as Deuteronomy 13:7 alludes to, there are good friends and there are regular friends. As the saying goes, "friends help you move, good friends help you move a body."
18. Jeremiah 12:6: "For even your kinsmen and your father's house, even they are treacherous toward you." As Olyan (pp. 85–86) notes, "Behavioral parity, in contrast to formal equality of social status, wealth, life stage, or other personal characteristics, is a broadly attested expectation of friendship across biblical texts, mentioned most frequently in the breach ... friends are expected to seek each other's welfare, support one another when times are bad, be loyal, and reciprocate appropriate behavior."
19. Genesis 47:29: "And when the time approached for Israel to die, he summoned his son Joseph and said to him, 'Do me this favor, place your hand under my thigh as a pledge of your kindness and loyalty: please do not bury me in Egypt.'"
20. See Deuteronomy 13:7, which lists close friends alongside family members, and Psalm 15:3, which also seems to group together friend and family.
21. See Genesis 31:23 where Laban takes his previously unmentioned "*aḥim*" to chase after Jacob. As Cynthia R. Chapman notes, "Words like 'brother' can mean uterine brother, half-brother, cousin, and ally." See her *The House of the Mother: The Social Roles of Maternal Kin in Biblical Hebrew Narrative and Poetry* (New Haven: Yale, 2016), 77.

While family and friends seem to share certain core character-istics, "the comparison of relatives to friends, *as if friendship were the paradigmatic relationship,* a phenomenon familiar to some contempo-rary Westerners – 'my brother/sister/child/parent/cousin is my best friend' – is unattested in biblical texts."[22] Rather, it is family that is the paradigmatic source of relationships in the Bible. Thus, Song of Songs uses that same root *rei'a* to refer to a lover (the *ra'aya*), who says about her male paramour, "If only it could be as with a brother, as if you had nursed at my mother's breast: Then I could kiss you when I met you in the street, and no one would despise me" (Song. 8:1). This passage offers a striking wish to modern ears, but illuminates an assumption of a shared emotional categorization between friend and family member that differs in degree, with the family serving as the baseline.[23]

> [Family members are] paradigmatic intimates…characterized by intimacy, harmony, loyalty, support (particularly in times of need), and respect for hierarchy, [they] serve as a model for rela-tionships, both voluntary and involuntary, that extend beyond the immediate family circle and larger kin group. Ties between a deity and his or her worshipers, a king and his people, human treaty partners, members of professional classes, and friends are all shaped by, at least in part, by the rhetoric and/or presuppositions of idealized familial relations.[24]

---

22. Olyan, 25. Emphasis mine.
23. As Olyan (89) observes:

> The use of friendship vocabulary for sexual intimates further complicates things…. Could it be that biblical constructions of friendship might potentially include a sexual dimension? Or is the friendship language used of husbands, wives, and lovers to be understood simply as metaphorical, intended to enrich the poetic imagery of the text in some way…by adding yet another axis of emotional intimacy to the portrait of the relationship… [maybe] it makes the portrayal of the relationship between the lovers more emotionally complex without suggesting anything about the nature of friendship per se.

24. Olyan, 11–12.

Unlike friendship, however, a family association is involuntary, and there are distinct formal obligations. Only family members display signs of mourning (though friends offer comfort when one of them is mourning over a family member);[25] only family members have an obligation to honor,[26] and there are multiple restrictions with respect to inter-family sexual relationships (see Lev., chapters 18 and 20). Other family-specific rituals include levirate marriage (*yibum;* see Deut. 25:5), burial (Gen. 47:30), redemption of a poor family relative who has sold himself into servitude (Lev. 25:47–49), and serving as a blood avenger (*go'el hadam*).[27]

THE PROBLEM OF FRIENDSHIP IN CHRISTIANITY

It is interesting to briefly note that, as Nehamas points out, friendship is a theologically problematic concept for Christianity, a faith premised on the belief that Jesus loves all of humanity equally.

> The love of an infinite being, who loves everything and everyone unconditionally, translated into the earth's finite realm, becomes love for everyone God loves. And that is absolutely everyone – including, in particular, one's enemies – in loving whom one ultimately loves God himself. *Friendship, though, unlike Christian love, involves loving some people more than the rest of the world,* toward which, though not necessarily ill-disposed, friends may remain more or less emotionally indifferent.[28]

According to the Christian theologian Søren Kierkegaard, "to distinguish one person from the rest of the world, to love one in preference

---

25. While Job's friends cry, tear their clothes, and throw dust (2:12), the text doesn't describe this as "mourning," contra "Jacob rent his clothes, put sackcloth on his loins, and observed mourning for his son many days" (Gen. 37:34). Similarly, "paying a *shiva* visit" is something friends do, while it is only the family members themselves who do the actual mourning.
26. Exodus 20:12: "Honor your father and your mother."
27. Numbers 35:12, which, based on other occurrences of the root "*go'el*" as well as ancient Near Eastern parallels, is assumed to refer to a blood relative.
28. Nehamas, 31. Emphasis mine.

to others, is 'a mockery of God.'"[29] This Christian principle appears to contrast with the very nature of "friendship... [which] is inconceivable without thinking that it is perfectly all right to treat some people differently from the way we treat everyone else, to give them preference and pride of place, simply because they are our friends."[30]

FRIENDSHIP IN RUTH: A CASE STUDY

Keeping in mind this brief survey of friendship as explored in Western conceptualizations and the Bible – its core components and expectations, and the overlap and distinctions between friendships and familial relationships – let us examine the Book of Ruth's portrayal of the nature of friendship, with a focus on the dynamic between Ruth and Naomi.[31] This friendship is a unique one, as it is the only biblical friendship between two named women, it spans the length of an entire book, and it consists of a dynamic between two individuals of vastly different cultural backgrounds and ages.

After the death of Ruth's husband, Mahlon, her association with Naomi becomes a voluntary one, lacking in any formal obligation or affiliation. Notably, Naomi actively attempts to dissuade Ruth and Orpah (the wife of Naomi's other deceased son) from joining Naomi on her journey back to Bethlehem:

> But Naomi said to her two daughters-in-law, "Turn back, each of you to her mother's house. May the Lord deal kindly with you, as you have dealt with the dead and with me!" (1:8)

With no remaining familial bond between the women, and thus no obligation or cultural expectation for them to stay together, Orpah is

---

29. *Works of Love*, trans. Howard and Edna Hong (Princeton: Princeton University Press, 1998), 37.
30. Ibid., 57, 59.
31. There are many other rich biblical narratives of friendship well worth analysis through the prism of friendship studies, including most famously David and Jonathan, as well as that of Job and his friends, and Jephthah's daughter and her friends (Judges ch. 11), among others.

persuaded to return home to her people.[32] And yet, Ruth clings to Naomi, a voluntary association which is arguably best categorized as a friendship:

> They broke into weeping again, and Orpah kissed her mother-in-law farewell. But Ruth clung to her. (Ruth 1:14)[33]

Though the meaning of the name "Ruth" is debated, some suggest it stems from that very same root *"rei'a,"* an etymological signal that Ruth is the quintessential friend. In fact, the *Peshitta*, the Syriac translation of the Bible, renders her name *Rei'ut*.[34] As theologian and novelist C. S. Lewis describes, friendship is "a sort of secession, even a rebellion... a pocket of potential resistance... [because friends] have in common some insight or interest or even taste which the others do not share."[35] Here we see this manifest – Ruth "rebels" against her native society, one which Orpah readily returns to, and aligns herself with Naomi and the Israelite people. Ruth demonstrates that "friends recognize in one another something they don't find in the rest of the world."[36] In essence, through friendship one testifies that:

> Our friendship promises – and continues to promise, as long as it lasts – a better future; but all that I can know about that future

---

32. Though the midrashic tradition has judged Orpah negatively for this decision (see Dr. Ziegler's chapter in this volume, "The Roots of the Book of Ruth," pp. 241–242), the text itself does not do so, and many readers of Ruth have noted that Orpah's decision is justifiable on moral grounds. In particular, Naomi told Orpah to go back home and former family members do not have formal obligations toward one another, neither in the Bible, nor in the modern era.

33. Olyan (p. 68) is quick to note that "the author's perpetuation of the in-law terminology [i.e., 'her mother-in-law'] may be intended to underscore the continuing importance of the two women's tie to the family of their dead husbands and to foreshadow future positive developments for them both in the context of that family."

34. I thank Alex Maged for noting this possible meaning of the name in personal correspondence. See Yael Ziegler, *Ruth: From Alienation to Monarchy*, Maggid Studies in Tanakh (Jerusalem: Maggid, 2015), 165, who suggests it while noting it is a "stretch." Scholars have not reached a consensus on the actual etymology of Ruth's name.

35. *The Four Loves*, cited in Nehamas, 203.

36. Nehamas, 51.

is that I can't approach it with anyone but you .... [T]he promise friendship makes can be very firm but, however firm it is, its fulfillment is never guaranteed: ready as I am to come to want new things and harbor new wishes because of your own desires and wishes, I also can't know what will become of me once these have a hand in shaping my life.[37]

Ruth then offers her loyalty to Naomi, pledged until death:

> But Ruth replied, "Do not urge me to leave you, to turn back and not follow you. For wherever you go, I will go; wherever you lodge, I will lodge; your people shall be my people, and your God my God. Where you die, I will die, and there I will be buried. Thus and more may the Lord do to me if anything but death parts me from you." (Ruth 1:16–17)

As Nehamas notes, "Dying for the sake of one's friend may perhaps be the noblest expression of friendship, and a friendship that leads to it may make the friends' lives altogether worth living."[38] This blurring of distinction between Ruth and Naomi, 'til death do them part, is a unique moral bond. Possibly, it is the ultimate manifestation of Leviticus' commandment to "love your fellow as yourself."[39] As contemporary scholar Laurie Zoloth-Dorfman elaborates:

> What makes the bond possible and, hence, moral and meaningful is that Ruth has recognized Naomi as a self, taken on the responsibility of the entire capacity of her being and in that moment truly has been able to be a self in the text. She sees herself as Naomi, as paired as surely as Adam and Eve were paired, a coupling of similar selves in the darkness of the world .... The moral encounter involves a decentering of being, an opening up

---

37. Ibid., 135.
38. Ibid, 69.
39. I thank Alex Maged for this suggestion.

to the plurality and, indeed, to the infinity of possibility in the presence of the other.[40]

The story continues when, after arriving in Bethlehem, Ruth happens upon the field of Boaz, a relative of Naomi's. He allows her to glean in the field, and advises her:

> Listen to me, daughter. Don't go to glean in another field. Don't go elsewhere, but stay here close to my girls. (Ruth 2:8)

It is the fellow females in the field best positioned to provide support to the mendicant Ruth as she strives to ensure economic support for herself and Naomi. "Feminism pays particular interest to friendship because it can be deeply liberating for those who don't fit well into society's existing structures: friendships can be agents of social change."[41] As in chapter 1, where it is the women of Bethlehem who address the returned Naomi, and in the later chapter 4, where the women bless Naomi upon the marriage of Ruth and Boaz and bestow a name upon the child born of that union, here, too, women play the crucial role of social support in a patriarchal context.[42]

Though Boaz allows Ruth protection and privileges in the field, he does not ensure her and Naomi's sustained financial viability. Thus, in chapter 3, Ruth, on the advice of Naomi, puts on special clothing and goes down to the threshing floor of Boaz. Naomi's instructions to Ruth on what she should do as she heads toward Boaz contain a few discrepancies between how the Hebrew words are read and how they are written. These discrepancies seem to blur the distinction between the two

---

40. "An Ethics of Encounter: Private Choices and Public Acts," ed. Elliot N. Dorff and Louis E. Newman, *Contemporary Jewish Ethics and Morality: A Reader* (Oxford: Oxford University Press, 1995), 226–227.

41. Ibid., 55.

42. Once, when teaching this chapter in my synagogue, Cong. Ahavath Torah in Englewood, NJ, an audience member suggested, only half in jest, that maybe the women of Bethlehem named the baby since they didn't trust Naomi to name it, given that she had named her own children Mahlon and Chilion, loosely translated as "Sickness" and "Destruction." The person who made this observation happened to be named Peretz, whose name is mentioned in the verse immediately preceding the marriage of Boaz and Ruth.

women, making it seem as if one is superimposed on the other, to the point where it's almost unclear who it is getting dressed and going to the threshing floor. These verses read:

> So bathe, anoint yourself, dress up, and go down [written: *and I will go down*] to the threshing floor. But do not disclose yourself to the man until he has finished eating and drinking. When he lies down, note the place where he lies down, and go over and uncover his feet and lie down [written: *and I will lie down*]. He will tell you what you are to do. (Ruth 3:3–4)

"'A friend is another self' [said Aristotle] … some of us think of our friends as a kind of mirror in which we can see and come to know ourselves as we couldn't possibly do on our own, as another self."[43] Contemporary scholar Rachel E. Adelman asks:

> Does Naomi intend Ruth to take along her mother-in-law's shadow as she wraps herself up in her garments and descends to the threshing floor? … is Ruth assuming an alternative identity, perhaps the identity of Naomi herself? Do these "slips of the tongue" and "pen" gesture at the older woman's desire to lie at the man's feet, to bear his child, to be the one who will redeem herself of widowhood…. Leah, Tamar and Ruth … each of the three women … pretends to be another woman in bed. While Leah simulates Rachel, and Tamar dresses up as a harlot, it is Naomi's identity that Ruth assumes.[44]

After Ruth succeeds in inspiring Boaz to take action, Boaz and Ruth are married. They bear a child, Obed, and the women of Bethlehem joyously react:

> And the women said to Naomi, "Blessed be the Lord, who has not withheld a redeemer from you today! May his name be

---

43. Nehamas, 11.
44. *The Female Ruse: Women's Deception and Divine Sanction in the Hebrew Bible* (Sheffield: Sheffield Phoenix Press, 2015), 116–117.

perpetuated in Israel! He will renew your life and sustain your old age; for he is born of your daughter-in-law, who loves you and is better to you than seven sons." (Ruth 4:14–15)

This encomium – in which God Himself is invoked – of Ruth's love for Naomi, a dynamic which long ago transitioned from daughter-in-law to friend, brings to mind the nineteenth-century American philosopher and poet Ralph Waldo Emerson's statement that "[friendship is] a select and sacred relation, which is a kind of absolute, and which even leaves the language of love suspicious and common, so much is this purer, and nothing is so much divine."[45]

The salvific effect Ruth has had on Naomi has reached its culmination. Just as Naomi regained her youth vicariously through Ruth's actions at the threshing floor, she now embraces Ruth's baby – the product, albeit indirectly, of that nighttime interaction – as its nurse (4:16). Though Naomi had claimed, upon her return after years in Moab, to be empty (1:21), she has been made full by Ruth. "Could our friends be irreplaceable because, just as with metaphors, we never fully know what their role in our life may be? Could our friends be, in the sense that metaphors are, inexhaustible?"[46] Ruth has elevated Naomi from bereft and bitter widow to woman renewed and redeemed. We never know what effect our friendships will have through the vicissitudes of life and on our personal development and fulfillment. After all:

> What we "really" are is not a hidden, unchanging nature that is from within us from the beginning, sometime unearthed and brought to light. It is something that we become – the result, but not the overall purpose, of countless activities and the vagaries of life…. Our love for our friends is also entwined with a sense that we haven't yet exhausted what's good in ourselves. "Friends bring out the best in one another."… Our friends also have an idea of what we are or should be – an idea that, given our friendship, we are apt to take seriously. That is what we see of ourselves in them:

---

45. *Essays and Letters*, cited in Nehamas, 12.
46. Nehamas, 125.

not, as Aristotle may have thought, our virtuous similarities but a picture, an interpretation of who we are to them that we can use – not uncritically – to guide our self-formation.[47]

Though Naomi and Ruth shared a history as mother-in-law and daughter-in-law, it was not these broken family ties that kept them together; rather, it was the bonds of friendship. In reflecting on his own lifelong friends, Nehamas offers what is a rather fitting conclusion for this analysis of the dynamic of Ruth and Naomi:

> When I realized that these people are who they have come to be, at least in part (and it is a large part) because of their friendship, I also realized that friendship, even when motivated by a desire to regain a common past, is also crucial in forging a different future.... Friendship is crucial to what most of us come to be in life.[48]

Of course, we will never know exactly what motivated Ruth to stick with Naomi despite their troubles and to make a choice different from Orpah's: Was Ruth's fealty and friendship premised on the shared past they had as members of a family? Was it inspired by Naomi's quiet faith despite the harshness of her circumstances? Was it born of admiration for Naomi's virtue? While we cannot know for sure, we do know that Ruth turned to Naomi and said, in essence:

> You got troubles, I've got 'em too
> There isn't anything I wouldn't do for you
> We stick together and see it through
> Cause you've got a friend in me.[49]

---

47. Ibid., 211–212, 223. Elie Wiesel, in his meditation on his life's work composed after undergoing heart surgery, remarked that "friendship contains an element of immortality." See *Open Heart* (New York: Schocken, 2015), 55.

48. Ibid., 3–4.

49. Many thanks to Alex Maged and Ilana Kurshan for their review of this chapter and their many helpful suggestions, and Prof. Christine Hayes for bringing the Piercy poem to my attention.

Love in the Time of Omer

Ilana Kurshan

The period of the Omer, the seven weeks that link the barley offering of Pesaḥ with the wheat offering of Shavuot, is bookended by two love stories. When we first begin counting the Omer, we read Song of Songs, a celebration of young love in all its joy and innocence. Seven weeks later, on Shavuot, we chant the Book of Ruth, a more sobering tale of two women who rebuild a family devastated by loss. In the period of the Omer, spanning Pesaḥ and Shavuot, we experience the shift from young love to mature love and from freedom to redemption.

Song of Songs is appropriate for Pesaḥ, and not just because it celebrates the blossoming of spring. In its description of carefree, unbounded lovers leaping over the hills and peering through the lattices, the book is its own feast of freedom: the freedom to love and be loved without any concerns or responsibilities. The lovers sing each other's praises in elaborate metaphors invoking fine gold, strings of jewels, and spangles of silver, adorning one another in verse after verse. As if in defiance of time itself, the entire book of Song of Songs – eight chapters in total – has no narrative progression and no plot development. The young man and woman appear frozen in time, like the lovers depicted in John Keats' "Ode to Grecian Urn":

Fair youth, beneath the trees, thou canst not leave
Thy song, nor ever can those trees be bare;
Bold Lover, never, never canst thou kiss;
Though winning near the goal – yet, do not grieve;
She cannot fade, though thou hast not thy bliss
Forever wilt thou love, and she be fair!

In this poem, Keats describes an ancient Greek vase whose surface depicts one lover running after another. Since they exist in the static immobility of sculpture, they will never catch up to each other and embrace. They are, as Keats says, "Forever warm and still to be enjoyed / Forever panting and forever young." Their love is eternal and timeless, like the lovers in the last verse of Song of Songs who are still hurrying off to the hills of spices.

The freedom of Pesaḥ gives way to the legal strictures of Shavuot, where we are bound – albeit also blessed – by the responsibility of observing the mitzvot of the Torah. We are no longer just a liberated people; we are a people consecrated unto God in a divine covenant. The contrast between the two holidays is evidenced also in the two books. Ruth, unlike Song of Songs, is a story of love but also of economics, politics, and history. From the very first verse, we are immediately situated in a particular geographic and chronological context: "In the days when the judges ruled, there was a famine in the land, and a man of Bethlehem in Judah, with his wife and two sons, went to reside in the country of Moab" (1:1). Unlike Song of Songs, the Book of Ruth unfolds sequentially over time, with a clear narrative progression: Elimelech's family travels to Moab to escape famine; Elimelech dies; Mahlon and Chilion get married; Mahlon and Chilion die; Naomi sets off on her own – from famine to death to marriage to moving, this book is filled with the stuff of real life.

Is the Book of Ruth a love story? Perhaps the most romantic scene takes place not between the characters who ultimately marry one another, but between Ruth and Naomi. In the book's opening verses, Naomi urges Ruth and Orpah to "turn back" to their mothers' homes, where they are likely to have better luck finding new husbands. "Have I any more sons in my body who might be husbands for you?" (1:11) she asks them, urging them a second time to "turn back." In Song of Songs, there is also a repeated exhortation to turn back, albeit for very different reasons: "Turn back, turn back, O maid of Shulem! Turn back, turn back, that we may gaze upon you" (7:1). The lover wants his maid to turn back so that he may feast his eyes on her beauty – on her rounded thighs like jewels, and the goblet of her belly.

Naomi, who has no babies and no food in her belly, does not want Ruth and Orpah to be saddled with her, and so she kisses them goodbye with bitter lips – unlike the kisses of the lovers in Song of Songs, which are sweeter than wine. But Ruth has no intention of turning back. She is devoted to her mother-in-law, and she declares in language arguably as passionate and poetic as Song of Songs: "Do not urge me to leave you, to turn back and not follow you. For wherever you go, I will go. Wherever you lodge, I will lodge. Your people shall be my people, and your God my God. Where you die, I will die, and there I will be buried. Thus and more may the Lord do to me if anything but death parts me from you" (1:16–17). The lovers in Song of Songs may declare, "Let me be a seal upon your heart, like the seal upon your hand, for love is as fierce of death" (8:6), but this rhetoric seems to be merely the well-meaning declarations of those whose love has never been put to the test. Ruth does not ask to be set as a seal on Naomi's heart; she actually does it, binding her destiny to that of her mother-in-law and demonstrating after the loss of her husband that she has already internalized the lesson that love is fiercer than death.

Ruth learns this lesson when it comes to Boaz as well. She understands that if she can win Boaz's love, she and Naomi will survive in Moab. And so for Ruth, courting Boaz is a response to the exigencies of the moment; it is something she must do to save herself and her mother-in-law from the dangers of being unattached women in a foreign land. Boaz's reapers are hard at work in the fields when Ruth arrives, and she gleans behind them, catching whatever they let fall. Keats invokes the pathos of her situation when he writes in "Ode to a Nightingale" of "Ruth, when sick for home, she stood in tears amid the alien corn." With the exception of her mother-in-law, no one knows her and she knows no one. She is a stranger in a strange land, and as Keats suggests, she is probably homesick.

The lovers in Song of Songs are not homesick but lovesick: "Refresh me with apples for I am sick with love" (2:5), one lover tells the other. They pluck myrrh and spices and linger in the fields embracing one another, as if they have all the time in the world. These are not lovers who need to support themselves or find a roof to put over their heads – they can sustain themselves with raisin cakes and fall asleep in the nut groves to the voice of the turtledoves. Ruth and Naomi, in contrast, are concerned with their sustenance and their survival: Naomi has come to Moab from Beit Leḥem, the "house of bread" where there is ironically no bread to eat, and Ruth is grateful when, at the end of a day of gleaning, Boaz hands her roasted grain and invites her to dip her bread in astringent vinegar.

While Ruth dines on vinegar-soaked bread, the lovers in Song of Songs eat honey from the honeycomb and celebrate the sweetness of the ripe fig and the budding vine, which are analogized to the blossoming of young love. These lovers celebrate one another's beauty by invoking the natural world around them: "Like a lily among thorns, so is my darling among the maidens" (2:2). In the Book of Ruth, though, there are no maidens. Naomi regards herself as past her prime: "I am too old to be married," she tells Ruth and Orpah (1:12). And while Ruth may be beautiful, her appearance is never mentioned in the text. We are not told what she looks like or whether Boaz finds her attractive. She finds favor in her kinsman's eyes not because of her beauty but because of her background: when Ruth asks Boaz why he is so kind to her, he responds, "I have been told of all that you did for your mother-in-law after the death of your husband, how you left your father and mother and the land of your birth and came to a people you had not known before. May the Lord reward your deeds" (2:12).

This is one of several blessings that appear throughout the Book of Ruth. Naomi blesses Ruth and Orpah; Naomi blesses Boaz for being kind to Ruth; and the townspeople bless Ruth and the baby born to Naomi through her. These blessings are intended to serve the practical purpose of conferring good fortune. In Song of Songs, though, the language is not one of blessing but of blazon: the lovers catalogue one another's attributes – the belly like a heap of wheat, the hair like a flock of goats. What is poetry in Song of Songs becomes practicality in the

Book of Ruth: the wheat is all being busily harvested in the fields and if there were any goats, they would probably be promptly milked, and not invoked in rich metaphors.

The wheat and barley fields are the setting for much of the Book of Ruth, whereas Song of Songs takes place in a garden. The female lover in Song of Songs is described as a "locked garden," perhaps a reference to her virginity and to all that about her which has yet to be discovered: "Let us see if the vine has flowered, if its blossoms have opened, if the pomegranates are in bloom" (7:13). In contrast, Ruth is not a locked garden or a "still unravished bride," as Keats would have it, but a widow who has already experienced hunger, loss, and dislocation. She cannot afford to play games, and so she doesn't waste her time hiding in the crannies of the rock or pretending to be hard-to-get like a scampering fox. She has no choice but to be more forward, and so she lets herself into the granary, lies down on the floor beside a sleeping Boaz, and asks him to spread out his robe over her.

"Do not awaken or rouse love until it please," adjures the lover in Song of Songs on three separate occasions, but Ruth does not have the luxury of waiting for the perfect spring day to get married. She cannot risk missing the knock of her beloved on her door merely because she does not want to soil her feet or don her robe. Instead, she holds out her shawl to Boaz after their tryst on the granary floor, and he counts out six measures of barley for her to take home. "If a man offered all his wealth for love, he would be laughed to scorn" (8:7), declare the naïve young lovers in Song of Songs, untutored in the harsh ways of the world; and yet this is exactly what Boaz does, and he is blessed by the townspeople and celebrated for it.

Boaz marries Ruth, but only after first offering her to someone else – as if to suggest that he is far more concerned about Ruth's welfare than about his exclusive relationship with her. In the final chapter of the Book of Ruth, Boaz summons an unnamed redeemer and asks is he is willing to redeem Naomi's late husband's land. At first the redeemer is amenable, but once he realizes that this entails marrying Ruth as well, he reneges. At that point Boaz rather gallantly declares before all the townspeople that he is acquiring both the field and the woman – in that order! – "so as to perpetuate the name of the deceased upon his estate" (4:10). He marries Ruth to protect her family's property, offering his love for the sake of her wealth. It is not exactly a fairy tale ending.

Did Boaz and Ruth live happily ever after? We do not know. As the Book of Ruth draws to a close, the image that lingers is not one of the newly married couple being congratulated by the townspeople, but of the young widow trying her luck on the threshing floor. It is an image reminiscent of Keats' "Ode to Autumn," in which the poet personifies Autumn as a female goddess sitting on a granary floor, her hair blowing in the wind:

> Sometimes whoever seeks abroad may find
> Thee sitting careless on a granary floor,
> Thy hair soft-lifted by the winnowing wind;
> Or on a half-reap'd furrow sound asleep,
> Drowsed with the fume of poppies....
> And sometimes like a gleaner thou dost keep
> Steady thy laden head across a brook;
> Or by a cider-press, with patient look,
> Thou watchest the last oozings, hours by hours.

This is a poem about labor not leisure, and about industry not idleness. The breath like the fragrance of apples from Song of Songs has been replaced with the oozings of the cider press. The blossoming Rose of Sharon has given way to the drowsy poppy. And the lover has become the gleaner. Ruth, who has tasted the bitter fruits of loss and hunger, knows that there is no Song of Songs for her to sing, a notion captured by Keats in the very next stanza:

> Where are the songs of Spring? Ay, where are they?
> Think not of them, thou hast thy music too,
> While barre´d clouds bloom the soft-dying day
> And touch the stubble-plains with rosy hue;
> Then in a wailful choir the small gnats mourn....
> The redbreast whistles from a garden-croft;
> And gathering swallows twitter in the skies.

It is these gathering swallows, and not the voice of the turtledove, that serve as harbinger of the Messiah. While the lovers in Song of Songs are still frolicking amidst the gardens and valleys, Ruth gives birth to the ancestor of David. Redemption comes not from the carefree freedom of Song of Songs, which we chant on the feast of freedom that is Pesah, but from a life bound by Torah and mitzvot, which we celebrate on Shavuot.

The holiday of Shavuot is often analogized to a wedding between God and Israel, with the Torah as the *ketuba* handed from bride to groom. The Talmud in Tractate Taanit (26b) interprets the mention of a wedding day in Song of Songs (3:11) as a reference to the day the Torah was given on Sinai. If so, then the Omer serves as a sort of engagement period: on Pesah we celebrate our relationship with God like young lovers, and on Shavuot we accept all the commitments that this relationship entails. In between these two festivals, the period of the Omer reminds us that perhaps the love into which we inevitably grow is not that of the fleeing lovers on the urn, but of the gleaners who winnow on the granary floor.

Betrothal and Betrayal in Biblical and World Literature

Alex Maged

Ifyou spend enough time studying the works of particular authors or playwrights, their storylines can start to feel familiar. Much of Sophoclean tragedy, for instance, involves a ruler or warrior of noble stock whose hubris incites the wrath of the gods and leads to his eventual demise. Conversely, Jane Austen's novels are dominated by the drama of young ladies of humble economic means who hope to win the hearts of gentlemen outside their social class. Franz Kafka's characters, meanwhile, suffer arbitrarily at the hands of uncaring, inaccessible bureaucrats. Chaim Potok's personalities struggle to strike the appropriate balance between tradition and modernity. Arthur Miller's subjects pursue in vain the "American dream." The list goes on.

In literary terms, "genre" is the word that we use to refer to a group of works that share the same basic form, style, or subject. Within a given genre, you can often identify one or more "stock characters" – stereotypical protagonists or antagonists whose personalities and behaviors are familiar to audiences by dint of their frequent recurrence. And the set of highly particular circumstances in which these characters inevitably find themselves are called "type-scenes."

Yet "type-scenes" do not belong exclusively to works of fiction. In a way, they are not even limited to literary contexts. If, as the saying goes, history does indeed "repeat itself," at least to some degree, then type-scenes exist independent of human contrivance. Indeed, they form the framework of human life, within which we exercise our freedom of will and chart our personal trajectories. Our "situations," in other words, are often remarkably similar to those of other people. But it is how we decide to act within those situations that distinguishes us as individuals.

Perhaps nowhere is this truth more poignantly expressed than in our Tanakh. Jewish and secular scholars alike have long been aware of the fact that many biblical episodes exhibit common narrative arcs – whether it's the younger brother who is chosen over the elder,[1] the husband who asks his wife to pretend that she's his sister,[2] or the woman who spends years agonizing to conceive before she finally becomes a mother.[3] Yet it was not until a few decades ago that the term "type-scene" was applied to these parallel plots, by the Jewish professor of Hebrew and comparative literature Robert Alter. Alter was also among the earliest scholars to articulate a methodology for mining from these type-scenes the full measure of their meaning.

In his book, *The Art of Biblical Narrative*,[4] Alter looks specifically at what he dubs the "betrothal scene." This scene generally features a man in a foreign land who meets his wife-to-be by a well of water and receives from her father an invitation to join the family for a meal. Obvious occurrences of the scene include Genesis 24 (Isaac, by proxy, and Rebecca); Genesis 29 (Jacob and Rachel); and Exodus 2 (Moses and Zipporah). From these scenes, and others like them, Alter constructs a case study to demonstrate how one ought to approach

---

1. For example, Hevel over Cain; Isaac over Ishmael; Jacob over Esau; Joseph over his brothers; and Ephraim over Manasseh.
2. For example, Abraham asking his wife Sarah to do so before Pharaoh; and again, before Avimelech; and Isaac, too, asking his wife, Rebecca, to do so before Avimelech.
3. For example, Sarah, Rebecca, Rachel, Tamar, Hannah, and Manoah's wife.
4. New York: Basic Books, 1981.

type-scenes throughout Tanakh. Of his many insights, three stand out in particular:

(1) *The similarities between type-scenes symbolically express the essential features of the situation.*

   Genesis 24, Genesis 29, and Exodus 2 all tell tales of men meeting their wives. In this context, the foreign land, on Alter's reading, symbolizes the foreignness of marriage; the well symbolizes the couple's fertility; and the invitation to join the father for a meal inside the home symbolizes the absorption of the husband into his new family.

(2) *The differences between type-scenes symbolically express the defining characteristics of their protagonist.*

   For example, in Genesis 24, the husband-to-be – Isaac – is not even present. It is his father's servant, Eliezer, who is responsible for choosing the wife on his behalf. This symbolizes Isaac's passive nature, which will continue throughout his life – and throughout his marriage, specifically – and cause him troubles later down the line.

   In Genesis 29, the well is covered with a giant boulder, which Jacob must remove before the flock can drink. This reflects the fact that Jacob does not receive anything easily. He must always overcome adversity in order to achieve what comes naturally to others.

   In Exodus 2, Moses is not greeted by one girl, but seven. His wife to-be, Zipporah, is never named; she never speaks; and she never interacts with Moses directly. This symbolizes the lack of attention that she will receive throughout her marriage. Moses, as a communal leader, is too consumed with "the masses" to dedicate himself to her individual needs.

(3) *The basic type-scene can be significantly altered, to produce a "reversal" scene.*

   In the Book of Ruth, for instance, Alter finds an inverse of the typical betrothal scene. Here it is not the man, but the woman, Ruth, who finds herself in a foreign land; it is not the maidens, but the lads, who draw the water; and it is not the husband who courts the wife, but she who courts him.[5] In a sense, then, the Book of Ruth constitutes a sharp reversal of the trend that weaves itself throughout the rest of Tanakh.[6] This is an idea to which we shall return later.

Needless to say, Alter's treatment of biblical type-scenes involves far more than the ideas presented here. Rather than reproducing Alter's study on type-scenes in its entirety, however, let us see if we can contribute to it another chapter. Specifically, our goal in this essay shall be to propose a type-scene that is closely related to the one examined by Alter, though which he never identifies in his work. It is not the "betrothal scene," but a scene that often comes immediately on its heels; we might term it the "betrayal scene."

The possibility of a "betrayal scene" is intimated as early as the second chapter of Genesis, as the first husband in human history beholds his newly created wife:

> And the man said: "This is now bone of my bones, and flesh of my flesh; she shall be called Woman, because she was taken out of Man." *Therefore shall a man leave his father and his mother,* and shall cleave unto his wife, and they shall be one flesh. (Gen. 2:3)

---

5. To Alter's observations we might add: Whereas the father of the daughter generally invites the son into the house to break bread, in the Book of Ruth it is Boaz's threshing floor into which Ruth invites herself. Ruth is entering at the first stage of the bread-making process; she does not receive the finished product (a detail that is especially ironic when one considers that the name of the city in which she finds herself is Beit Leḥem – literally, "the house of bread"). Indeed, the entire story unfolds during the wheat harvest, and it is in a wheat field that Ruth first meets Boaz. It seems that the replacement of bread/family home with wheat/threshing floor symbolizes the fact that neither Ruth nor Boaz enters this marriage with an extensive support system: Ruth is an immigrant widow, and Boaz has no close relatives either. Both are "starting from scratch," as it were.

6. More recently, Ezra Zuckerman Sivan has advanced the intriguing possibility of reading the sale of Joseph as a "reverse type-scene." See his "Intergenerational Fumbling: The Sale of Joseph as an Anti-Well Scene" in *Me'orei Ha'eish* (Brookline: Young Israel of Brookline, 2017). Yael Ziegler also revisits Alter's theory of "type-scenes" and its application to the book of Ruth in *Ruth: From Alienation to Monarchy,* Maggid Studies in Tanakh (Jerusalem: Maggid, 2015).

Adam sees Eve and is immediately struck by a sense of ontic belonging. Somehow, Adam intuits, he and Eve are meant to "be one." Yet even as Adam waxes poetic on the potential of the male-female relationship, the Torah interrupts with an ominous observation: for man to *cleave* to his wife, he must first *leave* his father and mother. His closeness with his partner costs him a measure of his closeness with his parents.

Whether this verse should be read descriptively ("this is how it is") or prescriptively ("this is how it ought to be") is, at this point in the Torah, difficult to discern. Notice, however, that the nature of man's relationship to his *other* set of parents – namely, his parents-in-law – is neither described *nor* prescribed in this passage. It is left for each individual to determine on his own.

This, then, is the genesis of the betrayal scene. If, as Alter teaches us, the betrothal scene ends when the father invites his new son into the family home, the betrayal scene begins when the son attempts to leave that home. There are at least six such "taking leave of the in-laws" scenes throughout Tanakh. Like all type-scenes, they vary, sometimes significantly, from one to the next. But the basic storyline is rather consistent. With that outline, let us now proceed to present our six proposed "betrayal scenes." In each case, we will cite the relevant passages at length, emphasize recurrent motifs, and offer a few brief notes of commentary.

1. ELIEZER AND BETHUEL (GENESIS)

And the servant said unto him: "*What if the woman will not be willing to follow me unto this land;* must I needs bring thy son back unto the land from whence thou camest?" And Abraham said unto him: "Beware thou that thou *bring not my son back thither* (Gen. 24:5–6)

And they [Abraham's servant and Rebecca's family] did eat and drink, he and the men that were with him, and *tarried all night*; and they rose up in the morning, and he said: "*Send me away unto my master.*" And her brother and her mother said: "*Let the damsel*

> *abide with us a few days, at the least ten; after that she shall go."* And he said unto them: *"Delay me not,* seeing the Lord hath prospered my way; send me away that I may go to my master." And they said: "We will call the damsel, and inquire at her mouth." And they called Rebecca, and said unto her: "Wilt thou go with this man?" And she said: "I will go." (Gen. 24:54–58)

Our first "betrayal scene" occurs when Abraham sends his servant – presumably Eliezer, though the text does not identify him as such – to find a wife for Isaac. As in its corresponding "betrothal scene," Isaac, the husband-to-be, is conspicuously missing here. Yet Eliezer wisely predicts that this convenient absence may not prevent a future father-in-law from attempting to keep Isaac close all the same. Precisely because Eliezer realizes how difficult it may be to extricate the daughter from her father's home does he inquire from the outset regarding how he ought to proceed should such a scenario unfold (as indeed it does). Apparently, then, the conflict underlying the "betrayal scene" was common enough that Eliezer understood that he should prepare for it.

So did Abraham. Indeed, Isaac's betrayal scene is unique in that it offers us the perspective not only of the in-laws, but also of the father, each of whom wants the son/daughter to stay with them. Abraham wants Isaac to continue the covenantal legacy of his father in Canaan. Rebecca's brother and mother, meanwhile, attempt to delay her departure – with the ultimate hope, no doubt, that she will in fact never leave, and that Isaac will journey to her instead. But Eliezer and Rebecca quash that plan immediately.

Part of this may have to do with the absence of yet another critical figure: Bethuel. Though present to meet Eliezer the previous evening, Bethuel curiously disappears the next morning. This scene, then, holds the distinction of being the only one in which not only the son-in-law, but also the father-in-law, are nowhere to be found. So it is no coincidence that Eliezer and Rebecca have a much easier time leaving the father's home than do most of the figures we will meet shortly; there is little conflict in this scene precisely because neither of the typical parties to that conflict is present to engage in it.

2. JACOB AND LABAN (GENESIS)

And Jacob said unto Laban: "*Give me my wife, for my days are filled, that I may go in unto her...*" (Gen. 29:21)

And it came to pass in the morning that, behold, it was Leah; and he said to Laban: "What is this thou hast done unto me? Did not I serve with thee for Rachel? Wherefore then hast thou beguiled me?" And Laban said: "It is not so done in our place, to give the younger before the first-born. Fulfill the week of this one, and we will give thee the other also for the service which *thou shalt serve with me yet seven other years.*" (Gen. 29:25–27)

And it came to pass, when Rachel had borne Joseph, that Jacob said unto Laban: "*Send me away, that I may go unto mine own place, and to my country.* Give me my wives and my children for whom I have served thee, and *let me go*; for thou knowest my service wherewith I have served thee." And Laban said unto him: "If now I have found favor in thine eyes – I have observed the signs, and the Lord hath blessed me for thy sake." And he said: "Appoint me thy wages, and I will give it." And he said to him, "You know how I have worked for you and how your livestock was with me. For the little that you had before me has increased in multitude, and the Lord blessed you upon my arrival; but now, *when will I, too, make for my own household?*" (Gen. 30:25–30)

And the Lord said unto Jacob: "*Return unto the land of thy fathers, and to thy kindred*; and I will be with thee." (Gen. 31:3)

So he fled with all that he had; and he rose up, and passed over the River, and set his face toward the mountain of Gilead. And it was told Laban on the third day that Jacob was fled. *And Laban took his brethren with him, and pursued after him* seven days' journey; and he overtook him in the mountain of Gilead. (Gen. 31:21–23)

Our second "betrayal scene" occurs when Isaac's son, Jacob, ventures to Haran and falls in love with Rachel. Like his father before him, Jacob seeks a mate from Haran who will join *his* family in Canaan. Yet Laban has seen this scene before, as it were, and is better prepared this time around. Thus, on the night Jacob is scheduled to marry Rachel, Laban substitutes Leah in her stead. This ensures not only that both daughters will find a suitable partner, but also that Rachel, and therefore Jacob, will have no choice but to extend their tenure in Haran – precisely as Laban had once hoped Rebecca and Isaac might.

So the sheer duration of Jacob's delayed return is unique, as far as betrayal scenes go. Indeed, Jacob lingers for a full twenty years in total: seven in return for Leah, seven in return for Rachel, and another six in service of Laban's flock. This is consistent with Alter's observation: things seem to come harder to Jacob than they do to others. Yet in other ways, Jacob's betrayal scene serves as the paradigm for all others. Thus, when Laban notes to Jacob that "Hashem has blessed me on your account," he is, in effect, articulating the position of fathers-in-law throughout these scenes: namely, that our sons add to the wealth and prestige of our household, and that we therefore do not want them to leave. And when Jacob, in turn, retorts "When will I too make for my own household?" he is essentially presenting the rejoinder with which all sons-in-law might counter: We are not content to enlarge the household of somebody else; we want to establish our own households.

3. MOSES AND YITRO (EXODUS)

> And it came to pass *in the course of those exceedingly many days* that the king of Egypt died; and the Children of Israel sighed by reason of the bondage, and they cried, and their cry came up unto God by reason of the bondage. (Ex. 2:23)

> And Moses went and returned to Yitro his father-in-law and said unto him: "*Let me go, I pray thee, and return unto my brethren that are in Egypt, and see whether they be yet alive.*" And Yitro said to Moses: "*Go in peace.*" (Ex. 4:18)

> And Yitro, Moses' father-in-law, came *with his sons and his wife* unto Moses into the wilderness where he was encamped, at the mount of God; and he said unto Moses: "I thy father-in-law Yitro am coming unto thee, and thy wife, and her two sons with her." (Ex. 18:5–6)

Our third betrayal scene involves Moses and Yitro – and, at first glance, it seems to defy the pattern we have until now observed. After all, when Moses requests permission to leave, his father-in-law blesses him to "go in peace." There seems to be no conflict between the two men. Having already witnessed the tension that these sorts of requests are liable to produce, however, we should know better by now than to accept this apparent magnanimity at face value.

Several observations justify such circumspection. Note, for instance, that Moses had by this point *already* tarried with Yitro for "exceedingly many days." Moreover, it seems that, even now, Moses is *not* asking to leave Yitro's home permanently; he is asking to go on a short trip to visit his family, from which Yitro fully expects that Moses will promptly return. In fact, this may explain why Moses' wife and children do not stay with him:[7] once it becomes evident that Moses will be in Egypt for longer than anticipated, Yitro apparently demands – or Moses offers – that Zipporah and the boys return to Midian. Had Yitro not decided to join the Israelites at Mount Sinai – bringing with him Moses' wife and sons – it is reasonable to assume that they would have remained in Midian, waiting patiently for Moses' return.

Indeed, one peculiarity regarding Moses which separates him from the protagonists of the other "betrayal scenes" we have examined thus far is the extent to which his children seem to fall out from under the orbit of his influence. Several biblical genealogies, for instance, omit mention of Moses' progeny (see Ex. 6 and Num. 31). One source even seems to identify his eldest son as the founder of an idolatrous cult (see Judges 18 and Bava Batra 109b). Such curiosities likely contributed to the midrashic view per which Yitro is imagined to have actively interfered in Moses'

---

7. See Exodus 18:1–4, which leaves it clear that Moses' children were not with him during the Exodus.

parenting, by extracting from him a commitment to raise at least one of his sons in accordance with Yitro's polytheistic way of life (see *Mekhilta DeRabbi Yishmael, Yitro*). Yet the earliest hints to such overbearance, of course, actually appear in the scene we are presently examining.

Simultaneously, our scene may also foreshadow Moses' later experience with Pharaoh. Like Yitro, the king of Egypt will also, at one point, permit Moses to depart from him, so long as he leaves behind the children (Ex. 10:11). Indeed, Pharaoh will prove masterful at giving the appearance of granting Moses' request, only to then tack on caveats which fundamentally alter the nature of his acquiescence. So Moses will have to be very clever about the way he negotiates with Pharaoh, and will have to make sure that he takes nothing for granted. In this respect, his tenure in the house of Yitro can be said to have prepared him well.

4. HOBAB AND MOSES (NUMBERS)

> And Moses said unto Hobab, the son of Reuel the Midianite, Moses' father-in-law: "We are journeying unto the place of which the Lord said: I will give it you; *come thou with us*, and we will do thee good; for the Lord hath spoken good concerning Israel." And he said unto him: "*I will not go; but I will depart to mine own land, and to my kindred.*" And he said: "*Leave us not, I pray thee*; forasmuch as thou knowest how we are to encamp in the wilderness, and thou shalt be to us instead of eyes. *And it shall be, if thou go with us, yea, it shall be, that what good soever the Lord shall do unto us, the same will we do unto thee.*" And they set forward from the mount of the Lord three days' journey. (Num. 10:29–33)

Interestingly, the identity of the protagonists in this scene is actually subject to interpretation. "Hobab the son of Reuel the Midianite Moses' father-in-law": depending on how you punctuate that verse, Hobab is either "Moses' father-in-law" or "the son of … Moses' father-in-law," i.e. Moses' brother-in-law.

Both options are intriguing. Either the conflict from the previous scene, left unresolved all these years, is finally drawing to a head here; this time, Moses tries to persuade Yitro to stay with *him*, and perhaps ensure thereby that it is *his* influence which prevails over his wife and children. Or, alternatively – and, in a twist of irony – Moses is now attempting to keep Yitro's *son* away from Yitro, in much the way that Yitro had once kept Moses' son away from Moses.

Also unclear is whether Hobab (be he father-in-law or brother-in-law) ultimately joins the Israelites, or returns to Midian – he responds with silence to Moses' final appeal, and by the next verse, the Israelites are already on their way.

It may be no coincidence that the scenes involving Moses' family are the ones which are the most ambiguous. In choosing not to devote detailed attention to the fate of Moses' family, the Torah is, in a sense, mimicking Moses himself; as leader of the entire nation, Moses, unfortunately, simply could not make his family the object of his near-exclusive focus the way that other patriarchs could. This parallels Alter's previously cited observation concerning the corresponding betrothal scene. Moses, uniquely, is surrounded by seven girls rather than one, and, for Alter, this represents the fact that Moses' interests are always on the collective. He is not one to devote disproportionate attention to any one particular individual – even the one whom he will go on to marry.

5. THE LEVI AND HIS CONCUBINE (JUDGES)

And it came to pass in those days, when there was no king in Israel, that there was a certain Levite sojourning on the farther side of the hill-country of Ephraim, who took to him a concubine out of Bethlehem in Judah. And his concubine played the harlot against him, *and went away from him unto her father's house* to Bethlehem in Judah, and was there the space of four months. And her husband arose, and went after her, to speak kindly unto her, *to bring her back*, having his servant with him, and a couple of asses; and *she brought him into her father's house*; and when the father of the damsel saw him, he rejoiced to meet him. *And his father-in-law, the damsel's father, retained him; and he abode with him three days; so they did eat and drink, and lodged there.* And it came to pass on the fourth day, that they arose early in the morning, and *he rose up to depart*; and the damsel's father said unto his son-in-law:

"Stay thy heart with a morsel of bread, and afterward ye shall go your way." So they sat down, and did eat and drink, both of them together; and the damsel's father said unto the man: *"Be content, I pray thee, and tarry all night,* and let thy heart be merry." *And the man rose up to depart; but his father-in-law urged him, and he lodged there again. And he arose early in the morning on the fifth day to depart; and the damsel's father said: "Stay thy heart, I pray thee, and tarry ye until the day declineth"*; and they did eat, both of them. And when the man *rose up to depart,* he, and his concubine, and his servant, his father-in-law, the damsel's father, said unto him: "Behold, now the day draweth toward evening; *tarry, I pray you, all night*; behold, the day groweth to an end; lodge here, that thy heart may be merry; and tomorrow get you early on your way, that thou mayest go home." *But the man would not tarry that night, but he rose up and departed*, and came over against Jebus – the same is Jerusalem; and there were with him a couple of asses saddled; his concubine also was with him. (Judges 19:1–10)

This is the longest "betrothal" scene, and also the most dramatic of them. It involves multiple attempts to leave on the part of the Levite, and, correspondingly, multiple attempts to keep him there. Also unique to this scene is its setting. It does not actually begin in the house of the father-in-law; only because his daughter runs back to him do we have a "betrayal scene" of which to speak.

These idiosyncrasies are probably best accounted for through recourse to a third: unlike the other women we have studied, our protagonist in this scene is not, in fact, a "wife" – she is a "concubine." As such, she is more likely than the others to have enjoyed greater rights and privileges as part of her father's household than she does as part of her husband's. Indeed, the sense we get is that this concubine was not particularly well treated by this "husband" – hence her desire to return.

Note also that the father-in-law, in this scene, never once voices as a motivation for his conduct a desire to make his own house greater by keeping the Levite there. His aims appear more urgent than that. This father, it seems, understands that his daughter is not faring well under her husband; like all fathers, he simply wishes to protect his child, and buys as much time as he can because he fears that returning with her husband may actually be dangerous for her. Tragically, of course, this premonition proves most prescient: on the very night that the Levite ultimately forces an exit from the father's house, he hands his concubine to a band of hoodlums for assault, before dismembering her himself the next morning.

6. HADAD AND PHARAOH (I KINGS)

> And [Hadad and the Edomites] arose out of Midian, and came to Paran; and they took men with them out of Paran, and they came to Egypt, unto Pharaoh king of Egypt, who gave him a house, and appointed him victuals, and gave him land. And Hadad found great favor in the sight of Pharaoh, so that *he gave him to wife the sister of his own wife,* the sister of Tahpenes the queen.... And when Hadad heard in Egypt that David slept with his fathers, and that Joab the captain of the host was dead, *Hadad said to Pharaoh: "Let me depart, that I may go to mine own country."* Then Pharaoh said unto him: "But what hast thou lacked with me, that, behold, thou seekest to go to thine own country?" And he answered: *"Nothing; nevertheless, let me depart in any case."*
> (I Kings 11:18–19, 21–22)

Our sixth scene is by far the most obscure. It constitutes little more than an editorial aside in the larger story of King Solomon's reign and, fascinatingly, does not even involve the king or anybody in his kingdom. In fact, its protagonists are both foreigners. This speaks, above all, to the ubiquity of the fundamental conflict captured by our various betrayal scenes.

Our scene also betrays just how elemental are the motives which drive said conflict. Asked point blank what he lacks in Egypt, Hadad readily admits that he wants for nothing at all. Nevertheless, Hadad insists on returning home; it is apparently little more than the desire to be in the place that he knows best – and the place where he is best known – which propels him to ask for his leave. This is a simple desire, but a common one.

Indeed, the exchange between Pharaoh and Hadad invites us to consider just how common the desire is. To that end, it should come as no surprise that the "betrayal scene," which we have studied until now as a biblical phenomenon, knows analogues in the annals of external literature as well. Consider, for reference, the following brief citations from the *Tale of Sinuhe* (Egypt, c. twentieth century BCE); from *The Odyssey* (Greece, c. eighth century BCE); and from *Sakuntala and the Ring of Recollection* (India, c. fourth century CE):

> And [Amunenshi] said to me: But look, you are here, and you will stay with me, and I shall do you good. He placed me at the head of his children. He joined me to his eldest daughter. He had me make my choice of his country, from the choicest of what was his.... It was a good land.... He appointed me the ruler of a tribe of the choicest of his country. Provisions and strong drinks were made for me, with wine as a daily supply, and cooked flesh, and roast fowl, as well as wild game.... I spent many years there.... The messenger who went north and south to the Residence would tarry for me. I would make all men tarry. (*The Tale of Sinuhe*, 160–186)

> Nausica said: "If only such a man would be called my husband, living here and content to stay. Well, go on, give him something to eat and drink..." And she told Odysseus: "I can just hear one of the townspeople saying, 'Well who's this tall, handsome stranger trailing along behind Nausica? Where'd she pick him up? She'll probably marry him, some shipwreck she's taken in from parts unknown. He's sure not local...' That's what they'll say, and it will count against me." Alcinous, Nausica's father said: "I would wish that you, being the kind of man that you are, would marry my daughter and stay here and be called my son. I would give you a house filled with possessions if you chose to remain. But no Phaeacian will ever keep you here against your will. As for your send off, you can be sure of it – it will be tomorrow." (*The Odyssey*, selected passage from book VI–VII)

Kanva said: My heart is touched with sadness since Sakuntala must go today; my throat is choked with sobs, my eyes are dulled by worry. If a disciplined ascetic suffers so deeply from love, how do fathers bear the pain of each daughter's leaving? (*Sakuntala and the Ring of Recollection*, IV, 146–154)

We thus observe that tension arising from the desire of children-in-law to establish their independence outside the orbit of their parents-in-law is practically a universal motif in both biblical and world literature.

There is, however, a significant exception to this rule which we must finally consider.

7. RUTH AND NAOMI (RUTH)

The Lord grant you that ye may find rest, each of you in the house of her husband. Then she kissed them; and they lifted up their voice, and wept. And they said unto her: Surely we will return with thee unto thy people. And Naomi said: Turn again, my daughters: why will ye go with me? Are there yet any more sons in my womb, that they may be your husbands? Turn again, my daughters, go your way; for I am too old to have a husband. If I should say, I have hope, if I should have a husband also tonight, and should also bear sons; Would ye tarry for them till they were grown? Would ye stay for them from having husbands? Nay, my daughters; for it grieveth me much for your sakes that the hand of the Lord is gone out against me. And they lifted up their voice, and wept again: and Orpah kissed her mother in law; but Ruth clave unto her. And she said: Behold, thy sister in law is gone back unto her people, and unto her gods: return thou after thy sister in law. And Ruth said: Entreat me not to leave thee, or to return from following after thee: for whither thou goest, I will go; and where thou lodgest, I will lodge: thy people shall be my people, and thy God my God: Where thou diest, will I die, and there will I be buried: the Lord do so to me, and more also, if ought but death part thee and me. When she saw that she was steadfastly minded to go with her, then she left speaking unto her. (Ruth 1:9–18)

This scene from the Book of Ruth is a familiar one. Even forgoing our current analysis, Ruth and Naomi's conduct within it strikes us as especially magnanimous. Yet their behavior is not merely rare; it is positively revolutionary. That is something which we can appreciate fully only within the literary paradigm of the "betrayal scene."

Against all odds which other scenes would by this point have conditioned us to expect, Naomi, the mother-in-law in this scene, actively petitions her daughter-in-law to *leave* her. She does so despite how dependent she is upon her daughter-in-law at this particular juncture in her life, because she knows that Ruth's happiness is likeliest to be found back in her own homeland, where she can rebuild her own life unburdened by the task of caring for Naomi.

Yet Ruth also overturns precedent, by insisting to *stay*. She knows, as Naomi does, that her prospects of establishing herself in Judea are slim at best. But this does not concern Ruth. Like Naomi, Ruth is not looking out for her own best interest; neither woman is motivated by building her *own* name. They are, instead, looking out for each other. In that way, this scene constitutes an "inverted" type-scene – just as, Alter claimed, Ruth's *betrothal* scene is inverted as well.

Nor is it likely a coincidence that this biblical book in particular is the one which reverses the trend. The story of Ruth, after all, is the story of founding Israel's monarchic line – and the monarchy is particularly liable to quick descent into the trivial pettiness of family feud, dynastic dispute, civil war, and other such dysfunctions. Such are the perils that proceed from focusing too intently upon asserting one's independence from others and carving out a personal legacy distinct from theirs.

This is not to imply any critique of those who felt the need to break away from the influence of their extended families, and who insisted on crafting legacies that did *not* build upon those of the previous generation. In many cases, they had good reasons to feel this way – and their doing so was indeed best for their families and the future of the Jewish nation.

Yet in establishing the seeds of Jewish monarchy, another model is required. To form an enduring and respected line of leadership, the progenitors must show themselves capable of coming together for the sake of the collective, of putting aside personal interest under the realization that we are ultimately one large family.

Ruth uniquely displays this sort of selfless awareness. Her aspiration is to contribute whatever individual accomplishments she may achieve to the national family which sustains her – not to break free from it and pursue merely her own personal destiny. Through her actions she communicates her desire to build a household and a legacy that carries forward not only her name, but that of the larger collective to which she belongs.[8]

8. Special thanks to Rabbi Dr. Stuart Halpern for helpful edits on the draft of this chapter and for inviting me to deliver an earlier version as part of his IBC course on the Book of Ruth. Thanks as well to the congregants of Ohev Sholom in Washington, D.C. for serving as the initial audience for this material in June 2014.

In Pursuit of Wholeness: The Book of Ruth in Modern American and Israeli Literature

Sarah Rindner

W hile not the most dramatic of all the biblical stories, the quietly moving Book of Ruth has had a concrete impact on later Western literature. Sometimes the references to Ruth are explicit, as when the Romantic poet John Keats invokes her in "Ode to a Nightingale": "Through the sad heart of Ruth, when, sick for home / She stood in tears amid the alien corn."[1] Yet generally, the influence of Ruth in English and Hebrew literature is more subtle and diffused. What we encounter instead are Ruth-like scenarios, in which the ingredients of the original story are rearranged to form a new story that either draws on or even undermines the spirit of the original with its central theme of *ḥesed*, or loving-kindness. For modern writers in particular, an engagement

---

1. See Kurshan's chapter in this volume, "Love in the Time of Omer."

with the Book of Ruth reveals the limits of *ḥesed*'s power to transform and elevate the complicated and often cruel world in which we live. The American novelists Marilynne Robinson and Jane Hamilton as well as the Israeli writer Meir Shalev invoke the Ruth story in order to convey biblically infused narratives in which many of the themes of the Ruth story are present, yet without the redemptive overlay. In contrast, the Israeli writer S. Y. Agnon is able to draw upon the Book of Ruth in the manner of a modern writer, yet offers a formula by which the transformative spirit of the biblical narrative can inform our experience in the present. Appreciating how these varied writers understand the Book of Ruth can provide a heightened appreciation for how remarkable, and rare, the triumphs of Ruth and Boaz in the biblical account truly are.

MARILYNNE ROBINSON'S MIGRANT RUTH

In 1980, the American novelist Marilynne Robinson burst onto the literary scene with her critically acclaimed novel *Housekeeping*.[2] *Housekeeping* is the story of a young girl named Ruth who, along with her sister Lucille, is abandoned by their mother and left with a chain of relatives, finally ending up in the care of their eccentric Aunt Sylvie. This aunt and the two girls have all been abandoned by their closest relatives, and they try to create a home for themselves together. As is often the case in Robinson's fiction, echoes of the Bible are everywhere. Ruth, in considering her own yearning for the restoration of her family, reflects:

> Cain murdered Abel, and blood cried out from the earth; the house fell on Job's children, and a voice was induced or provoked into speaking from a whirlwind; and Rachel mourned for her children; and King David for Absalom. The force behind the movement of time is a mourning that will not be comforted. That is why the first event is known to have been an expulsion, and the last is hoped to be a reconciliation and return. (192)[3]

---

2. New York, Picador.
3. Page numbers taken from the 2004 Picador reprint edition.

Here Ruth considers the many places in the Hebrew Bible where a loss of family and pursuit of restoration propels the narrative forward, the Book of Ruth being no exception. Robinson's Ruth is similar to the biblical Ruth in her fierce loyalty to her aunt, in contrast to her sister Lucille who, like Orpah, ultimately rejects both of them in favor of a more conventional existence. In the Bible, Ruth achieves a stunning level of success in restoring Naomi's family to life through her union with Boaz, redeeming their family name and helping to forge the destiny of the nation of Israel.

Restoration is far more elusive in Robinson's novel. The home that Sylvie builds for herself and Ruth is described in delicate detail and beauty, but it is provisional in nature. Whereas Ruth gleans in foreign fields out of necessity for Naomi and herself, Sylvie and Ruth are drawn to the trappings of an itinerant lifestyle out of some kind of unfulfilled inner need. Sylvie sleeps with her shoes on every night and identifies with the migrants who pass through their remote Western town. Whereas in the Bible Naomi seeks a home for Ruth, "Daughter, I must seek a home for you, where you may be happy" (3:3), Sylvie believes that Ruth's happiness lies with Sylvie and in the temporary home they fashion together. At times it feels like Robinson is in dialogue with the Book of Ruth, imagining what would have happened if Ruth never had the luck of running into Boaz the redeemer, and instead had stayed together with Naomi and fashioned a life for the two of themselves together, away from the busybodies of the city of Bethlehem.

Yet Sylvie and Ruth pay a great price for their excommunication from polite society, and that is the sense, in contrast to the great genealogy following the Book of Ruth, that they will be forgotten. Early on in the novel Ruth meditates on the wife of the biblical Noah and wonders whatever happened to her:

> She was a nameless woman, and so at home among all those who were never found and never missed, who were uncommemorated, whose deaths were not remarked, nor their begettings. (172)

Soon, Robinson's Ruth finds herself entering this sisterhood of nameless women, as she and Sylvie quietly slip out of their hometown into an anonymous vagrant lifestyle that will provide some solace and well as a lingering sense of incompleteness. This, in a way, is the Ruth that could have been, an alternate literary universe which throws the greatness of Boaz and the serendipity of the biblical account into even greater relief.[4]

MEIR SHALEV'S WOUNDED RUTH

This anxiety about genealogy – and about being forgotten – colors another modern novel in dialogue with the Book of Ruth, *Two She-Bears* (*Shetayim Dubim*), published in Hebrew by Israeli writer Meir Shalev and translated into English by Stuart Schoffman.[5]

Two She-Bears is the story of two Ruths. One, Ruth Tavori, endures a difficult marriage with a complicated man named Zev in British Mandate Palestine. The second, her granddaughter Ruth, called Ruta, is a high-school Bible teacher in the same Yishuv her grandparents helped build. The connections with the biblical Book of Ruth are both explicit and implicit, as the narrator writes in regard to the younger Ruth:

> She was called Ruth Tavori in proper Hebrew: Rut Tavori, with a dignified pause in between, like at a state ceremony. But if you say the name without a proper space it comes out sounding "Ruta Vori." Try it, Varda, say it out loud. You see? Just like Ruth the Moabite. You pronounce it formally, she's the great-grandmother

---

4. Incidentally, Marilynne Robinson, whose 1980 Ruth never experiences a homecoming along the lines of her biblical namesake, and spends her days wandering in a kind of backwards version of the biblical book, returns to some of the concerns of *Housekeeping* in her 2004 novel called *Gilead* (New York: Picador). *Gilead* is the fictional memoir of the elderly pastor Reverend John Ames. Ames lives most of his life alone, after the tragic death of his young wife and infant daughter, until well into old age. He meets an itinerant woman much younger than himself, and they implausibly marry and have a child. Ames is as shocked that his wife would be interested in someone as old as he is just as she is startled that someone from civilized society would consider, or even look upon, someone as impoverished and unlearned as herself. While it's not clear that Robinson means to directly engage with the Book of Ruth in *Gilead*, though at one point Ames' wife does tell him that "you're just like all them old men in the Bible," Lila and John's mutual *ḥesed* toward each other seems to, in a way, fill in the void left empty by her earlier treatment of Ruth.
5. New York: Schocken, 2016.

of King David – but "Rutamoaviah" is the one who spent the night with Boaz on the threshing floor. (32)

As figures who are involved in building the State of Israel from its inception, the elder Tavoris live their lives in a biblical key. The narrator asks, "Who wasn't a woman of valor in the history of the Yishuv?" (34). Yet the characters break under the burdens they carry – their sense that they are participating in something of great historical importance contrasts with the dissolution of their private lives and relationships. ("You hear that, Grandma Ruth? You were a woman of valor even if you cried for no reason" [Ibid.].) The novel contains some explicit parallels with the Book of Ruth – two strong women, "she-bears," who endure huge losses and strive to move on amid a pastoral agricultural landscape in the Land of Israel. However, in Shalev's story there is also a pronounced contrast. The Book of Ruth seems to hover as a specter in this novel to remind us of the characters' limitations, particularly in the realm of reproduction. Early on in the novel, the narrator reflects:

> As you may or may not know, history in the Bible is inseparable from genealogy, all those long lists of people who begat and begat and begat, this one begat that one who begat that one who begat that one, because that is what's really important and not all the Zionist slogans about coming to the Land of Israel and founding a village and forming committees and plowing the first furrow – what's really important are names, births, deaths. (35)

We will soon learn that the house of Tavori is plagued from its inception by a certain impotence, both literal and figurative, and all of the characters need to make a kind of peace with the question of what will endure after them. One child dies by snakebite, another is cruelly murdered only a week after she's born. In exploring all of these traumatic events from her family history, the younger Ruta seeks a narrative where they can have some kind of redemptive meanings. Here and there she finds a moving note of consolation, but overall there is a sense that this family has removed itself from the biblical train of who "begat" whom, and the connections with the biblical Ruth remain ironic at best.

Perhaps the one aspect of Ruth that is most difficult for a modern author to adopt or incorporate in his or her novel is the motif of *ḥesed*. This is a key element of the Book of Ruth, which the sages teach was written only "to teach how much reward comes to those who act with loving-kindness" (Ruth Rabba 2:14). In the hardscrabble world in which Marilynne Robinson's Ruth resides, Christian neighbors can at best offer a bland and conventional kind of assistance. They don't truly help Ruth and Sylvie, and, once the townsfolk recognize the depth of Sylvie's non-conventional ways, the neighbors' interest in the protagonists is ultimately weaponized against them. In *Two She-Bears*, the patriarch of the family, Zev Tavori, does not possess the humility that characterizes the biblical Boaz. Whereas Boaz essentially effaces himself by enabling *yibum*, the continuation of the family line, Tavori turns to murder over accepting any sort of imperfect family situation in which he is not securely situated at the head.

JANE HAMILTON'S RUTH IN A MEAN WORLD

In 1988, Jane Hamilton published the novel *The Book of Ruth*[6] where the eponymous heroine also partakes in a dysfunctional family arrangement and oversees a gruesome murder, after which she begins to pick up the pieces of her life. While the connections between the novel and the biblical book are more tenuous than in the previous two examples, the opening lines in the novel are illustrative, if only by way of contrast with the biblical version: "What it begins with, I know finally, is the kernel of meanness in people's hearts. I don't know exactly how or why it gets inside us; that's one of the mysteries I haven't solved yet."

For Hamilton's Ruth, who has lived a more difficult life than most, kindness is not a given, but it may be possible to minimize a natural cruelty, "A person has to fight the meanness that sometimes comes with you when you're born" (326), and at times her readings of the Bible help her get there. This kind of provisional victory over evil is the best that Hamilton's Ruth can hope for in the world in which she lives, which makes the biblical vision of *ḥesed* appear all the more radical in contrast.

---

6. New York: Anchor Books.

AGNON'S REDEMPTIVE RUTH

One novelist willing to explore that unique and irreductive quality of *ḥesed* that is at the heart of the Book of Ruth is S. Y. Agnon. In his short novella, "In the Prime of Her Life,"[7] first published in 1923, Agnon touches on key themes of the Ruth story, particularly the concept of *yibum* and how radical *ḥesed* might play out in the context of a bereaved family.

"In the Prime of Her Life" is narrated by a young woman named Tirza whose own mother Leah died "in the prime of her life" (age 31) of a "heart illness" (*maḥalat halev*) and who now lives with her businessman father. Tirza is consumed by thoughts of a sensitive poet and teacher named Akaviah Mazal, who once loved her mother and whom her mother loved in turn. Tirza's mother was barred from marrying Akaviah for economic reasons related to her poor health, and after her death Tirza finds a journal written by Akaviah that includes his delicate reflections on his affection for Leah. Agnon, in his typical subtle fashion, suggests a connection to the Book of Ruth without making it explicit: "And in those days I read from the Books of Joshua and Judges, and at that time I found a book among my mother's books, may she rest in peace" (197). The Book of Ruth also opens with "In those days of the Judges," and thus Agnon clues in the Jewishly literate reader that there may be some connection between Tirza's mother and the story of Ruth.

As Tirza broods upon the loss of her mother, she increasingly feels a kinship with Mazal, with whom her mother had such a strong connection. She concludes that, in a manner that recalls S. Ansky's *Dybbuk*, "Mazal has been wronged. He seemed to me to be like a man bereft of his wife and yet she was not his wife" (201). Tirza thinks of Akaviah for years; she attends a school for teachers where he is employed even though she is ill-suited for the teaching profession, and finally courageously approaches him on her own one evening, in a clandestine fashion that also reminds us of Ruth. Once there, she learns from Akaviah that he was born to a family of converts, once again bringing to mind Ruth as the prototypical convert, though in Akaviah's case they had

---

7. Trans. Gabriel Levine, in *8 Great Hebrew Short Novels*, ed. Alan Lelchuk and Gershon Shaken (Jerusalem: Toby Press, 2005).

begrudgingly converted to Christianity for reasons of livelihood. Akaviah's mother sought to return to the Jewish people, despite the downgrade in her financial and social status, and Akaviah continues this trajectory:

> He had yearned with all his heart to complete what his mother had set out to accomplish upon returning to the God of Israel, for he had returned to his people. Yet they did not understand him. He walked as a stranger in their midst – they drew him close, but when he was as one of them they divided their hearts from him. (226)

While Agnon invokes the ingredients of the Ruth story, they do not map out on his characters in a straightforward fashion. While Tirza reminds us of Ruth in some ways, as with her clandestine visit to a much older man, Akaviah also is a Ruth- or perhaps Naomi-like figure in his outsider status among the Jewish community to which he has returned. Even in the Ruth story itself, some of this inversion of roles exists. When Ruth prostrates before Boaz in his Bethlehem field she thanks him for the kindness he has shown to her, a foreigner. Yet when she comes before him in the middle of the night it is he who thanks her: "Be blessed of the Lord, daughter! Your latest deed of kindness (*ḥesed*) is greater than the first, in that you have not turned to younger men, whether poor or rich" (Ruth 3:10). *Ḥesed* does not stream in one direction in the Book of Ruth – Ruth and Boaz each provide *ḥesed* and are recipients in turn, thus collapsing the hierarchy between them. Tirza longs for Akaviah and for the connection to her mother that he can provide. Akaviah will urge Tirza to pursue a man who is younger and more appropriate for her but she refuses. Ultimately, the story suggests, in the spirit of *yibum*, that past wrongs can be redeemed and a broken family can be mended, particularly through the unrelenting dedication of one young woman.

"In the Prime of Her Life" concludes with the idyllic though subtly discomfiting scene of Tirza married to Akaviah and pregnant with their first child. Akaviah had warned Tirza before their marriage that she is still young, and that he had "come to the age where all I desire is some peace and quiet" (234), perhaps also recalling the multiple references to *menuḥa*, peaceful rest, in the Book of Ruth. Akaviah's hesitation, as well as the reservations of those around her, do not deter Tirza, and she pursues this unlikely union faithfully even if it is not the romantic love story for which other girls her age may hope. Their newlywed bliss is soon punctured by some misgivings on Tirza's part – her husband is busy writing a history of the Jews of their town, and she finds herself resentful of her domestic duties and rather lonely. Nevertheless, the rooms of the newlywed couple are "suffused with warmth and light" (244), and Tirza is heartened by the close relationship that grows between her husband and her father who visits them each evening. While this is not a literal *yibum* situation, it shares in the spirit of *yibum*, wherein someone who has lost his beloved (in this case Akaviah) marries her next of kin. It also evokes the *yibum*-esque scenario of Megillat Ruth, where Boaz marries Ruth as a kinsman of her deceased husband and father-in-law.

While Tirza's life with Akaviah is far from a perfect relationship, she senses, as does the reader, that her unconventional choice is imbued with larger significance. Together they mend a rift that had been breached first with Leah's broken engagement to Akaviah and then with Leah's own death. Tirza's father and Akaviah should be at odds with one another, as one replaced the other with respect to Leah. Yet Tirza's marriage to Akaviah unifies the two men and thus closes a circle. Toward the end of the story Tirza gazes upon her husband and father and writes:

> Now I glance at my father's face and now at my husband's. I behold the two men and long to cry, to cry in my mother's bosom. Has my husband's sullen mood brought this about, or does a spirit dwell in womankind? My father and my husband sit at the table, their faces shining upon me. By dint of their love and compassion, each resembles the other. Evil has seventy faces and love has but one face. (244)

This sentiment, "evil has seventy faces and love has but one face," offers a creative iteration of underlying spirit of *yibum*, through which one husband can virtually morph into another and in which ḥesed makes family restoration possible even after tragic loss. This is part of the triumph of Megillat Ruth – Ruth the Moabite, whose ancestor Lot was once banished from Abraham's tent, now returns to the Jewish

Sarah Rindner

people. The family line of Elimelech and Naomi, once threatened with dissolution, is also symbolically maintained through the union of Ruth and Boaz. Even writing in 1923, Agnon would be all too familiar with the modern individualism that would have made such a sentiment feel hopelessly outdated. Even in the world of the Book of Ruth such *ḥesed* was not ubiquitous, as testified to by the horrors of the contemporaneous Book of Judges. Through fiction Agnon is able to do something that few other novelists engaging with the Book of Ruth want, or perhaps are able, to do. Agnon brings the unlikely *ḥesed* of Ruth to life in a nuanced manner that suppresses none of the strangeness of the not-quite-*yibum* predicament depicted in both stories, which are each infused with a hint of the same eternal quality.

The dissolution of families and relationships is an immutable part of the world in which we live. Modern Western societies, with their strong emphasis on individualism, have been particularly susceptible to this dynamic, and as such scores of modern novels explore these themes. The Book of Ruth presents an account of familial dissolution but importantly, restoration as well. Agnon's invocation of the book, notwithstanding its irony, is a rare example in modern literature that mines the biblical story to its full depth. Ruth's travails alongside Naomi, their exile and their exclusion from civilized society are a natural fit for modern novelists like Robinson, Shalev, and Hamilton. The inexplicable acts of goodness that drive men and women like Boaz, Naomi, and Ruth are harder to find, in literature and in life.[8]

---

8. The book *Rising Moon* (Modi'in: Renana Publishers, 2015), by Rabbi Moshe Miller, influenced my understanding of the way in which *ḥesed* and *yibum* are at the heart of the Book of Ruth. Rabbi Jeffrey Saks' brilliant reading of the Agnon story, "In the Prime of Her Life," available at http://www.webyeshiva.org/course/midrash-agnon-in-the-prime-of-her-life/, enriched my appreciation of the story. Finally, a lecture by Professor Ilana Pardes of Hebrew University gave me the idea to place "In the Prime of Her Life" in dialogue with Ruth in the first place (https://www.youtube.com/watch?v=WYgNSrXz59Q).

Conversion and Peoplehood

Border Crossings:
A Tale of Two Converts

Dr. Ronnie Perelis

The Torah enjoins the Israelites upon their entrance into the Land of Israel to love the stranger thirty-six times. Moses gives the people a historical context to this commandment; he reminds them to love or in some instances to not oppress the stranger "for you were a stranger in the land of Egypt."[1]

This thread of commandment and of memory woven throughout the Torah argues that the memory of displacement, disenfranchisement, and oppression should inspire an attitude of care and concern for those on the margins of society, those without the socioeconomic networks that would protect them in times of need and the family networks that would give emotional and physical protection from the vagaries of life. In biblical times this stranger – the *ger* – was a foreigner who found his way to the Land of Israel and sought shelter among the People of Israel.

---

1. For a penetrating psychological reflection on these verses see Yisroel Campbell's performance at the "Jerusalem Sermon Slam," December 22, 2013, https://youtu.be/q48ivlmVuSc.

The Torah does not define the religious status of this foreigner; instead it focuses on the responsibility of those on the inside, of those firmly rooted within the social matrix of power and security, to make space for this stranger. Those who are rooted are enjoined both to not harm the strangers, and to go one step further and to actually love them.[2]

I want to stop and consider the ways this powerful moral injunction, which is grounded in an appeal to the past, to the foundational nation-building experience of slavery and redemption, enlightens, inspires, and complicates the experience of those who seek entrance into the community. History can only go so far in helping us understand the present. And yet, how else do we understand the pedigree of our ideas? Through historical analysis we can see that things are both more similar and more different than we assume – we make the familiar strange and the strange more familiar.

I want to use the example of two pre-modern converts to Judaism to think about the ways that outsiders can find their way into the heart of a new community. In doing so I hope to explore the ways that bonds of faith can complicate and break through barriers of blood and tribe. In both cases we have people whose ethnic origins are not only foreign but often considered hostile to the community they desire to integrate into. Both individuals had to leave the comfort and familiarity of their homes and the privilege of their class to follow their search for religious truth and forge a new sense of belonging.

In this way they follow in the footsteps of the prototypical "righteous convert," Ruth. Ruth's Moabite origin placed her on the short list of nations whom the Israelites were enjoined to avoid. In fact, it is the case of Ruth that establishes the rabbinic ruling that the prohibition against allowing Moabites to enter into the Congregation of Israel applies only to Moabite men, not women. She leaves the comfort of her homeland, her family, and all that was familiar to follow her widowed mother-in-law who had nothing to offer her to a land she did not know and to live

---

2. Rabbi Jeremy Wieder discussed the intricacies of these laws in both their biblical and rabbinic contexts during the panel dedicated to "Immigration and Identity" at Yeshiva University (May 2018) where this chapter had its earliest iteration. My chapter does not propose a halakhic or concrete policy regarding outsiders seeking entrance into the community, but I hope these historical meditations can provide much-needed context and nuance to this charged issue.

at the behest of people who would at best look at her with suspicion. Ruth is well aware that her mother-in-law cannot provide children to wed or money or land to provide for her needs. Her decision to follow Naomi is not based on "anything of this world."

> But Ruth replied, "Do not urge me to leave you, to turn back and not follow you. For wherever you go, I will go; wherever you lodge, I will lodge; your people shall be my people, and your God my God. Where you die, I will die, and there I will be buried. Thus and more may the Lord do to me if anything but death parts me from you." (Ruth: 1:16–17)

For Ruth her connection to Naomi is inextricable from her willingness to embrace Naomi's nation and to make her God her own. It is hard to detangle Ruth's religious motivation from her attachment to Naomi. The Book of Ruth does not have her call out to the God of Israel or receive prophecy or brave martyrdom; it's her selfless dedication to her mother-in-law that is a key factor that brings her to the attention of her eventual "redeemer," Boaz. Boaz takes her as a wife and restores her and Naomi's fortunes. More fundamentally, the narrative ends with a genealogy which begins with Ruth the Moabite, a stranger with a checkered past, but ends with David the King of Israel and the root of the Messiah. So the foundational narrative of the righteous convert is threaded with kindness and self-sacrifice and transcends blood-lines, allowing for an outsider to be the mother of the nation's redemption.

Despite the focus on caring for the stranger, and even the celebration of the righteous convert in the story of Ruth, there are many factors that dampened and complicated the Jewish embrace of the stranger in the pre-modern period. In the diaspora, Jews were a tolerated minority whose tolerance was partially based on their respect for the religious hegemony of their hosts. So there would be no conversion of Christians in the lands of Christendom and no conversion of Muslims in the lands of Islam. To be involved with any part of such a conversion was punishable by death. These laws developed with the rise of Christianity as the official religion of the Roman Empire in the fourth century and were in force up to the modern age.

Another complicating factor facing the would-be convert lies at the heart of Judaism's identity as both a national and a religious community. You are born into Judaism and yet Judaism is a set of ideas, beliefs, and most importantly actions.

Anyone who embraces those ideas and deeds can join, regardless of their ethnic or national origin. Conversion is a fundamental avenue of entry and thus the tribe, where bonds are formed through blood and family and a shared past, paradoxically can always be expanded to include members who do not share any of those tribal bonds.

The Jews are referred to as the Children of Israel – the descendants of Abraham, Isaac, and Jacob, whose name was changed to Israel. Yet what does it mean to be a child of Israel? Is it in the blood or is there something else that makes up Israelite paternity?

The twelfth-century Andalusian-Egyptian polymath Maimonides received a query from a convert who felt that because he could not trace his lineage back to the forefathers of the Jewish people he could not invoke their names in his prayers. We know a little about this intrepid religious searcher from documents uncovered in the Cairo Geniza. He left behind a budding career in the church and the comfort and wealth of his father's home in Italy. He traveled to the Middle East to freely investigate Judaism. He studied in Baghdad and passed through Syria, eventually making his way to Cairo. Upon his conversion he took the Hebrew name of Ovadia, "Servant of God."[3]

Maimonides tells Ovadia the convert that Abraham, Isaac, and Jacob *are* his fathers because he follows their teachings. Ovadia left his family and home behind in search of religious truth just like Abraham who left behind all that was familiar to follow God's voice. Maimonides identifies the convert's commitment to the right ideals and sacrifice on behalf of those ideals as the mark of inclusion in the group. By discounting the power of blood, Maimonides welcomes this outsider in.

---

3. The letter to Ovadia the proselyte is presented in English translation in Isadore Twersky, *A Maimonides Reader*, ed. Isadore Twersky (Behrman, 1972), 475–476. For more on Ovadia's background see the website dedicated to his life and work: https://johannes-obadiah.org/index.html.

He writes:

> Because since you have come under the wings of the Divine Pres-
> ence and confessed the Lord, no difference exists between you
> and us, and all miracles done to us have been done as it were to us
> and to you. Thus is said in the Book of Isaiah, "Neither let the son
> of the stranger, that has joined himself to the Lord, speak, saying,
> 'The Lord has utterly separated me from His people'" (Is. 56:3).
> There is no difference whatever between you and us. You shall
> certainly say the blessing, "Who has chosen us," "Who has given
> us," "Who have taken us for Your own," and "Who has separated
> us": for the Creator, may He be extolled, has indeed chosen you
> and separated you from the nations and given you the Torah.

Belief in the One God, sacrifice, and commitment to Divine Law is
what secures Ovadia the convert's place within his new community.
His foreignness, his gentile blood, is no longer relevant because he has
embraced the ideals of his new community and thus has forged his place
within their fold. Maimonides is unable to provide a robust family net-
work for this foreigner but he can assure him a spiritual space among
his religious brethren.

In the early modern period we find another example of an outsider, tormented by the weight of his foreign blood, with all that it con-
jures up in the racially charged Atlantic world of the seventeenth century.
Manuel Cardoso de Macedo was born into a well-to-do Old Christian[4]
family in the Azores and through a surprising series of religious transfor-
mations – he first embraces Calvinism while living in England and then
discovers Judaism during his time in the prisons of the Lisbon Inquisition – he found his way to the Jewish community of Amsterdam where
after a formal conversion he lived out the rest of his life as a devout Jew.[5]

---

4. Old Christian describes those Iberian Catholics who did not come from recent
   Jewish or Muslim converts and the descendants of converts known as Conversos
   or New Christians. These distinctions arose out of anxiety about the assimilation
   of Jewish and (to a lesser extent) Muslim converts into Iberian society.
5. Cardoso is the central figure in chapter 5 of my recent book, *Narratives from the
   Sephardic Atlantic: Blood and Faith* (Bloomington: Indiana University Press, 2016).

Cardoso de Macedo adopts the Jewish name of Abraham Pelegrino Guer – Abraham the convert, the pilgrim, the wanderer. He wrote an eloquent spiritual autobiography about his religious journey that he begins with a fundamental question: "How can it be that I – who descend from such vicious Jew-haters, have a place beneath the wings of the Divine Presence?"[6] He talks about how deeply his father and his whole Portuguese society sought to destroy all vestiges of Judaism. He says that for his father "there would not be enough wood to burn all of the Jews"! Confronted with the weight of his blood, Cardoso seeks to retrace his steps toward the Law of Moses and the People of Israel in his autobiography and somehow write his way into the Jewish fold.

Cardoso focuses on two essential features of his religious journey and his decision to convert: his commitment to the truth and his self-sacrifice on behalf of his new coreligionists. His story begins in England where his father sent him to study and apprentice with some of his mercantile partners in the textile and dyestuffs trade. There the teenage Cardoso is fascinated by the variety of Christian sects and decides to explore them. He goes to London and buys "seven books of seven different sects and resolved to see which one was *closest to reason*." He settles on Calvinism. While in England he is quite brash about his new religious commitment; when he meets fellow Spanish and Portuguese expatriates he does nothing to hide his rejection of the Catholic faith and slowly word makes it back to the bishop of his town in the Azores. On a return trip home he is interrogated about his heretical dabbling and he declares to the bishop: "I am a Calvinist and a Calvinist I will die, unless you can show me my errors through reason." Intellectual curiosity and bravery are hallmarks of his religious quest.

His defiance gets him sent to the prisons of the Lisbon Inquisition where he, by chance, meets a New Christian, Henrique Dias Milão, who was accused of a full list of Judaizing heresies. Cardoso, whose Protestant

---

6. This fascinating document survived in an eighteenth-century manuscript copy and was transcribed and edited by the Dutch historian Bernard Teensma. I am currently working on an English translation of the text. To consult the Portuguese original see *La vida del buenaventurado Abraham Pelengrino*, ed. B. Teensma, *Studia Rosenthaliana* vol. x (1976): 1–36.

heresy was all about the centrality of the Bible, is shocked to actually meet someone who was (at least accused of) practicing the laws of the Holy Bible. This threw into doubt his faith in Calvinism – he realized that if the Bible was central then certainly the laws of the Bible should be practiced. He resolves to learn more about Judaism.

He is penanced at the Auto da Fe of April 5, 1609, and then sent to a reform school along with other penanced heretics. There he seeks out other Conversos who were accused of secretly practicing Judaism and furtively seeks to learn more about Judaism from his fellow heretics. However, this is not only an intellectual quest. In discovering information about Judaism he becomes close to Jews of flesh and blood, and grows connected to their plight. He tells the reader that he "began to feel affection for the Nation." He helps organize an escape for some of the Dias Milão family. The plan was foiled and all were arrested, but Cardoso would not turn on his Converso accomplices. He withstood the abuse of the inquisitors and shielded his co-conspirators from further persecution. He made a second attempt at escape and eventually, together with a group of Conversos, made it to the religious liberty of Hamburg where he finished his process of conversion within the embrace of the small Sephardic community. But his travails were not over. He finds work with a son of his former cellmate, a member of the Dias Milão family, in the port of Danzig, helping to manage the family's sugar refinery. The family were accused of ritually murdering one of their Christian servants and a riot was forming against them. Cardoso urged his bosses to flee and said that he would stay behind to watch over the property. Cardoso was beaten by the angry mob and then thrown into prison after the house was ransacked. He declares that he would take a month in the Inquisition over a day in that terrible prison. He leaves prison with a limp that he will live with the rest of his life. He makes it to Amsterdam and becomes part of the growing Sephardic community in that bustling center of trade. And it is there, in the security of Amsterdam, that he writes his autobiography, which if read carefully reveals a portrait of a religious searcher who found the truth but who is left uneasy about his place within the community of the faithful. He rehearses his acts of sacrifice on behalf of the Nation to convince himself and his readers that despite his past, despite the legacy of Jew-hatred he inherited from his father, he belongs with the Children of Israel.

He ends his journey by invoking the same words of Isaiah (56:6–8) that Maimonides used in his letter to Ovadia over four hundred years before. Cardoso ends his narrative by calling out to the "children of the strangers" – the outcasts of society – who find their way to God's law:

> And children of the strangers, those who join unto A[donay], in order to serve Him and in order to love the name of A[donay], in order to be His servants, guarding the Sabbath from profaning it, holding fast to My covenant, Lo, I will bring them to My holy mountain, and I will rejoice with them in My house of prayer…. For My house will be called a house of prayer; so says A[donay] God, to all of the nations, the oppressed of Israel will be gathered, I will still gather unto Him his oppressed ones.[7]

In this remarkable document we can see Manuel Cardoso transform himself into Abraham Pelegrino Guer, a stranger but one who can find his place on God's mountain. Cardoso uses his autobiography as a way to write himself into the Jewish people. He showcases his passion for religious truth, his investigation of multiple religious paths, his sacrifice for his beliefs, and his suffering on behalf of other Jews whom he shielded from inquisitorial persecution and other assaults. He earns his place within the community because his heart was pure, his commitment was strong, and his dedication to his new community was tested by sacrifice. He overcomes the powerful barriers of family and blood that organized both his original community of Catholic Portugal and the Sephardic community of Amsterdam. He integrates himself into his chosen community by his acts of self-sacrifice on behalf of fellow Jews and by his devotion to Judaism. By emphasizing his commitment to the ideals of Judaism and to the welfare of his adopted community, Cardoso, like Maimonides and like Ruth, discounts the

---

7. This is my translation of Cardoso's Portuguese version which may either be based on the Spanish translation commonly used in Amsterdam or on his own rendering from the Hebrew. These verses are part of the *haftara* recited on the Shabbat of Repentance that falls between Rosh HaShana and Yom Kippur according to the Western Sephardic custom. These are not obscure verses, but ones with living resonance for Cardoso's readers.

power of blood, and claims a space for himself based on what he can share with his fellow Jews; this allows him to transcend his past and the weight of his blood.

Mutatis mutandis. . .

Ovadia and Cardoso found their way to cosmopolitan centers of global trade – twelfth-century Cairo and seventeenth-century Amsterdam – where people from all over the world came and went with their shipments of goods and which allowed for a degree of anonymity, freedom of movement, and self-expression. Neither of these spiritual wanderers had to contend with being considered "undocumented," let alone "illegal" people, but they did have to find their place within tightly knit communities based on strong family ties and ethnic solidarity. The experience of these two individuals cannot be translated seamlessly into policy for a modern nation state; rather, their examples serve to highlight an ethical and psychological dimension. In both cases we can see that bonds of blood, family networks, and the psychic weight of ethnic identities are real; often enough they are felt more strongly by the outsider trying to enter than those already situated securely within the ethnic matrix. The outsider asks, "Can I ever fully be part of the new community?" The communities where the stranger has sought refuge, however, have to stretch themselves beyond their comfort to let this person in, to see him as one of their own, and to ease their doubts.

Cardoso and Maimonides uphold Abraham, the first Jew, as the model for the ideal convert with his mixture of personal sacrifice, courage, and devotion to the truth. However, the Rabbis of the Talmud turn to Ruth as their model for the process of conversion. For example, according to some rabbinic opinions a convert is supposed to be discouraged from joining the Jewish people, just like Naomi discouraged Ruth.[8] In this exegetical model, perhaps we can draw another lesson for welcoming outsiders. Not only can outsiders become integral members of the community; perhaps they, like Ruth, can bring with them the unexpected promise of redemption.

---

8. For an in-depth analysis of the variety of legal positions regarding converts to Judaism see Isaac Sassoon's *Conflicting Attitudes to Conversion in Judaism, Past and Present* (Cambridge: Cambridge University Press, 2017).

Ruth and Contemporary Conversion: Lessons in *Ahavat HaGer*

Rabbi Zvi Romm

The biblical story of Ruth has been frequently mined for insights, both halakhic and ideological, into the conversion process. The Talmud (Yevamot 47b) cites Ruth's words to Naomi as examples of the type of mitzva acceptance (*kabbalat ol mitzvot*) necessary for conversion. Later rabbinic literature attempts to pinpoint the stage at which Ruth converted. Contemporary voices in Jewish life debate the extent to which Ruth's conversion process is similar or dissimilar to the present-day procedure; these debates typically are heavily polemic in nature.

As much as there is ample room for using Ruth as a lens through which to view the conversion process, the focus of the biblical story is on Ruth's life post-conversion. As such, I believe the primary conversion-related lessons to be drawn from the Book of Ruth have less to do with the convert's embrace of Judaism and more to do with the Jewish community's embrace of the convert.

It is striking – and profoundly moving – to contemplate how Ruth is welcomed into the Jewish community with warmth and love. The Midrash (Ruth Rabba 2:14) teaches us that Megillat Ruth was composed to teach us "the reward given to those who perform acts of kindness." The kindness shown to Ruth is meant to impress upon those of us who are born Jewish how much responsibility we bear to create a seamless transition for converts into the Jewish fold.

One of the Torah's 613 mitzvot is *ahavat hager* (love of the convert). The mitzva is codified in Deuteronomy (10:10): "You shall love the stranger, because you were strangers in the land of Egypt." The stranger is this context is traditionally understood to refer to the convert, who abandoned his or her former life and attempts to become part of a foreign people. This positive mitzva is linked to a parallel negative mitzva which prohibits *onaat hager* (paining a convert). According to the Talmud (Bava Metzia 59b), the concept of dealing sensitively with a convert is mentioned thirty-six (or forty-six) times in the Torah, underscoring its importance.

What follows is a brief presentation of ways in which we can emulate the kindness shown to Ruth in our contemporary world, putting the lofty ideals of *ahavat hager* into practice.

WE NEED TO SPEAK MORE ABOUT CONVERSION IN OUR COMMUNITIES

Growing up, I confess that I thought of converts as exotic. One would read the occasional story of someone from a very different culture embracing Judaism, but it was not something which I saw as a common phenomenon.

My own work with converts and conversion candidates has impressed upon me that this is a fiction. Converts are very much a part of the contemporary American Orthodox community. This is not only true in communities and synagogues which are outreach-oriented, in which one would expect to find many people of diverse backgrounds. It is even true in synagogues in which the average worshipper is assumed to be "*frum*-from-birth." It is true in modern Orthodox as well as "*yeshivishe*" synagogues.

In truth, it is not surprising that there are so many converts who are part of the fabric of our communities. The RCA-affiliated Manhattan Beth Din for Conversions alone oversees close to one hundred conversions every year. Most of these converts live in very robust Orthodox communities in the New York area and participate fully in the life of the community.

I think it is important that people stop viewing conversion as exotic and begin to view converts as yet another standard subset within the Orthodox community. In light of how many converts are already part of the Orthodox community, the mitzva of *ahavat hager* needs to be a topic which is regularly addressed in public. *Shiurim* and talks can and should be devoted to this important biblical mitzva, which is far more relevant than people think it is.

More often than not, public discourse within the Orthodox community on the topic of conversion tends to focus on the halakhic and political dimensions of conversion standards. While these discussions are important, discussing standards exclusively can potentially objectify the convert. In contrast, speaking about *ahavat hager* humanizes the convert, reminding the rest of the community that conversion is not only about the obligations the convert has to God and Torah but also includes the obligations the Torah community has toward the convert.

I believe that it is also important to include in our public discourse expressions of admiration for converts and the choices they have made to lead a Torah lifestyle. Sadly, people sometimes express disbelief that anyone would choose an Orthodox lifestyle. This attitude not only disrespects the convert; it also sends a debilitating message to our own children: we only practice Torah because we were born this way. You'd have to be crazy to actually choose to do this!

On a public level, we need to remind our constituents that we pray explicitly for the welfare of converts three times a day in *Shemoneh Esreh*. Indeed, we mention converts in the same breath with "the righteous, the pious, and the elders of the Jewish people." We need to publicly share stories about the nobility and self-sacrifice of converts – both past and present – and describe how our great leaders went out of their way to show honor and respect to those who had made the courageous decision to join the Jewish people.

WE NEED TO RESPECT CONVERTS' PRIVACY

Speaking about conversion more frequently in public creates an environment of *ahavat hager*, as long as we speak about the mitzva conceptually and abstractly. At the same time, individual converts in our communities are entitled to their privacy, which we should guard zealously.

Some converts are very open about their status. Others prefer to keep a low profile. This is especially true when the convert was raised with a Jewish identity but was not halakhically Jewish. It goes without saying that a major part of *ahavat hager* includes respecting a convert's wishes to not publicize his or her status. Beyond that, *ahavat hager* requires us to be sensitive to the fact that people we interact with may well be converts, unbeknownst to us, and we should be careful to not act in a way which makes them uncomfortable.

A seemingly innocuous activity which has made many a convert – and *baal teshuva* – squirm is the favorite Orthodox pastime known as "Jewish geography." For those who grew up or have spent many years in the Orthodox community, Jewish geography is a fun way to instantly establish a connection between two people. For a convert, it can be torture. If the convert desires – as is his or her right – to keep the facts of his or her life pre-conversion private, "Jewish geography" forcibly "outs" the convert and compels him or her to reveal a non-Jewish background. We should be very careful when hosting to stay away from questions about the person's past; if such questions come up around a Shabbat table, we should do our best to redirect the conversation.

On the topic of Shabbat meals, it is imperative that we, as a community, ensure that converts are regularly invited for Shabbat meals. In most cases, they have no Jewish or observant family to host them. Many will feel shy about proactively requesting meals. For that reason, we need to be proactive in searching out converts we know before Yom Tov and making sure that they need not spend the holiday alone.[1]

---

1. There are potential halakhic issues, which are beyond the scope of this chapter, involved in inviting a conversion candidate to a Yom Tov meal that is not on Shabbat.

THE WORST SIN: RAISING THE
SPECTRE OF NULLIFICATION

Some years ago, a born Jew whom I know was involved in a financial dispute with someone who had converted to Judaism years beforehand. The born Jew called me up with (what he thought) was a halakhic question: in light of what he perceived as the unethical way the convert was acting in their dispute, was there some way that the conversion could be retroactively revoked? I was shocked, and quickly told the questioner that not only could no nullification take place, but that even the sugges- tion of such was a terrible sin of *onaat hager*!

This story should give us some insight into the sense of uncertainty many converts live with, and the supreme importance of helping to create an environment which alleviates those fears. The feeling that the conversion can be "undone" or "revoked" for any reason is terrifying for a convert. It is a terrible violation of *ahavat hager* to imply – or certainly to state explicitly – that a convert's conversion could potentially be nullified. Born Jews would tremble if they felt their Jewish identity could be taken away due to religious or ethical lapses on their part.

The average layperson needs to realize that he or she is not a *beit din* and should not be deciding whether a particular convert is legitimate. It is wrong and extremely hurtful to quiz converts to get a sense of their sincerity, knowledge, or observance levels, and to make decisions based on that information as to whether the conversion was valid. Examining a conversion candidate is solely the job of the *beit din*. Once a candidate is converted legitimately, it is a violation of *ahavat hager* for community members to constantly scrutinize the convert.

NO DIFFERENT THAN ANYONE ELSE

An important part of *ahavat hager* is making the *ger* feel like he or she is fundamentally no different than anyone else in the Orthodox com- munity. Some *gerim* enjoy their unique status as *gerim* and are anxious to share their stories; that is certainly their right. Many others, however,

---

One should discuss with a halakhic authority how to negotiate these issues. Typically, a halakhically appropriate solution can be found to help a conversion candidate feel embraced during the Yom Tov period.

prefer to blend in and not call attention to the fact that they are different in any way.

A question of interest to converts is how to relate to the morning blessing "*Shelo asani goy*," thanking God for having not created one as a gentile. Obviously, this is not literally true for a *ger*. Halakhic opinions differ as to whether one should omit the *berakha*, recite a variant ("*She'asani ger*" – "Who has made me a convert"), or recite the *berakha* with the understanding that the convert is thanking God for his or her present status as a Jew.[2]

During the course of my work with converts, I posed the question to Rabbi Mordechai Willig. Rabbi Willig generously and selflessly volunteers many hours to serve as a *dayan* on the *beit din* for conversions; I consistently marvel at how he has gone to extraordinary lengths – in contexts far removed from the public eye – to help make converts feel comfortable and accepted in the Orthodox community. His response was immediate: of course the convert should recite "*Shelo asani goy*." He should not feel different than anyone else in *shul*. That is the mitzva of *ahavat hager*!

A similar approach applies to helping converts deal with the loss of a close non-Jewish relative. Although a convert is not halakhically obligated to sit *shiva*[3] or say Kaddish[4] for a non-Jewish relative who passes, many converts find comfort in doing so. Not only are these time-hallowed practices therapeutic, but observing them helps the convert feel fundamentally similar to other members of the community who turn to these practices in their time of grief. Conversely, not observing *shiva* or not saying Kaddish may reinforce the convert's feeling of being a community outsider. It is important to realize that a halakhic exemption from these practices is not synonymous with a prohibition to observe them. Rabbis should reach out to converts in their communities with halakhically appropriate options to deal with their grief.

---

2. See *Shulḥan Arukh Oraḥ Ḥayim* 46:4 and *Ba'er Hetev* 8.
3. *Shulḥan Arukh Yoreh De'ah* 374:5.
4. See *Zekan Aharon* II:87 who suggests that the convert may, indeed, be obligated to say Kaddish.

Some converts, especially those who are private about their status, may not wish to sit *shiva* after the passing of a close relative. They are anxious about the well-meaning questions which will be asked of them during the *shiva*, forcing them to reveal more about their past lives than they feel comfortable doing. This position, too, needs to be respected. Caring rabbis and close friends need to think of alternative ways to acknowledge the convert's grief and pain when *shiva* is not desired.

"MY DAUGHTER, I SEEK A HAVEN FOR YOU" (RUTH 3:1)

In the Book of Ruth, the pinnacle of the concern Naomi shows toward Ruth is manifest in her successful effort to help her remarry. In the contemporary world, as well, the ultimate display of *ahavat hager* is to help converts marry and build observant Jewish families.

Finding a marriage partner is often challenging even for those who grew up in the Orthodox community. Converts may experience additional hurdles: most female converts become Jewish at an age when they are already considered "older" by some in the Orthodox community. Some born Jews may feel uncomfortable marrying someone without Jewish family. (Ironically, numerous converts have expressed to me that they would rather not marry a convert, as they want to have a Jewish extended family.) Some born Jews may feel uncomfortable with a convert who looks ethnically different as a marriage partner.

Precisely because of these challenges, we as a community must make a special effort to introduce converts to potential marriage partners. While it may be tempting to suggest matches based on superficial similarities, we should do our best to suggest matches who share common goals and personalities, even if the backgrounds are radically different from one another. Even if our efforts are not met with immediate success, converts are encouraged, knowing that the community cares about them.

It is worth noting that sometimes the sudden introduction of a newly-minted Jew into the marriage arena opens up new *shiddukh* possibilities. I know of several born Jews who went years without finding a marriage partner. They then met someone who had converted at an age close to their own; this new Jew, who had not been a marriage option only a short time before, proved to have the qualities which had been lacking in previous relationships. These couples are now happily married. Both the born Jew and the convert in the relationship had almost despaired of finding that marital "haven" which Naomi sought for Ruth.

AHAVAT HAGER: NOT JUST FOR CONVERTS

I have argued that converts are far more pervasive in our communities than we often assume, and, as such, there is a need to promote the mitzva of *ahavat hager*. Beyond that fact, highlighting the mitzva of *ahavat hager* helps sensitize us to the many other "strangers" in our communities, even those who were born Jewish. Consider the powerful words of the medieval author of *Sefer HaḤinukh*:

> We should learn from this precious mitzva to extend ourselves to anyone in our communities who is far from his place of origin and family. We should not simply pass him by when we discover him all alone, without those who can help him. We see that the Torah commands us to extend ourselves to someone who needs support. (Mitzva 431)

There are so many "strangers" in our communities: couples in crises, children who feel lost, older singles, people struggling emotionally, religiously, financially – the list goes on and on. Our public discourse on the topic of *ahavat hager* – narrowly defined – will help us develop and sharpen a sensitivity to those who are part of the broader definition of *ahavat hager*, as described by *Sefer HaḤinukh*. The development and implementation of that sensitivity carry with them great blessings, as described in that same passage:

> When we develop these character traits, we merit having God extend His mercies to us, and the blessings of Heaven descend upon us.

The sensitivity shown to Ruth ultimately paved the path to the birth of King David. May our sensitivity to converts in the contemporary community also yield blessed results.

Ireland and "The People"

Dr. Seamus O'Malley

Ｉn 2016, the Irish Taoiseach (equivalent to a Prime Minister), Enda Kenny, met with President Donald Trump at the White House, for what most thought would be a pro forma and innocuous visit. Instead Kenny used the opportunity to aggressively defend immigrants against Trump's policy threats, pointing out that St. Patrick was an immigrant, that many Irish had to flee their country because of the Potato Famine, and that America had always served as a symbol of hope: "Four decades before Lady Liberty lifted her lamp, we were the wretched refuse on the teeming shore. We believed in the shelter of America, in the compassion of America, in the opportunity of America. We came and became Americans."[1]

Kenny's words won praise internationally, but for many Irish critics his speech was pure hypocrisy, given Ireland's traditionally hostile reception to its own immigrants. In 2004 an amendment to the Irish constitution passed, with 80 percent of the vote, that prohibited children

---

1. *Irish Times*, March 19, 2017. www.irishtimes.com/news/ireland/irish-news/30-million-views-and-counting-enda-kenny-s-st-patrick-s-speech-goes-viral-1.3016419.

born on Irish soil from becoming citizens if both of their parents were foreign nationals.[2]

One would think a place like Ireland would welcome immigrants in an attempt to bring it back to pre-Famine population levels. But immigration and populism have proved lifelong antagonists, and populism, in many forms, has been a strong current in Irish discourses for two centuries. Evidence for this trend can be found in the repeated use of the loaded phrase "the people," two words that do much of the heavy lifting for populist movements. If the spirit of openness to newcomers is best expressed by the Book of Ruth (1:16) – "for whither thou goest, I will go; and where thou lodgest, I will lodge: thy people *shall be* my people" – such a welcoming set of words clash with "the people," a phrase that erects walls.

Enlightenment political discourse revolved around the contradictions within the phrase. Writers like John Milton, John Locke, or Thomas Paine, usually signaled the educated – Enlightened – upper middle classes when they mentioned "the people," as opposed to the "vulgar," mostly uneducated manual laborers.[3] Such usage reached fruition in America with the US Constitution, which declared power for "We the People." "The people" in that document meant white male Protestant landowners, and was never intended to signal "the populace" at large. Yet the radical nature of its concepts grew, and in the United States and United Kingdom, the franchise was slowly expanded. Various movements and referendums eventually welcomed women, Catholics, and African Americans into the official citizenry of those two nations.

In Ireland, by contrast, history witnesses a different narrative. At the same time as the American Revolution, there was a similar phenomenon in Ireland, with Patriots arming themselves, complaining about British rule, and promising a government "by the people and for the people." These Patriots, however, could not match radical deeds to their radical words, as when they looked around they saw an island teeming with hostile Catholics, with whom they had no intention of sharing power in any form, especially the vote. Instead, "the people" as

2. *The Guardian*, June 12, 2004. www.theguardian.com/world/2004/jun/13/ireland.
3. See Paul Hammond, *Milton and the People* (Oxford: Oxford University Press, 2014).

a radical Protestant rallying cry died, on January 1, 1801, the first day the Act of Union went into effect, joining Ireland to the United Kingdom.

Phase two of "the people" emerged from Continental Europe. The French Revolution, despite its rational Enlightenment origins, spawned a more primordial, irrational, and mystic attachment to France as a nation, embodied in *le peuple*. German thinkers, inspired by the Romanticism birthed by the Revolution, turned to the *Volk*, whose supposed attachment to the soil gave legitimacy to various cultural activities. Populist nationalism was born.

There were just as many contradictions inherent in nationalism's conception of "the people" as there were in its Enlightenment forms, but they were of a different kind: nationalism used language, culture, local customs, etc., to delineate and define "the people." This inevitably meant asserting who were not "the people," and even who were the "enemies of the people" (hence the centrality of rejuvenated secular anti-Semitism during the emergence of nationalism).

These Continental ideas trickled across the waters, interestingly not finding fertile soil in England, but welcomed by Irish thinkers, who looked to "the people" – now the Catholic peasants, especially of the poor rural west. By the time of the Irish Renaissance (launched by W. B. Yeats, J. M. Synge, Lady Gregory, etc.), "the people" had become its own opposite. The Protestant landowners of the 1780s would not have recognized the new discourse.

It is crucial when examining a text that invokes "the people" to ask: Who are "the people"? Who are not? How are such definitions employed? What assumptions does it display? Is the text a critique of populism, or an endorsement? It is my belief that "the people" do not exist, but are powerful nonetheless. They are not out there waiting to be found; they are created anew every time someone groups communities together and calls them *the* people. They are made by language and discourse.

Yeats is an important figure for me, as he goes through so many phases. In his early, *Celtic Twilight* phase of the 1890s, he wants to go to "the people" of the Catholic, Irish-speaking West, to get away from the supposedly sterile cosmopolitanism of Dublin and London. He sees Irish culture in need of rejuvenation; he initiates the Renaissance by getting in touch with Irish soil, traditions, buried myths that are housed, hidden even, in the minds of the poor. Such an approach pays good cultural dividends for a decade, but eventually he gets restless. He reads Ibsen, Nietzsche. Both declared themselves "enemies of the people" to showcase their avant-garde credentials. Yeats too wants to be avant-garde, but to be the "enemy of the people" in Ireland means you are… a British bureaucrat, an absentee landlord, a police informer. This challenge sends Yeats into some rhetorical gymnastics. His Nietzschean, rebellious nature starts to bridle, as any true avant-gardist must, against popular culture – "the crowd," as they are increasingly called. "The crowd" and "the masses" dominate early twentieth-century thinkers, haunt them even. Mass culture is a new formulation, and many modernists reacted in horror.

Yeats, however, could not shake his commitment to "the people" as easily as, say, T. S. Eliot or Ezra Pound. He cleverly decided that "the people" are not "the masses": the latter prefer popular poetry, "the people" do not.[4] Yeats thus severs "the people" from the popular, forging an anti-populism out of a bizarre alliance of rural dwellers and the cultural elite. In these writings Yeats discovers his true enemy, the middle classes, whom he would blame for the world's ills for the rest of his life. Such gestures allow him to still champion "the people," while also becoming a spokesperson for high culture and a hostile critic of mass culture.

This second phase also lasts about a decade. The great poet eventually realizes something he had been denying all along: "the people" are Catholic, they are not different from "the crowd," they will never like his poetry or identify with his politics. Coincidentally or not, he then went on to produce his best poetry. But first he had, just like the world is now, to wrestle with the debates as to who are "the people," and who are not.

---

4.   See his 1901 essay "What is 'Popular Poetry'?" in *Early Essays* (New York: Scribner, 2007).

Immigration, Law, and Identity

Immigration:
A Perspective from Biblical
Narrative and Law

Rabbi Saul J. Berman

Perhaps it is no accident that the citizens of El Paso, Texas, their political leaders both Democrat and Republican, and their religious leaders, have been at the forefront of the national resistance to inhumane policies related to immigrants and border walls.[1] On the side of the mountain high above the Mexican city of Juarez, in letters thirteen stories high, visible across the border in El Paso, Texas, are painted the words, "*La Biblia es la verdad. Leela.*" In English, "The Bible is the truth. Read it."[2]

The attitudes of individuals toward immigrants and immigration are shaped by many factors such as family history, personal experience,

---

1. See *El Paso Times* Editorial Board, July 22, 2017, at https://hurd.house.gov/media-center/in-the-news/el-paso-leads-immigration-issues-editorial.

2. See Nash Jenkins, "Beto O'Rourke Is on a Long, Hard Road," *Time Magazine*, May 22, 2018. http://time.com/longform/beto-orourke-texas-democratic-senate-race/.

religious values, economic interests, and ethical convictions. The purpose of this chapter is not to displace those factors, nor to suggest that they are insignificant, but is simply an attempt to add another weighty factor to the deliberations of people who take biblical narrative and law seriously as sources of ethical values, personal virtues, and principles of social justice.

A. IMMIGRATION IN BIBLICAL NARRATIVE

The first component of my proposal is that we need to view the Book of Genesis, from chapter 12 until the end, as having a single central theme – the human experience of being immigrants. More than half of all the narratives in that portion of the Bible constitute a systematic attempt to describe the motives for immigration, the challenges which immigrants confront, and the varied ways in which our biblical ancestors attempted to meet those challenges. The stories themselves are well known to all readers of the Bible and need not be described in great detail. But outlining each of these narratives specifically from the perspective of the issues dealt with by immigrants may grant us new perspectives on the patterns implicit in the texts, and an opportunity to then see biblical legislation in the later books in a very different light.

1. Abraham's Experiences with Immigration
1:1 Abraham emigrates to Canaan
We are told in Genesis 11:31 that Terah the father of Abraham had begun a family journey from Ur of the Chaldees, intending to go to the land of Canaan, but that they stopped in the city of Haran. We are told nothing of the motive of that emigration, nor of any of the experiences which the family had during the journey or at the destination to which they had arrived. But at the start of chapter 12, God instructs Abraham to complete the journey which the family had begun.

> Now *Adonai* said to Avram, "Get yourself out of your country, away from your kinsmen and away from your father's house, and go to the land that I will show you. I will make of you a great nation, I will bless you, and I will make your name great; and you are to be a blessing. I will bless those who bless you, but I

will curse anyone who curses you; and by you all the families of the earth will be blessed." So Avram went, as *Adonai* had said to him, and Lot went with him. Avram was 75 years old when he left Haran. Avram took his wife Sarai, his brother's son Lot, and all their possessions which they had accumulated, as well as the people they had acquired in Haran; then they set out for the land of Kena'an and entered the land of Kena'an.[3] (Gen. 12:1–5)

Did Abram really require the incentives of the six blessings offered by God in verses 2 and 3? Was this not yet the Abraham who was later capable of submission even to the inexplicable divine command to sacrifice his beloved son, Isaac? It is striking that in verse 4 we are not told that Abraham went as the Lord had "commanded" him, but that he went as the Lord had "spoken" to him. Indeed, the implication is that it was not solely the divine command which motivated Abraham, but that the additional divine promises were themselves intended to serve as incentives, and in fact served in that capacity in his decision. Thus as we look in this passage at the question of what motivated Abraham to immigrate, we are pointed toward the conclusion that he had received a vision of great success in store for him in the land of Canaan – that there he would achieve both material wealth and personal greatness, that he would be the founder of a nation and a source of blessing for all of humanity. Who could resist such a vision?

Then perhaps, we are led in this direction not because Abraham himself needed such incentive, but because throughout human history such grand visions of streets paved with gold, of the opportunity to flourish in spiritual and material realms, would continue to generate vast movements of people, people who were neither prophets nor saints, and that we need to understand and respect such motivation. But numerous intense challenges were yet to be confronted by Abraham and by his descendants in the subsequent chapters of the Book of Genesis.

---

3. Translations in this section are based on the *Complete Jewish Bible* (CJB) as found in https://www.biblegateway.com.

1:2 *Abraham emigrates to Egypt*

In verse 10 of that very chapter, Abram is confronted by the need to emigrate again, this time due to a famine in the land of Canaan.

> But there was a famine in the land, so Avram went down into Egypt to stay there, because the famine in the land was severe. When he came close to Egypt and was about to enter, he said to Sarai his wife, "Here now, I know that you are a good-looking woman; so that when the Egyptians see you, they will say, 'This is his wife,' and kill me but keep you alive. Please say that you are my sister, so that it will go well with me for your sake, and so that I will stay alive because of you." (Gen. 10–14)

The motive for Abram's second emigration is clear and unequivocal – there was a famine in Canaan. But there is an anomaly here. Abram recognizes that he will experience a severe challenge in his flight into Egypt – the Egyptians will attempt to take his wife, and if he resists they will kill him. How precisely did Abraham know this about Egypt? He had not read Fodor's *Guide to Egypt,* nor did he Google "vacationing in Egypt." We need to consider the possibility that the feared conduct of Egypt was quite well known, even to strangers who were coming all the way from Ur of the Chaldees. We might further need to consider the possibility that such expected conduct would have been a reality virtually wherever Abraham and his family would have wandered over 3,000 years ago.

In any case, recognizing this challenge, Abram instructs his wife to lie about her marital status in order to maximize their protection. A close reading of the text suggests that Sarah herself actually did not lie, but that Pharaoh, after suffering a plague and connecting that to his having taken Sarah, accused Abraham of having directly lied about the identity of Sarah (Gen. 12:19).[4] Jewish commentators debated intensely the question of whether Abraham was morally justified in placing Sarah at risk through this stratagem. Thus, Nahmanides actually perceives

---

4. See *Ramban (Nachmanides): Commentary on the Torah,* translated and annotated by Rabbi Dr. Charles B. Chavel (New York: Shilo Publishing House, 1971), vol. 1, p. 176.

here a double sin on the part of Abraham: first his lack of faith in divine protection in leaving the Promised Land due to a famine, and then in "bringing his righteous wife to a stumbling-block of sin on account of his fear for his life."[5] Most, however, justify Abraham on the dual grounds of it not being right to rely on miracles and the permissibility of lying as a defense against an aggressor.[6]

1:3 The countercultural model: Abraham and family

Our next meeting with Abraham around the issue of treatment of migrants is the passage in Genesis 18:1–8, 16.

> *Adonai* appeared to Avraham by the oaks of Mamre as he sat at the entrance to the tent during the heat of the day. He raised his eyes and looked, and there in front of him stood three men. On seeing them, he ran from the tent door to meet them, prostrated himself on the ground, and said, "My lord, if I have found favor in your sight, please don't leave your servant. Please let me send for some water, so that you can wash your feet; then rest under the tree, and I will bring a piece of bread. Now that you have come to your servant, refresh yourselves before going on." "Very well," they replied, "do what you have said." Avraham hurried into the tent to Sarah and said, "Quickly, three measures of the best flour! Knead it and make cakes." Avraham ran to the herd, took a good, tender calf and gave it to the servant, who hurried to prepare it. Then he took curds, milk and the calf which he had prepared, and set it all before the men; and he stood by them under the tree as they ate.... The men set out from there and looked over toward S'dom, and Avraham went with them to see them on their way.

---

5. Ibid., 173–174.
6. See ibid., Hebrew version, p. 79, footnote to Gen. 12:10, s.v. *bishgaga*. Albeit it is still worth noting the ingenious approach of E. A. Speiser, "The Wife-Sister Motif in the Patriarchal Narratives," *Biblical and Other Studies* I (Cambridge: Brandeis University Press, 1963), 15–28. He summarizes his position in his notes to *The Anchor Bible: Genesis* (New York: Doubleday and Co., 1964), 91–94.

It is clear that the Torah is here positing the conduct of Abraham as a countercultural model for dealing with the arrival of strangers – unconditionally welcoming them, offering them water to wash themselves, a place to rest, and food to eat, and then accompanying them along the way in their departure. The passage further emphasizes that Abraham did not singly perform all of these actions, but that in addition to his personal efforts, he engaged his wife and their household staff in extending hospitality to the strangers. Rabbinic Midrash places great emphasis on the fact that this passage follows immediately upon the fulfillment by Abraham of the commandment of circumcision (Gen. 17:24), suggesting that his altruistic welcoming of the strangers was performed despite the fact that he was still in intense pain in consequence of the circumcision.[7] In addition, the opening verse of the chapter indicates that God Himself had appeared to Abraham at that moment in time,[8] yet Abraham apparently leaves God in the lurch in order to welcome the strangers, leading to an interpretation of verse 3 as an aside by Abraham to God requesting Him to wait while he greets the guests. This understanding leads the sages to suggest that "It is greater to welcome strangers into your home than to greet the Divine Presence."[9]

1:4 The countercultural model: Lot

The suggestion that such behavior in welcoming strangers was in fact a countercultural model, distinctive to the family of Abraham, is further emphasized at the start of the next chapter (Gen. 19:1–11), in the reaction of the citizens of Sodom to the behavior of Lot, the nephew of Abraham.

> The two angels came to S'dom that evening, when Lot was sitting at the gate of S'dom. Lot saw them, got up to greet them and prostrated himself on the ground. He said, "Here now, my lords, please come over to your servant's house. Spend the night, wash your feet, get up early, and go on your way." "No," they answered,

---

7. Bava Metzia 86b.
8. To manifest the Godly virtue of visiting the sick according to *Midrash Tanḥuma* to Gen. 18:1, and Sota 14a, as cited in Rashi to Gen. 18:1.
9. Shevuot 35b, cited by Rashi as an alternative interpretation of Gen. 18:3.

"we'll stay in the square." But he kept pressing them; so they went home with him; and he made them a meal, baking *matzah* for their supper, which they ate. (Gen. 19:1–3)

But before they could go to bed, the men of the city surrounded the house – young and old, everyone from every neighborhood of S'dom. They called Lot and said to him, "Where are the men who came to stay with you tonight? Bring them out to us! We want to have sex with them!" Lot went out to them and stood in the doorway, closing the door behind him, and said, "Please, my brothers, don't do such a wicked thing. Look here, I have two daughters who are virgins. Please, let me bring them out to you, and you can do with them what seems good to you; but don't do anything to these men, since they are guests in my house." "Stand back!" they replied. "This guy came to live here, and now he's decided to play judge. For that we'll deal worse with you than with them!" Then they crowded in on Lot, in order to get close enough to break down the door. But the men inside reached out their hands, brought Lot into the house to them and shut the door. Then they struck the men at the door of the house with blindness, both small and great, so that they couldn't find the doorway. (Gen. 19:4–11)

Let's focus first on the conduct of Lot. The Torah uses almost identical words and phrases to describe Lot's bodily stance, his urging of the strangers to accept his hospitality, and his offering of food (Gen. 19:1– 3) as it had previously used in describing Abraham's similar actions (Gen. 18:1– 5). Both are sitting at the beginning of the story; both see and then arise to greet the unknown guests and bow to them; both plead with the strangers to stay for while before moving onward; both offer rest, water to wash feet, and a feast. Lot is thus located in the narrative as the family member of Abraham, representing the same social value as his uncle. The narrative is also clear that the accepted standard of conduct of the city of Sodom is the sexual exploitation of strangers. Lot had to be aware that he was taking a risk in rejecting the suggestion of the Messengers that they would remain in the street overnight. Lot was, after all, not himself a native citizen of Sodom and thus becomes the target of the natives' critique when he attempts to protect his guests – "he himself is only a resident alien and he presumes to pass judgement over us!" (paraphrase of Gen. 19:9.)

While presumably recognizing the vulnerability of his status in Sodom, Lot apparently assumes that he will be able to negotiate for the protection of his guests. His negotiating stance is bizarre, offering up his daughters in place of the two strangers, but perhaps he thinks that he and his family are sufficiently integrated into the community that his offer will be perceived as sufficiently ludicrous to preclude its actual acceptance. But that assumption is demonstrated to be false and the ire of the citizenry is simply raised to an even more vicious level. Interestingly, there had been no suggestion of the strategy of negotiation with the ruler of Egypt on the part of Abraham.

A further significant contrast with the narrative about Abraham's welcoming strangers is that Lot's family members are not brought into the process of participation in the virtuous conduct. It is then not accidental that Lot's married daughters and their husbands refuse to believe Lot's warning and simply remain to be destroyed with Sodom (Gen. 19:14); that his wife turns back yearningly during their flight and is herself turned into a pillar of salt (Gen. 19:26); that his two unmarried daughters subsequently commit incest with their father and bear children who are the ancestors of other nations (Gen. 19:31–38), cousins to Israel – but leaving no members of the family of Lot in direct association with the future Israelite people. Is it then already the case that a distinctive attitude of generosity to strangers is an essential virtue for inclusion within the Israelite nation?!

1:5 *The messengers of rescue in Sodom*

Abraham's emigration to Canaan was motivated by his vision of a blessed and successful life; his emigration to Egypt was motivated by the famine in the land of Canaan. The arrival of the two messengers in Sodom was motivated by their service of a divine mission to rescue Lot and as many righteous citizens of Sodom as they might discover. But their mission itself did not provide protection against the evil intentions and practices of the citizens of Sodom. We need, therefore, to pay attention here also to the defensive response to the vulnerability to which they were exposed – to their own homosexual rape and murder, and to the rape and murder of those whom they were charged to rescue. The verse is clear about what they did; they used violence, but only to achieve the protective purpose which would still allow the performance of their mission. They could presumably have killed the attackers, but instead they blinded those who were attempting to break into Lot's home so that they would be unable to find the entrance and to perform the evil deeds which they had intended. It was, as it were, a proportional use of violence as a deterrent to the violence the citizens of Sodom had threatened.

1:6 Abraham's flight to Gerar (Gaza)

After the violent upheavals in the grazing land through the central plains of Canaan as a result of the destruction of Sodom, Abraham had to seek other grazing lands for his flocks. He apparently, therefore, traveled east toward the Mediterranean coast to the land of Gerar. There, a partial repeat of the occurrence in Egypt took place, described in Genesis 20:1–11, 14–15.

> Avraham traveled from there toward the Negev and lived between Kadesh and Shur. While living as an alien in G'rar, Avraham was saying of Sarah his wife, "She is my sister"; so Avimelekh king of G'rar sent and took Sarah. But God came to Avimelekh in a dream one night and said to him, "You are about to die because of the woman you have taken, since she is someone's wife." Now Avimelekh had not come near her; so he said, "Lord, will you kill even an upright nation? Didn't he himself say to me, 'She is my sister'? And even she herself said, 'He is my brother.' In doing this, my heart has been pure and my hands innocent." God said to him in the dream, "Yes, I know that in doing this, your heart has been pure; and I too have kept you from sinning against me. This is why I didn't let you touch her…. Then Avimelekh called Avraham and said to him, "What have you done to us? How have I sinned against you to cause you to bring on me and my kingdom a great sin? You have done things to me that are just not done." Avimelekh went on, asking Avraham, "Whatever

could have caused you to do such a thing?" Avraham replied, "It was because I thought, 'There could not possibly be any fear of God in this place, so they will kill me in order to get my wife.'... Avimelekh took sheep, cattle, and male and female slaves, and gave them to Avraham; and he returned to him Sarah his wife. Then Avimelekh said, "Look, my country lies before you; live where you like."

The similarities in this narrative to that of Genesis chapter 12 are obvious. Upon entering Gerar, Abraham feared that his wife would be taken and he would be killed, and so he, as well as Sarah according to Avimelech's defense to God, lied about their relationship. But so are the distinctions obvious.

In this instance Abraham was not confronting a life-threatening famine, but was apparently motivated by the desire to achieve greater economic success, and nevertheless put himself and Sarah into the situation of needing to lie in self-defense.[10] But other differences are even more significant. In the earlier narrative, Pharaoh asks Abraham why he lied instead of telling him the truth, and then does not even wait for an answer, but in the very same sentence, returns Sarah to Abraham, instructs him to leave the country, and assigns guards to escort them out of Egypt (Gen. 12:18–20). In the situation in Gerar, Avimelech asks the same question of Abraham (Gen. 20:9), but then adds another element in pressing Abraham to tell him what he has seen in Gerar that would have led him to fear rape and murder at their hands (Gen. 20:10.) To that question Abraham replied, "It was because I thought, 'There is not any fear of God in this place, so they will kill me in order to get my wife'" (Gen. 20:11). At that response by Abraham, Avimelech falls silent, as if in admission of the fact they might well have done exactly what Abraham feared. Abraham's response in this instance is a form of chastisement, which Avimelech fails to take to heart, now and later.

As this narrative resumes in Genesis chapter 21, after the account of the birth of Isaac and the expulsion of Hagar and Ishmael, Avimelech

---

10. Indeed, Nahmanides in his commentary to Gen. 20:12 views Abraham's conduct in Gerar as even more reprehensible than his conduct in Egypt.

and his general, Phichol, approach Abraham and request that he enter into a treaty with them not to deal falsely with them, their sons, or grandsons (Gen. 21:22–23). Abraham consented, but requested that they first resolve an outstanding matter between them; he rebuked Avimelech over the fact that Avimelech's servants had robbed a well dug by Abraham (Gen. 21:25). The Torah in fact here uses the very same word, "rebuked," which it uses in Leviticus 19:17 in legislating the requirement of rebuke against one who has wronged another. But Abraham's rebuke is of no avail. Avimelech responds with a total denial of any responsibility: "Avimelech answered, 'I don't know who has done this. You didn't tell me, and I heard about it only today'" (Gen. 21:26). Abraham now realizes what he had previously only suspected, that he has no effective legal protection for his rights to property, that even direct address to the king will not yield anything but denial of responsibility. Even as Avimelech petitions Abraham to enter into a treaty with him, Abraham remains a stranger, an outsider, not protected by the law of the land, by the very principles of truth and kindness to which Avimelech appeals and expects Abraham to honor in his own conduct in the treaty into which they about to enter.

1:7 Abraham's negotiations in Hebron
With the death of Sarah in the city of Hebron, Abraham needs to acquire a burial cave for his wife, and his family. E. A. Speiser puts it as follows:

> The Promised Land was a spiritual grant from God. But the best practical safeguard in terms that everyone could recognize and accept was a clear legal title to the land. The living could get by as sojourners; but the dead required a permanent resting ground. The Founding Fathers, at least, must not be buried on alien soil. The spot had to be theirs beyond any possibility of dispute…tradition had to insist on a title which no law-abiding society would dare to contest and upset.[11]

---

11. E. A. Speiser, *The Anchor Bible*, Genesis, op. cit., comment to chapter 23, at pp. 171–172.

The extremely detailed record of the negotiations leading to the purchase of the Cave of Machpelah by Abraham is founded entirely on the vulnerability of his status as a resident alien. He declares that status to the town's community council at the outset and then insists that all aspects of the negotiations leading to the sale take place in public in the presence of the council and with their consent (Gen. 23:3–16). Abraham had learned well the lesson of his relationship with Avimelech in Gerar. The local authorities could not be left with the excuse that they did not know in advance of the claim that Abraham had to the land. His defensive response to his vulnerability as an alien was precisely his preemptive inclusion of the council in every detail of the transaction, his need for a separate burial cave, the location of the cave, the current property owner, the boundaries of the field within which the cave was found, the price requested by the vendor, the coinage with which it was paid, and even the standard by which that coinage was valued.

One must wonder what psychic price is paid for the vigilance that must be maintained by the migrant as to his or her economic and social vulnerability in every sphere of life, and the degree of planning and detailed execution needed in order to achieve any reasonable degree of protection from exploitation. Is that what the Torah is attempting to convey, in informing us that Abraham had to rise up from his mourning and weeping for Sarah in order to negotiate as a resident alien with the local council of the children of Het (Gen. 23:2–4)?

1:8 Abraham's search for a wife for Isaac

The longest single chapter in the Book of Genesis, consisting of sixty-seven verses, is devoted to a single event, the search for a wife for Isaac.[12] Abraham charged his senior servant with the task of selecting a bride for Isaac, with a single condition, that she be of Abraham's own family from his ancestral home. The servant,[13] upon his arrival in the City of Nachor in Aram Naharayim, apparently understood that Abraham had

---

12. In the Hebrew original this is also a single chapter uninterrupted by paragraph divisions. In the synagogue reading on the Sabbath this chapter is divided into four readings.

13. Identified in rabbinic tradition as Eliezer of Damascus, based on his role in Abraham's household described in Genesis 15:2.

in mind as a wife for Isaac not just any member of his tribe, but a bearer
of a particular personal virtue.

> Toward evening, when the women go out to draw water, he had
> the camels kneel down outside the city by the well. He said, "*Ado-
> nai*, God of my master Avraham, please let me succeed today;
> and show your grace to my master Avraham. Here I am, stand-
> ing by the spring, as the daughters of the townsfolk come out to
> draw water. I will say to one of the girls, 'Please lower your jug,
> so that I can drink.' If she answers, 'Yes, drink; and I will water
> your camels as well,' then let her be the one you intend for your
> servant Yitz'chak. This is how I will know that you have shown
> grace to my master." (Gen. 24:11–14)

The servant does not even ask for God to assure that the woman be of the
family of Abraham, the condition which Abraham had demanded, but
that she manifest the quality of welcoming strangers, of offering drink to
persons and camels, and of inviting them into the family's home. Obviously the servant did not expect there to be a mass rush by the women
at the well to serve him in this manner, because he understood that this
was a countercultural characteristic. That's exactly what he understood
Abraham to be looking for in order to assure the continuity of this quality in the household of his son, Isaac.

The centrality of this virtue in the formation of the households of
the descendants of Abraham is emphasized by the fact that this description of the servant's expectation, and then of its fulfillment by Rebecca,
is described in identical detail four times in the course of this chapter:
when the servant petitions God for it, when Rebecca fulfills it, and
when the servant describes his petition and Rebecca's conduct to Laban.

The rabbinic understanding that this quality of kindness to strangers was fundamental to Abraham for the families of all of his offspring
is powerfully indicated by a passage in Midrash[14] which describes

---

14. *Pirkei DeRabbi Eliezer*, ch. 30. https://www.sefaria.org/Pirkei_DeRabbi_
Eliezer.30?lang=bi. I am indebted to Rabbi Jacob J. Schacter who first introduced
this midrashic text to me in another context.

Abraham visiting the home of his son Ishmael to find that his wife, in Ishmael's absence, refuses to provide Abraham with bread and water. Abraham sends a message to his son to "Exchange the threshold of thy house, for it is not good for thee." Ishmael gets the message, divorces his wife, and marries another who exhibits appropriate hospitality and of whom Abraham approves.

Thus far then, we have found in the biblical narratives about Abraham and his family multiple elements that reflect more generally on the experiences of immigrants. We discovered many motives for immigration: having a vision of a blessed life, escaping famine, being messengers on a divine mission, seeking greater economic success, and more specific needs such as the burial of a relative or finding a wife. We took careful note as well of the multiple vulnerabilities which strangers/ immigrants confront: threat of sexual abuse and threat to life, risk of rejection, economic exploitation, and absence of legal protection. Thirdly, we have taken note of the variety of strategies which Abraham and others utilized in the attempt to meet these challenges: lying, negotiation, violence, rebuke, entry into treaty, insisting on public acknowledgment of one's rights, and extreme vigilance.

Beyond all of this, we recognized in these biblical narratives about Abraham the emergence of a countercultural model in his life and in the lives of Abrahamic families, which propounds the moral need to welcome strangers, immigrants, and wanderers; to be responsive to their physical and emotional needs; to secure their safety and their economic security. These patterns will be further enhanced and fleshed out as we turn from Abraham to the next three generations of his descendants, Isaac, Jacob, and Joseph.

	Cases	Genesis	Motive for Immigration	Vulnerabilities	Defensive Response
Abraham	1:1	12:1–5	vision of blessed life		
	1:2	12:10–20	famine → Egypt	threat of rape and murder	Abraham mad and asked Sarah to lie

	Cases	Genesis	Motive for Immigration	Vulnerabilities	Defensive Response
	1:3	18:1–8		welcoming strangers as countercultural model	engaged his family
Lot	1:4	19:1–3		welcoming strangers at risk of rejection	negotiation
Messengers	1:5	19:4–26	on divine mission	homosexual rape and murder	violence and escape
Abraham	1:6	20:1–15	economic success → Gerar	threat of rape and murder	Abraham and Sarah lie; chastisement
	1:7	21:22–32		theft of wells – no legal protection	rebuke and entry in treaty
		23:1–20	needs burial cave for wife → Hebron	deception – revocation of sale	public negotiation of contract; vigilance
	1:8	24:14	sends Eliezer to Haran for wife for Isaac	need to preserve welcoming strangers as countercultural model	search for wife with those qualities

2. Isaac's Experience as an Immigrant

2:1 Isaac flees to Gerar

The Torah appears to present three narrations of the Forefathers emigrating due to famine, experiencing a threat of rape and death, lying in self-defense, and then departing. Why this apparent redundancy? The Torah presents us with two such accounts of Abraham emigrating due to economic conditions. The first is in chapter 12 when, due to famine, Abraham flees to Egypt, discovers that there is a threat to body and life, asks Sarah to lie, lies himself, is enriched, his lie is discovered, and he departs. In the second account, in chapter 20, the narrative repeats the same fundamental elements – economic crisis leads Abraham to remove himself and his family to Gerar; under perceived threat of rape and death, Abraham lies, but his lie is discovered. Then another layer of the story emerges. When Pharaoh, ruler of Egypt, asked Abraham why he lied, he did not even await an answer, but ordered Abraham to depart, and ordered his officers to immediately deport Abraham and his family (Gen. 12:18–20). By contrast, when Avimelech, ruler of Gerar, asked Abraham why he lied, he actually awaits an answer. In response, Abraham rebukes Avimelech for the absence of fear of God in his land which led him to think that risk of rape and death was realistic (Gen. 20:9–11). Avimelech does not repudiate Abraham's chastisement, but enriches him and invites him to settle anywhere in Gerar. Thus, while in these two accounts the motive for emigration is similar, and the vulnerabilities are identical, in the second narrative Abraham seizes on an opportunity for an additional layer of defensive response, direct rebuke of the ruler, and that is apparently successful in reducing the risk of sexual assault and of death.

However, as the narrative in chapter 20 about Abraham and Avimelech resumes in the latter part of chapter 21, a new vulnerability of Abraham as an immigrant emerges with great force, as the servants of Avimelech laid claim to and dispossessed Abraham of the wells which he had dug. Abraham bides his time until Avimelech approaches him with the offer that they enter into a treaty. Then Abraham returns to his previously successful strategy of rebuke, but Avimelech completely rejects any responsibility for the misappropriation of the wells by his servants (Gen. 21:22–27). Thus, Abraham then discovered that he had no legal protection against this economic exploitation, and so he tried a further new strategy, entering into a specific treaty with Avimelech about the particular well which Abraham had dug at Beer Sheba (Gen. 21:28:32). Thus, the second narrative about Abraham as a resident alien is not simply a repetition of the first, but is a layering on of a second account which then extends our understanding both of the vulnerabilities experienced by the immigrant, and of the defensive strategies which they utilize in confronting those challenges.

Now, as we turn to the third account of this sort, Isaac's flight to Gerar, we need to watch closely for the new elements of recognition of vulnerabilities experienced, and defensive responses implemented by immigrants, which are introduced in this third narrative layer. Isaac confronts a famine, in response to which he emigrates to Gerar. Fearing that the locals will kill him to take Rebecca, he lies and tells them that she is his sister. The ruler, Avimelech, apparently already had his eyes on Rebecca, but sees Isaac pleasuring her and understands that they are husband and wife. Avimelech confronts Isaac with the fact and asks him why he had lied. Isaac responds that he feared for his life (Gen. 26:6–9). Avimelech's response is telling:

> And Abimelech said, "What is this you have done to us? One of the people might soon have lain with your wife, and you would have brought guilt on us." So Abimelech charged all his people, saying, "He who touches this man or his wife shall surely be put to death." (Gen. 26:10–11)[15]

Avimelech does not deny the reality base of Isaac's fear. In fact, he seems to suggest that he himself was about to take her (with or without her consent). And he understands that it is in fact necessary for him as ruler to command his people not to abuse Isaac or Rebecca under threat of the death penalty. Clearly their status as strangers would leave them with no protection without the declaration of the royal edict. Thus far the elements are identical to those of the preceding two accounts regarding Abraham.

But the story continues. Isaac prospered in Gerar and as he did so:

> ...the Philistines envied him. Now the Philistines had stopped up all the wells which his father's servants had dug in the days of Abraham his father, and they had filled them with earth. And Abimelech said to Isaac, "Go away from us, for you are much mightier than we." Then Isaac departed from there and pitched his tent in the Valley of Gerar, and dwelt there. And Isaac dug again the wells of water which they had dug in the days of Abraham his father,

---

15. The translation here, and hereafter, is slightly modified from that of the New King James Version, as found at https://www.biblegateway.com.

for the Philistines had stopped them up after the death of Abraham. He called them by the names which his father had called them. Also Isaac's servants dug in the valley, and found a well of running water there. But the herdsmen of Gerar quarreled with Isaac's herdsmen, saying, "The water is ours." ... (Gen. 26:14–20)

Isaac's economic success, despite or because of the fact that he was an alien, generated envy on the part of the local citizens. So much so that they stuffed up his family's wells, despite the fact that the success of both agriculture and herding was dependent upon open wells and cisterns. Even Avimelech knew that he could not stop this antagonism toward the stranger and could not guarantee him any economic justice and so he tells Isaac to simply move on. But Isaac is determined to meet this challenge with persistent effort, perhaps thinking that he could eventually persuade the local citizens that they might also benefit from his success and that they might cease being jealous and antagonistic toward him. But his moving within Gerar does not solve the problem; wherever Isaac re-excavates the wells that his father had dug, the locals claim the water as their own; Isaac lacks any legal protection against their economic exploitation of him, and he has to move yet again.

The immigrant's vulnerability to economic exploitation was already evident in the second story about Abraham, but the awareness of the jealousy of the local citizens as a new challenge, and the determination to overcome both the economic challenge and the emotional vulnerability through persistence in living amongst them and of maintaining the same level of economic efforts, are new elements which only appear in this third layer of narrative. The culmination of this stage of our understanding of the experiences of the immigrant appear in the next verses:

Then Abimelech came to him from Gerar with Ahuzzath, one of his friends, and Phichol the commander of his army. And Isaac said to them, "Why have you come to me, since you hate me and have sent me away from you?" (Gen. 26:26–27)

Here Isaac confronts the emotional assault against himself as a stranger, head on. He does not hide his anger, but acknowledges his awareness of hatred toward himself. But he remains in control, agrees to enter into treaty with Avimelech, and ends the relationship by sending them away, as they had previously sent him away (Gen. 26:30–31).

	Cases	Genesis	Motive for Immigration	Vulnerabilities	Defensive Response
Isaac	2:1	26:1–24	famine → Gerar	threat of rape and murder	Isaac lied
		26:14–23		hated by government	persistence, pride
		26:26–29			acknowledged hatred; rebuke; entry into treaty and flees

3. JACOB EMIGRATES AND RETURNS AS AN IMMIGRANT

3:1 Jacob flees to Haran

After Jacob steals the blessing which their father Isaac had apparently intended to give to his brother, the latter, Esau, threatens to kill Jacob. Rebecca, upon being informed of Esau's intentions, instructs Jacob to flee to the home of her brother, Laban, in Haran until the fury of Esau would subside (Gen. 27:45). Jacob meets and loves Rachel, and is welcomed into Laban's home with an exuberant declaration as to Jacob's place in the family: "And Laban said to him, 'Surely you are my bone and my flesh.' And he stayed with him for a month" (Gen. 29:14). By the end of the month, Laban's true attitude toward his refugee nephew begins to emerge in four consecutive rejections and deceptions.

First: A rejection. The intensity of Laban's claim of loving connection to Jacob is reflected in the fact that his welcome is an echo of the words of Adam upon the discovery of the woman created for him, "This at last is bone of my bones and flesh of my flesh" (Gen. 2:23). While not a spouse, Laban seems to be suggesting that Jacob shall be unto him as a son, his own offspring. Yet, thirty days later: "Laban said to Jacob, 'Because you are my relative [brother], should you therefore serve me for nothing? Tell me, what should your wages be?'" (Gen. 29:15). Note how Laban has here demoted Jacob's place in his family from son to brother, or possibly even just to relative – like nephew.[16] As a possible son, Jacob might have seen himself as entitled eventually to some significant share in the property of Laban. As an employee, he is clearly entitled only to whatever his salary is. But despite this rejection, putting Jacob back in his place as a stranger with limited entitlements, Jacob does not react negatively, because he has a plan. He intends to marry Rachel and thereby his status in the family, at least as a son-in-law, will be assured. He asks for the hand of Rachel as payment for seven years of work, to which Laban accedes.

Second: A deception. This all sets the stage for the second betrayal as Laban substitutes Leah for Rachel on the wedding night. When Jacob, in the morning, objects to the deception, Laban's response is unequivocal – you are only an immigrant here, if you had been a citizen you would have known that "such is not done in our country, to give the younger daughter [in marriage] before the firstborn" (Gen. 29:25–26). But Laban has something else in mind. He has the opportunity to exploit Jacob's desire to marry Rachel by offering to give her also to Jacob in exchange for another seven years of labor. While having objected to the deception, Jacob does not further decry the economic exploitation, nor does he pause in his response; he has a strategy that will get him what he wants – he will simply work harder, even longer than originally planned, another seven years, in order to get Rachel as his wife; and so he does (Gen. 29:27–30.)

Third: Further deception. During those fourteen years, Laban's wealth had grown enormously due to the efforts of Jacob and the divine

---

16. For use of the Hebrew word *aḥikha*, brother, to refer to more distant relatives, see Num. 20:14 and Deut. 23:8. This shift in the attitude of Laban is noted by Maimonides in his commentary to Gen. 29:15. It is also worth considering the possibility of an alternate translation of Laban's comment, as: "Are you then my brother, that you would work for me for free?" In this case, the echo would be to Cain's rejection of responsibility for his brother, "Am I my brother's keeper?" (Gen. 4:9).

blessing of his labors. But now Jacob wanted to be able to establish himself independently. And so he negotiated a new agreement with Laban as to his compensation (Gen. 30:25–34). However, Jacob later explains to his wives that during the additional six years that he worked for an agreed-upon salary, Laban had constantly changed the terms of their agreement, and that it was only divine intervention which enabled him to become wealthy:

> And you know that with all my might I have served your father. Yet your father has deceived me and changed my wages ten times, but God did not allow him to hurt me. If he said thus: "The speckled shall be your wages," then all the flocks bore speckled. And if he said thus: "The streaked shall be your wages," then all the flocks bore streaked. So God has taken away the livestock of your father and given them to me. (Gen. 31:6–9)

In fact, Jacob later declares that he had throughout this time worked self-sacrificially in the face of Laban's repeated deceptions. That seems to have been Jacob's systematic response to the economic exploitation by Laban:

> Then Jacob was angry and rebuked Laban…. "These twenty years I have been with you; your ewes and your female goats have not miscarried their young, and I have not eaten the rams of your flock. That which was torn by beasts I did not bring to you; I bore the loss of it. You required it from my hand, whether stolen by day or stolen by night. There I was! In the day the drought consumed me, and the frost by night, and my sleep departed from my eyes. Thus I have been in your house twenty years; I served you fourteen years for your two daughters, and six years for your flock, and you have changed my wages ten times. Unless the God of my father, the God of Abraham and the Fear of Isaac, had been with me, surely now you would have sent me away empty-handed. God has seen my affliction and the labor of my hands, and rebuked you last night." (Gen. 31:36, 38–42)

Fourth: Another rejection. As Jacob had negotiated a successful agreement with Laban as to his salary for shepherding his flocks (Gen. 30:25– 43), the separate wealth of Jacob increased. It was then that he took note of the deep jealousy toward him on the part of his brothers-in-law, which was producing a similar shift in attitude toward him on the part of their father, Laban:

> Now Jacob heard the words of Laban's sons, saying, "Jacob has taken away all that was our father's, and from what was our father's he has acquired all this wealth." And Jacob saw the countenance of Laban, and indeed it was not favorable toward him as before. (Gen. 31:1–2).

Despite having been rejected, deceived, and cheated, Jacob only loses total hope in his ability to remain in Haran when he experiences the jealousy of his brothers-in-law, and the corrosive effect that has on whatever positive feelings still existed in his relationship to Laban. Then, after a vision in which God instructs Jacob to return to Canaan, and with the consent and support of Rachel and Leah, he packed up his family and began his travel back to the land of his forefathers (Gen. 31:3–21).

In that final stage, however, the Torah itself testifies to a double deception perpetrated against Laban, one by Rachel, the other by Jacob:

> Now Laban had gone to shear his sheep, and Rachel had stolen the household idols that were her father's. And Jacob stole away, unknown to Laban the Syrian, in that he did not tell him that he intended to flee. (Gen. 31:19–20)

These deceptions set the stage for a closing confrontation between Jacob and Laban in which Laban accuses Jacob of deception and theft by his sneaking away with Laban's daughters and grandchildren without informing him, and of stealing his household idols. Jacob responds to each accusation in turn. As to why he withheld his plan to leave, Jacob spoke in language precisely reminiscent of the language of his ancestors Abraham and Isaac in their confrontations with Pharaoh and Avimelech – they failed to disclose the truth because they feared that their wives would be taken from them (Gen. 12:12; 20:11; 26:7) – so too, Jacob says that he feared that Laban would take his wives from him by force (Gen. 31:31).[17] In fact, this parallel between the three prior stories of lying or withholding truth is already emphasized by the language of Laban in his charge against Jacob, saying, "What have you done.... Why did you...not tell me..." (Gen. 31:26– 27). Such was precisely the accusatory language of Pharaoh and Avimelech in the prior three stories (Gen. 12:18; 20:5, 9; and 26:9–10) – suggesting, of course, that all of them, including Laban, were knowingly lying about what they might have done had they actually known the truth. Truly, in all four of these stories, layered upon one another, the depths of the vulnerabilities of the immigrant are manifested and emphasized.

A further element in the parallel between these four narratives is that each concludes with entry into a treaty despite the absence of resolution of the distrust between the parties. But there is yet more to come.

3:2 Jacob returns and contends with Esau

Jacob returning to Canaan understands that he still needs to resolve the twenty-year-old conflict with his infuriated brother in order to achieve his desire for a peaceful life. His fear of Esau is palpable in Genesis chapters 32 and 33. Perhaps Jacob realized that his lack of fear in his earlier emigration to the home of his uncle, Laban, had left him truly unprepared for the challenges which his inferior status had exposed him to, and that this time he was going to be superbly prepared, perhaps even overprepared. His first layer of preparation was a verbal message of appeasement in which he adopts a distinctively subservient stance: "Speak thus to my lord Esau, 'Thus your servant Jacob says: I have dwelt with Laban ... and I have sent to tell my lord, that I may find favor in your sight'" (Gen. 32:4–5). When his messengers return with the news that Esau is coming toward him with a contingent of 400 men, Jacob realizes that a second layer of preparation is necessary, a defensive strategy which will at least assure the rescue of some part of his camp if there is

---

17. While Laban's accusations were of theft (*ganav*) – taking by deception, Gen 31:26, 27, and 30, Jacob responds by accusing Laban of robbery (*gazal*) – taking by force, Gen. 31:31.

a battle with the forces of Esau. Thus, "he divided the people that were with him, and the flocks and herds and camels, into two companies. And he said, 'If Esau comes to the one company and attacks it, then the other company which is left will escape'" (Gen. 32:7–8).

Jacob then turns to prayer and addresses God in what became for both biblical and rabbinic liturgy one of the standard sequences in the composition of compound prayers.

> Then Jacob said, "O God of my father Abraham and God of my father Isaac, the Lord who said to me, 'Return to your country and to your family, and I will deal well with you': I am not worthy of the least of all the mercies and of all the truth which You have shown Your servant; for I crossed over this Jordan with my staff, and now I have become two companies. Deliver me, I pray, from the hand of my brother, from the hand of Esau; for I fear him, lest he come and attack me and the mother with the children. For You said, 'I will surely treat you well, and make your descendants as the sand of the sea, which cannot be numbered for multitude.'" (Gen. 32:9–12)

Jacob begins with praise, acknowledging God as the Lord of his ancestors and of himself (Gen. 32:9) – which remains to this day the standard introduction to all blessings, as praise of God's entry into covenant with the Jewish people. He then expresses gratitude for the unearned kindness of his enrichment during his period of exile (Gen. 32:10). This is followed by his petition for delivery from the threat of his brother Esau (Gen. 32:11). And to close, Jacob returns to the expression of gratitude for God's promise that he will have numerous descendants (Gen. 32:12).[18] [19]

Having completed his prayer, Jacob initiates a fourth layer of preparation, the offering of tribute (a monetary bribe), the magnitude

---

18. This sequence, with the first three elements in that order, is anticipated in the order of sacrifices presented in Lev. chapters 1–5; and is fully replicated in the order of the four blessings of the traditional Grace after Meals.

19. Both Rashi, in his comment on Gen. 32:8, and Nahmanides, in his commentary to Gen. 32:4, refer to the element of prayer in Jacob's preparation, albeit for Nahmanides, prayer is the first of three elements while for Rashi it is only second of three. In the simple understanding of the text it in fact appears to be third of four.

of which is to be emphasized by the detailed mode of extended delivery in which Jacob instructs his servants (Gen. 32:13–21).

The brothers then meet, Jacob manifests his subservience, Esau manifests love of his brother and astonishment at his wealth and the size of his family, but eventually accepts the tribute offered by Jacob (Gen. 33:3–10). The text is thus equivocal as to whether a true resolution between them is arrived at. But clearly, Jacob's fear is not fully relieved. He begs off traveling together with Esau; he even avoids traveling with accompaniment offered by his brother, and, despite his having said that he will travel to Seir to be with Esau, he heads off in the opposite direction (Gen. 33:12–17). Thus the story of these brothers which began with Jacob's deception of Esau, seems to be closing with another act of deception, this time out of Jacob's sustained fear and suspicion of his brother's intentions, and the realization of his own continued vulnerabilities as a stranger in the very land of his birth.

3:3 The rape of Dinah
The literature on the story of the rape of Dinah is voluminous, in Midrash and rabbinic commentaries, as in fiction and in contemporary feminist literature. Our attention to this story is important because in biblical narratives, rape is the single most common factor in the vulnerabilities experienced by immigrants; whether by Sarah twice, by the divine messengers in Sodom, by the daughters of Lot, by Rebecca, here by Dinah, and later on by Joseph. Whatever ancient and contemporary writers speculated about what had preceded the rape and what had followed the rape, the biblical text itself leaves unequivocal two facts: first, that a forcible rape had in fact occurred, and second, that in the Bible's mind even love and desire to marry following the rape should not exonerate the perpetrator from guilt for the rape. The only struggle in the narrative is around the question of how an immigrant family could and should respond to the victimization of its member by no less than a prince of the land.

Jacob responded in a manner fully consistent with his flight from Esau, his long-standing submissiveness to Laban, and his fear of, and subservience to, Esau upon his return to Canaan. His moments of confrontation and expression of righteous indignation were rare. No surprise then that, "with his sons out with the livestock in the field, Jacob kept silent until they returned" (Gen. 34:5). Hamor, ruler of the City of Shechem, and his son, the rapist Shechem, make what they consider to be a reasonable post facto offer – entry into a treaty between the city and this tribe of strangers. The sons of Jacob recognize in this offer that neither Hamor nor the city will hold Shechem accountable for his crime, and so deceitfully negotiate and enter into a treaty, and then two of Dinah's brothers, Simon and Levi, war against the city and kill all of the males (Gen. 34:6–29). Jacob protests against the behavior of his sons, but purely on prudential grounds: "the Canaanites and the Perizzites … will gather themselves together against me and kill me. I shall be destroyed, my household and I" (Gen. 34:30). The generational difference could not be more vivid as the two brothers of Dinah respond out of righteous indignation: "Should he treat our sister like a harlot?" (Gen. 34:31). To submit to evil treatment out of fear of the repercussions to one's entire tribe, or to take even violent action in defense of justice – to stand up for one's rights despite the possible consequences – is a dilemma with which immigrants are regularly confronted.

The Bible does not fully resolve this controversy between Jacob and his sons. In this chapter the sons are granted the last word and, indeed, the other local tribes do not attempt to exterminate the tribe of Jacob as he feared they would. Nevertheless, at the very end of the Book of Genesis, Jacob, blessing his sons, still has harsh words for the brothers who in anger acted with violence which risked the lives of the entire tribe in the pursuit of justice: "Cursed be their anger, for it is fierce; And their wrath, for it is cruel!" (Gen. 49:5–7, at 7).

	Cases	Genesis	Motive for Immigration	Vulnerabilities	Defensive Response
Jacob	3:1	27:41–45	threat to life → Haran		
		29:14–15		demotion in the family	marries a local woman
		29:16–28		deceived as to marriage	works harder

Cases	Genesis	Motive for Immigration	Vulnerabilities	Defensive Response
	30:25–43		deceived as to compensation	self-sacrifice, and plans for departure
	31:7–9, 38–42		homosexual rape and murder	violence and escape
	31:1–7		jealousy of Laban's sons and of Laban	flight
	31:20–21 31:36–42		false accusation of theft	righteous indignation, rebuke, and entry in treaty
3:2	32:1–8, 13-21	returns to Canaan to find peaceful life	fear of Esau	verbal appeasement, offer of tribute, prayer, defensive action
3:3	34:1–7 34:24-26		rape of Dinah by Shechem	negotiation, violence by sons
	34:30–31		fear of war	Jacob – subservience attitude

4. JOSEPH AND HIS BROTHERS AS IMMIGRANTS IN EGYPT

4:1 The sale of Joseph into slavery

The longest narrative about a single individual in the Book of Genesis is about Joseph – his relationship to his father and his brothers; his sale as a slave into Egypt and his ascent there to a position of power; his rescue of Egypt from famine and his moving the family of Israel to Egypt. In all of that we are exposed to a further series of experiences of immigration, by Joseph and by his brothers and extended family. These further narratives add more rich layers to what we have already learned about why people emigrate, the challenges they confront, and their responses in meeting those challenges.

Joseph enters Egypt as a slave, sold by his own brothers (Gen. 37:23–28). He meets early success as a servant in the household of Potiphar, who totally trusts Joseph and promotes him to overseer of all of Potiphar's properties. But Joseph's rejection of the sexual overtures of Potiphar's wife leads her to falsely accuse him of attempting to rape her, and Joseph is imprisoned (Gen. 39:1–20). Joseph is neither given an opportunity to respond to the charges, nor would he be heard – he was, after all, just a slave, with no voice and no legal protection – silent acceptance of the injustice was all that was allowed to him. Joseph rose to a position of responsibility in the prison and interpreted the dreams of two of the prisoners. He asked one of them, the chief butler, to remember him favorably when, as Joseph predicted, he would be restored to his position of authority. Joseph emphasized that he had been kidnapped from the land of the Hebrews, was innocent of any wrongdoing, and deserved to be released from his unjust imprison-ment (Gen. 39:21–40:15). But the text immediately testifies that when he was released, "the chief butler did not remember Joseph, but forgot him" (Gen. 40:23). After all is said and done, the Bible informs us, in the mind of the rescued political authority, no debt, no gratitude, is owed to an immigrant, a foreigner, let alone a slave.

When it served the purpose of the chief butler to remember Joseph, he mentioned him to Pharaoh as someone who could accurately interpret dreams. Just to bring him before Pharaoh, in a portent of what was to come, Joseph had to be shaved and clothed in appropriate garb (Gen. 41:14). When Joseph's interpretation of the dreams, and his counsel, were accepted by Pharaoh, and Joseph was appointed as regent over Egypt, second only to Pharaoh himself, further transformation of Joseph needed to be made.

> Then Pharaoh took his signet ring off his hand and put it on Joseph's hand; and he clothed him in garments of fine linen and put a gold chain around his neck. And he had him ride in the sec-ond chariot which he had; and they cried out before him, "Bow the knee!" So he set him over all the land of Egypt. Pharaoh also

> said to Joseph, "I am Pharaoh, and without your consent no man
> may lift his hand or foot in all the land of Egypt." And Pharaoh
> called Joseph's name Zaphnath-Paaneah. And he gave him as a
> wife Asenath, the daughter of Poti-Pherah priest of On. So Joseph
> went out over all the land of Egypt. (Gen. 41:42–45)

The empowering of Joseph within Egyptian society required that Joseph
be transformed into an Egyptian. He could not be accepted as a foreigner, as an immigrant. He needed to wear garments of fine Egyptian
linen, and jewelry that befit an Egyptian leader that would appropriately
accompany the signet ring which signified his power. Joseph needed to
ride in a vehicle appropriate to his station and have a crier to demand
subservience to him. He also needed to have an Egyptian name and to
be married into Egyptian aristocracy; what better wife than a daughter of
a priest in a society in which only the priesthood shared ultimate power
with the king? In this manner, Joseph came to be assimilated into the
society. To escape the under-class status of an immigrant, a foreigner,
let alone a slave, one might be willing to give up the marks of his or her
prior identity. The melting pot makes intense demands. Life became
good for Joseph, no, for Zaphnath-Paaneah.

4:2 Jacob's sons go to Egypt for food

The severe famine which afflicted Egypt after the seven years of plenty
also affected the surrounding lands. Jacob sent all of his remaining sons
except Benjamin to purchase grain in Egypt. Joseph, directly administer-
ing the sale of grain, recognizes his brothers and accuses them of being
spies, enemies of Egypt seeking out its weaknesses (Gen. 42:1–9). This
trope is familiar to us. Jacob was accused of being a thief, Joseph was
accused of being a rapist, and now the ten brothers are accused of being
a fifth column, a band of foreign immigrants who are in reality enemies
of the state. The brothers defend themselves:

> "We are all one man's sons; we are honest men; your servants are
> not spies…" And they said, "Your servants are twelve brothers,
> the sons of one man in the land of Canaan; and in fact, the young-
> est is with our father today, and one is no more." (Gen. 42:11, 13)

But Joseph denies their claim and eventually agrees that he will allow them to leave with their purchased provisions, but only if they leave one brother behind as a hostage, until they return with the alleged additional brother (Gen. 42:12–20).

What an extraordinary dilemma. Should they leave one brother behind, at the mercy of an absolute ruler, to provide food for the rest of the family in Canaan, with the hope that they will be able to eventually extricate the hostage by bringing Benjamin to Egypt? Or, should they... what? Was there a realistic alternative? The brothers immediately agree, and Joseph selects Simeon from amongst them and binds and imprisons him as the hostage (Gen. 42:20–24).

A further severe challenge awaits them as they leave Egypt and return to Canaan. They discovered that the money which they had paid to purchase grain for their family has mysteriously reappeared in their sacks of food, and they were afraid (Gen. 42:25–35). They had protested to the ruler of Egypt that they were honest men. When the ruler allowed all but one of them to leave with a promise of return, he had said that it was because they were honest men. This the brothers had even reported to their father upon their return to Canaan (Gen. 42:11, 19, 31–34). Now they were vulnerable to the accusation that either they had stolen the food without paying, or they had stolen the money back after having purchased the food. If their safety in Egypt was dependent on their being "honest men," then their safety was now deeply challenged. Should they now simply give up on getting Simeon back, and not return to Egypt at all? This alternative might be necessary anyway since Jacob was refusing to allow them to put Benjamin at risk by taking him to Egypt (Gen. 42:36 and 38). The dilemmas of balancing the lives of many against one had now become even more complicated – there were no simple answers.

4:3 Jacob's sons return to Egypt for food

But their hands were forced by the intensification of the famine. Once again Jacob instructed his remaining sons to return to Egypt to purchase grain. Jacob still resists sending Benjamin with them but Judah indicates that without their bringing Benjamin the entire family in Canaan will die, and he offers to personally guarantee Benjamin's safety. Jacob agrees to allow Benjamin to be taken and offers counsel on how to achieve the appeasement of the ruler of Egypt – in ways similar to how he had succeeded in achieving the appeasement of Esau – with tribute and prayer (Gen. 43:1–14).[20]

The tension for the brothers on their second venture into Egypt continued to play itself out. On one hand they were invited to the home of Joseph, and the steward declined their offer to return the money found in their food sacks. On the other hand, weird things were happening. They were greeted in the manner of the house of Abraham, given water and having their feet washed and having their donkeys fed, and having bread and meat served to them. And they were seated in their birth order, and Joseph blessed Benjamin and gave him a fivefold portion (Gen. 43:16–34). Was this all a way to induce anxiety in immigrants suddenly exposed to inexplicable kindness surrounded by mystery. What relief they must have felt when finally their bags were packed and they left Egypt, all eleven of them, for the trip back to Canaan. But soon after their departure, they are pursued and an accusation is leveled against them, that they had stolen the ruler's silver goblet. The brothers respond as Jacob had, when accused by Laban of having stolen his household deities – with denial in righteous indignation, and with the declaration that if it be found, the one who stole it should die while all of the others should become slaves to the ruler. The cup is found where it had been planted, in the food sack of Benjamin, and upon their return to Joseph's home, Judah attempts to protect Benjamin by suggesting that all of them would now be slaves to Joseph, which Joseph rejects saying that only Benjamin will remain a slave and the others are free to leave (Gen. 44:1–17). Thus, their state of fear and anxiety remains unrelieved – they continue to be confronted with the dilemma of choosing between the protection of an individual and the well-being of the many – the hostage situation continues.

The seventeen-sentence monologue by Judah, the longest thus far in the Book of Genesis, in which he makes a passionate plea to Joseph on behalf of Benjamin in the interest of the emotional well-being of Jacob,

---

20. He does not add the suggestion of words of appeasement, but such is implied as Jacob suggests that they take double the money found in their sacks of food, and that "perhaps it was an oversight" – obviously suggesting that as an approach to explaining how come the money was still with them. The brothers indeed explicitly suggested that explanation, but it was dismissed by Joseph's steward (Gen. 43:18–23).

and offers to himself remain a slave in place of Benjamin, breaks through Joseph's facade and he reveals his true identity to his brothers. Judah's sensitivity to the emotional condition of his father from whom he is now separated, his willingness to sacrifice his own well-being in protection of his younger brother who, as far as he knows, has committed the crime of which he is accused, are the qualities of a true leader – and are virtues often found in immigrants confronting fear and anxiety derived from the tension between defense of a single weak link and the interest of the group as a whole.

While this concludes the essential corpus of immigration narratives in the Book of Genesis, there are a few footnotes on this matter which the text continues to reveal to us before it ends. First, despite Joseph's immense power in the land of Egypt, he does not expect his newly arrived extended family to be welcomed with open arms by the populace, and so he attempts to protect them by settling them off the beaten path, in the region of Goshen (Gen. 46:31–34). Second, despite the fact that Jacob then continues to live in Egypt until his death seventeen years later, he failed to recognize Joseph's sons born and raised in the diaspora (Gen. 48:8–9). And finally, despite Joseph's complete reorganization of the economy of Egypt, and his laying the groundwork for its longer-term economic security, memory of him was clearly not preserved in the history of Egypt, as the Bible itself testifies (Ex. 1:8) – was that because in the final event he was a stranger?

	Cases	Genesis	Motive for Immigration	Vulnerabilities	Defensive Response
Joseph	4:1	39:1–20	sold as slave	sexual seduction; false accusation of rape; no legal rights no debt or gratitude owed to him	silence – his social position allowed him no response
		40:14–15			
		41:9–14 41:39–45		pays the price of entry into the culture	shaves, changes clothes and jewelry, and signs of social status, marriage to an elite local woman
	4:2	42:1–24	famine – 1st trip to Egypt	false accusation – that they are enemies	persuasion, leave a hostage to save family
Jacob's sons and Jacob	4:3	42:25–28		money planted in their food bags	fear to return; endanger Benjamin to rescue Simeon
		43:1–14	famine – 2nd trip to Egypt	false accusation of theft	
		44:1–34		arrest of Benjamin	Judah endangers himself to rescue Benjamin
		45:26–28 46:1–7 48:1–11	family reunification (Jacob with Joseph)	does not recognize his grandchildren	blesses them

B. THE STATUS OF THE *GER*, THE IMMIGRANT,
IN BIBLICAL LEGISLATION

Biblical legislation encompasses approximately thirty-six instances in which it explicitly applies a particular law to the stranger, the alien, the *ger*.[21] Many of those instances appeared to require the *ger* to comply with biblical religious requirements such as those related to the observance of Holy Days, the compliance with food restrictions, and the participation in particular sacrificial practices. On the other hand, many relate to the nature of the civic duties of strangers, and of the duties of citizens and of the state toward them. But who exactly is this *ger*, this stranger whose rights and duties are being codified in the Torah?

Jewish tradition always understood that the term "*ger*" was in fact a multi-vocal term having two distinct meanings. On one hand, the term "*ger*" was a reference to the non-Jewish resident alien in the Land of Israel, in contrast to its Jewish citizens. On the other hand, the term "*ger*" appeared to be a reference to a non-Jew who had converted to Judaism and thereby became fully a member of Jewish society. The commonality of these two groups is not difficult to understand – they are all immigrants: some are geographic immigrants, the others are spiritual immigrants. It is striking that the Torah chooses to use the same word to describe both of those groups, as if reminding us that the vulnerabilities of the two groups in their disparate attempts to assimilate into a new and different world are ultimately quite similar. In the perception of the established "citizen," and in the newcomers' perception of themselves – they are strangers, immigrants from a different reality.[22]

But how then was the application of the law to be determined? Could one argue that all of the Torah's legislation related to the *ger* was applicable to both categories of immigrants? If so, why should the non-Jewish resident alien be required to observe Jewish ritual practices, and why should the law need to be redundant in indicating the inclusion of

---

21. Talmud, Bava Metzia 59b: "It has been taught: R. Eliezer the Great said: Why did the Torah warn against [the wronging of] a proselyte in thirty-six, or as others say, in forty-six, places?"

22. It is in this spirit that I understand the brief comment of Rashi to Ex. 22:20, s.v. *Ki gerim heyitem*, "Every use of the word '*ger*' refers to a person who was not born in that country, but came from a different country to reside there."

the convert in those and in the civil laws since s/he is fully Jewish by virtue of the conversion and is therefore included in the categories of *"ezraḥ"* (citizen), or simply "Israel"? While such a case might, with some strain, be made,[23] the direction of Jewish understanding of these passages was that Revealed Oral Law had determined that some of these laws pertain solely to converts, others pertain solely to non-Jewish resident aliens, and yet others to both categories. While some of the attributions were clearly and unequivocally accepted in Jewish law, others were subject to intense debate and shifting consensus over the centuries. Full explication of the parameters of this discussion goes far beyond the purposes of this chapter.[24]

What is of primary concern to us is the question of how biblical legislation deals with the vulnerabilities of the immigrant which the biblical narratives had so clearly and consistently identified. We will therefore examine the passages which regulate the conduct of Israelite society toward the *ger* in regard to the following vulnerabilities: threat to life, threat of sexual assault, threat of economic exploitation, lack of legal protection, and threat to emotional well-being. I will argue that the biblical legislation related specifically to the civil condition of the *ger* is entirely focused on these five areas and that these passages amount to radical re-ordering of the legal and cultural relationship to immigrants in which the *ger* is specifically granted protection of his life, of his sexual well-being, his economic security, his right to legal protection, and his right not be emotionally assaulted. Let's look at each of these in turn.

1. Protection of the Life of the Immigrant

The criminality of the taking of any human life is foundational to the Torah. It derives conceptually from the insistence that God created only a single couple in His image, from whom all of mankind is descended (Gen. 1:27). This fundamental equality of all of humankind means

---

23. For example, by the contention that the biblical expectation was that the non-Jewish resident alien should be required to comply with the fundamental religious practices of the dominant religion and would be expected eventually to fully enter into the Jewish religion through conversion.

24. For one recent treatment of this issue see Isaac Sassoon, *Conflicting Attitudes To Conversion in Judaism, Past and Present* (Cambridge: Cambridge University Press, 2017), ch. 2, 20–26.

that when God condemns Cain for the killing of his brother, Abel (Gen.4:8–15), there is no distinction that can be made between the taking of the life of one human or that of any other. Lest there be any uncertainty about the fundamental brotherhood of all of humanity and the consequent criminality of any person taking the life of any human, God makes the principle explicit when, after the Flood, he permits Noah and his descendants to kill animals for food, but declares the impermissibility of taking any human life:

> Surely for your lifeblood I will demand a reckoning; from the hand of every beast I will require it, and from the hand of man. From the hand of every man's brother I will require the life of man. Whoever sheds man's blood, By man his blood shall be shed; For in the image of God He made man. (Gen. 9:5–6)

For this reason, the declaration of the sixth commandment is unqualified as to the identity of the victim. "You shall not murder!" it declares (Ex. 20:13).[25] It makes no difference whether the victim is a citizen or a stranger, a man or a woman, a permanent resident or an illegal immigrant. Two additional times the Torah emphasizes that neither the identity nor the status of the victim or of the perpetrator modify the criminality of and the penalty for the act of homicide, and in each instance it specifies the applicability of this law to the *ger*. Thus, in regard to the capital crime of direct murder, the Torah says:

> Whoever kills any man shall surely be put to death. Whoever kills an animal shall make it good, animal for animal. … And whoever kills an animal shall restore it; but whoever kills a man shall be put to death. You shall have the same law for the stranger and for one from your own country; for I am the Lord your God. (Lev. 24:17–18, 21–22)

---

25. The ancient and contemporary debate as to whether the more correct translation is as above or should be "You shall not kill!" need not concern us here.

And, in regard to accidental murder where the penalty is exile, the Torah declares:

> Speak to the children of Israel, and say to them: "When you cross the Jordan into the land of Canaan, then you shall appoint cities to be cities of refuge for you, that the manslayer who kills any person accidentally may flee there…. These six cities shall be for refuge for the children of Israel, for the stranger, and for the sojourner among them, that anyone who kills a person accidentally may flee there." (Num. 35:10–11, 15)

Even the homicide of a non-Jewish slave is punishable by the same penalty and is treated explicitly and emphasized precisely because that position was so totally contrary to the practice of the surrounding ancient societies in which a slave was no more than property: "And if a man beats his male or female servant with a rod, so that he dies under his hand, he shall surely be punished" (Ex. 21:20).[26]

In contrast to the experience of Abraham, Lot and the messengers, Isaac, and Jacob, all of whom feared death as a central aspect of their vulnerability as immigrants, the Torah prescribes that the right of the immigrant to the protection of his life must be identical to that of any citizen in the society formed by the laws and values of the Bible.

2. Protection of the Immigrant from Sexual Assault

It is clearly not accidental that the lengthy passage in Leviticus chapter 18 which legislates against sexual crimes, particularly incest and adultery, is prefaced and concluded by an injunction against acting in a manner like unto the citizens of Egypt and Canaan.

---

26. As for the identity of the punishment as capital punishment for intentional homicide and exile for unintentional homicide, see *Mekhilta Nezikin*, #6; *Sifre* to Numbers, #117, and Maimonides, *Mishneh Torah, Laws of Homicide and Protection of Life* 2:10. While biblical and rabbinic law recognized the monetary interest of a master in his slave, that did not entitle the master to kill or even physically abuse his servant with impunity.

Then the Lord spoke to Moses, saying, "Speak to the children of Israel, and say to them: 'I am the Lord your God. According to the doings of the land of Egypt, where you dwelt, you shall not do; and according to the doings of the land of Canaan, where I am bringing you, you shall not do; nor shall you walk in their ordinances.... (Lev. 18:1–3)

'Do not defile yourselves with any of these things; for by all these the nations are defiled, which I am casting out before you. For the land is defiled; therefore I visit the punishment of its iniquity upon it, and the land vomits out its inhabitants. You shall therefore keep My statutes and My judgments, and shall not commit any of these abominations, either any of your own nation or any stranger who dwells among you (for all these abominations the men of the land have done, who were before you, and thus the land is defiled), lest the land vomit you out also when you defile it, as it vomited out the nations that were before you. For whoever commits any of these abominations, the persons who commit them shall be cut off from among their people.'" (Lev. 18:24–29)

Nor is it insignificant that the parallel passage in Deuteronomy chapter 22, which repeats, and expands in casuistic form, the legislation criminalizing adultery and rape, providing capital punishment for consensual adultery, has the three-fold refrain of "you shall extirpate the evil from your midst" (Deut. 22:21, 22, 24).

In both of these passages, the law of the Torah intersperses laws which hearken back to the narratives of Genesis, describing events in both Egypt and in Canaan in which sexual acts were either threatened or committed which are now being declared to be illicit whether or not they were so viewed earlier.

Thus, Lev. 18:7, "The nakedness of your father or the nakedness of your mother you shall not uncover," may refer to either homosexual rape of father or incest with mother, as the unspecified conduct of Ham for which his father Noah curses Ham's son Canaan (Gen. 9:20–27).

Lev. 18:8, "The nakedness of your father's wife you shall not uncover; it is your father's nakedness," reminds us of the conduct of

Reuben in taking his father's concubine, Bilhah, of which Jacob hears but to which he does not respond (Gen. 35:22).

Lev. 18:9, "The nakedness of your sister, the daughter of your father, or the daughter of your mother, ... their nakedness you shall not uncover." This is a prospective prohibition against conduct which Abraham claimed was permissible in his defense to Avimelech, of referring to Sarah as his sister (Gen. 20:12).

Lev. 18:15, "You shall not uncover the nakedness of your daughter-in-law – she is your son's wife – you shall not uncover her nakedness." This is responsive to the conduct of Judah in having sex with Tamar, albeit without knowing her true identity (Gen. 38:13–26).

Lev. 18:17, "You shall not uncover the nakedness of a woman and her daughter." Despite the omission of father-daughter intercourse from the incest list, we are reminded of the narrative of Lot and his daughters (Gen. 19:30–36) by this clause which bans even the taking of stepdaughters.

Lev. 18:18, "Nor shall you take a woman as a rival to her sister, to uncover her nakedness while the other is alive." Thus, the conduct of Jacob in marrying both Rachel and Leah (Gen. 29:22–28) is rejected as unacceptable.

Lev. 18:20, "Moreover you shall not lie carnally with your neighbor's wife, to defile yourself with her." This was precisely what Pharaoh of Egypt and Avimelech king of Gerar were expected to do by Abraham (Gen. 12:12 and 20:11) and by Isaac (Gen. 26:6). It was also what Joseph withheld himself from doing as a slave in Egypt, resisting seduction by the wife of Potiphar (Gen. 39:7–12).

The casuistic passages in Deuteronomy 22 related to rape (Deut. 22:25–29) serve as a legal and emotional resolution of the conflict between Jacob and his sons as to whether Shechem deserved to be killed for his rape of Dinah (Gen. 34:1–7, 25–31). The passage is complex because the biblical process of marriage had two stages. The first stage is the entry into contract of marriage by the parties, called "*eras*," usually mistranslated as "betrothed." The usual meaning of the word "betrothed" is "engaged to be married, or promised/pledged in marriage." That is not the meaning of the status of *eras*. Rather, the couple who have so entered into a contract of marriage in Jewish law by mutual agreement are already married to each other from the time of *erusin*, so that adultery is forbidden and termination of their marriage would require a divorce. Despite the fact that they are married to each other, cohabitation between them is not yet permissible.

The second stage is the ceremony initiating the permissibility of consummation of the marriage, referred to as "*lakaḥ*," meaning "taken in marriage." In early Jewish practice these two stages might be separated by many months while the detailed arrangements for the couple to live together are made, and while courtship between the parties already married to each other proceeds prior to inception of their full sexual relationship. Thus, in regard to exemptions from military service in discretionary wars the Torah speaks of, "And what man is there who is betrothed to a woman (*eras isha*) and has not married her (*lekaḥa*)? Let him go and return to his house, lest he die in the battle and another man marry her (*yikaḥena*)" (Deut. 20:7). To this day the traditional Jewish wedding ceremony consists of those two components, now known as "*erusin*" (or "*kiddushin*") and "*nissuin*." For hundreds of years now, the two ceremonies are performed in immediate succession, without any time gap in between them, but separated by the reading of the *ketuba*, which is a post-nuptial, unilateral contract providing for the financial security of the wife in case of dissolution of the marriage by death of the husband, or by divorce, and its delivery from the husband to the wife.

With this legal process in mind we can understand the rabbinic interpretation of the legal provisions of Deuteronomy 22. The passage presents the following legal rules embedded in the sequence of cases:

a. Consensual sexual relations between a married woman from the time of *erusin* and any man other than her husband is a capital crime, with both parties punishable (Deut. 22:22).
b. If immediately after consummation of the marriage the husband accuses his wife of having committed adultery in the time since the *erusin*, then:
   1. if her adultery can be proven, she will be found guilty;
   2. if her virginity as of the time of *nissuin* can be proven, the husband will be flogged, he will be required to pay a monetary fine for the defamation, and he will lose the privilege of ever divorcing his wife (Deut. 22:13:19).

3. The text does not specify what happens in a third possible situation, where there is neither sufficient evidence to prove adultery, nor to prove her virginity. There would then be no judicial resolution of their conflict and the parties would have to decide whether they want to remain married or get divorced.

c. If a married woman after *erusin* engages in an act of intercourse with a man other than her husband and she claims she was raped while the man claims it was consensual, then:

1. if the act took place in "the city" (under circumstances where she could have cried out for help and have been rescued), then, given her failure to cry out for help, the law will presume that the act was consensual (Deut. 22:23–24);

2. if the act took place in "the countryside" (under circumstances where even had she cried out no one would have been there to rescue her), then the law will presume that she was raped, and the rapist alone is put to death for his "adulterous" rape. For emphasis the Torah then adds,

> But you shall do nothing to the young woman; there is in the young woman no sin deserving of death, for just as when a man rises against his neighbor and kills him, even so is this matter. For he found her in the countryside, and the betrothed young woman cried out, but there was no one to save her. (Deut. 22:26–27)[27]

d. If a man rapes an unmarried woman, he is to pay a fine to the family for its disgrace, is required to marry his victim (if she so desires), and he will lose the privilege of ever divorcing his wife (Deut. 22:28–29). In addition to which he will be liable for the usual civil liabilities consequent upon his assault, such as for pain and shame.[28]

---

27. The emphasis here may be an explicit condemnation of an ancient practice which continues to this day in some cultures, in which the victim of rape is viewed as being a disgrace to the family and is then doubly victimized by being punished with expulsion from the family or even death (so called "honor killings").

28. Talmud, Ketubot 32b–33a, based on a close reading of Deut. 22:29.

Now to return to the case of the rape of Dinah by Shechem; the Torah seems to validate the emotional outrage felt by Dinah's brothers when it equates rape in the countryside to homicide,

> ...just as when a man rises against his neighbor and kills him, even so is this matter. For he found her in the countryside, and the betrothed young woman cried out, but there was no one to save her. (Deut. 22:26–27)

One can understand the feeling of the brothers that had they been present when Dinah was taken, they would have rescued her even at the expense of the life of Shechem, as if he were a murderer threatening her life.[29] But while they were not there then, they were present now and since she was still being held by Shechem, they needed still to rescue her even by taking the life of her rapist.

On the other hand, the biblical legislation actually sides with Jacob in not equating the rape of an unmarried woman with the rape of a married woman, insisting that it is only in the latter situation that a capital crime is being committed so that the life of the rapist is forfeited and may be taken in order to rescue the victim.

Given the intense connection between these legal passages related to adultery and rape and the prior biblical narratives of sexual crimes in both Egypt and Canaan, one can well understand the Torah's insistence that these laws need to be applicable to all persons present within the country, whether, "any [citizen] of your own nation or any stranger who dwells among you." For neither the identity or status of the perpetrator nor of the victim matter when it comes to abominations which defile the land and cause the expulsion of its inhabitants.[30] It is because of the great threat which such actions create to the very continued survival of

---

29. In fact, the Talmud, Sanhedrin 73a, asserts based on this passage that rescue of a married woman from a rapist could be done even at the expense of the life of the rapist if that were necessary.
30. See Lev. 18:24–28.

the nation in the land that the Torah insists on the citizenry assuming the responsibility to "extirpate such evil" from their midst.[31]

Once again then, in contrast to the experiences of Abraham and Sarah, the Messengers, Isaac and Rebecca, Jacob, Dinah, and Joseph, all of whom confronted sexual abuse as a central aspect of their vulnerability as immigrants, the Torah prescribes that the right of the immigrant to the protection of his or her sexual integrity must be identical to that of any citizen in the society formed by the laws and values of the Bible.

3. Protection of the Immigrant from Economic Exploitation

We have earlier clearly documented the presence of a recurrent theme in the biblical narratives about immigration in the Book of Genesis related to the economic vulnerability of the immigrant. Abraham finds his wells "stolen" by the servants of Avimelech in Gerar. He further fears that he will be exploited in his attempt to purchase a burial cave for his wife and family in Hebron, and takes extraordinary steps to assure the stability of that purchase. Isaac finds that the citizens of Gerar had simply stuffed up all of the wells which his father Abraham had dug, attempting to bar him from the use of the commonly held resource. Jacob was repeatedly deceived about the compensation due him for his labor. It is quite striking that the biblical legislation related to protection of the economic well-being of the *ger*, of the immigrant, falls precisely within the parameters of the three areas of economic threat and vulnerability identified in the narratives of the Book of Genesis.

First, as to security of ownership rights, which were denied to Abraham by the citizens of Gerar, and which he felt were insecure in his purchase of the burial cave in Hebron. The Torah prescribes that if a fellow Jew falls on hard times and is sold as a servant to a wealthy non-Jewish resident alien, that the Jewish servant has a right to redeem himself, and others of his family and community have a right to redeem him (Lev. 25:47–49). The Torah then goes on to detail precisely how that purchase from the immigrant owner of the servant should be negotiated:

---

31. See Deut. 22:21, 22, and 24.

Thus he shall reckon with him who bought him: The price of his release shall be according to the number of years, from the year that he was sold to him until the Year of Jubilee; it shall be according to the time of a hired servant for him. If there are still many years remaining, according to them he shall repay the price of his redemption from the money with which he was bought. And if there remain but a few years until the Year of Jubilee, then he shall reckon with him, and according to his years he shall repay him the price of his redemption. (Lev. 25:50–52)

It is clear that the Torah recognizes the vulnerability of the non-Jewish owner of the Jewish servant and fears that the attempt to gain his release from servitude might lead Jews to demand that the servant be freed without adequate compensation to the owner. It therefore details how the price will be established – by determining how much the purchaser had paid for the servant's services, dividing that by the number of years he was to serve until the Jubilee year, which would mark the termination of servitude, thereby establishing an annual value, and multiplying that by the number of years still remaining until the Jubilee year. This focus on details is clearly intended to prevent any economic exploitation of the *ger*, or any deprivation of his monetary rights in the service of his servant.

    This same principle is reflected in a set of two verses which constrain the economic oppression of the stranger: "You shall neither mistreat a stranger nor oppress him, for you were strangers in the land of Egypt" (Ex. 22:20)[32] and "Also you shall not oppress a stranger, for you know the heart of a stranger, because you were strangers in the land of Egypt" (Ex. 23:9). Rashi, commenting on this latter verse, noting the redundancy of this prohibition against theft[33] or other forms of economic oppression of the stranger, included in the term "*tilḥatz*,"

---

32. In the NKJV this is identified as verse 21, because the chapter opens with what is more generally numbered as the last verse of the preceding chapter.
33. Rashi to Ex. 22:20, s.v. *velo tilḥatzeno*.

translated as "oppression," cites a lengthy passage in Talmud which offers a number of explanations for the distinctive vulnerability of the stranger.[34]

A second element of the economic vulnerability of the stranger relates to the payment of his salary, as was the case with Jacob. The Torah directly addresses the issue of the payment of salary to the *ger*.

> You shall not oppress a hired servant who is poor and needy, whether one of your brethren or one of the aliens who is in your land within your gates. Each day you shall give him his wages, and not let the sun go down on it, for he is poor and has set his heart on it; lest he cry out against you to the Lord, and it be sin to you. (Deut. 24:14–15)

A somewhat broader passage which encompasses both the element of theft and the affirmative mandate of payment of day laborers in a timely manner, is as follows:

> You shall not steal, nor deal falsely, nor lie to one another. And you shall not swear by My name falsely, nor shall you profane the name of your God: I am the Lord. You shall not cheat your neighbor, nor rob him. The wages of him who is hired shall not remain with you all night until morning. You shall not curse the deaf, nor put a stumbling block before the blind, but shall fear your God: I am the Lord. (Lev. 19:11–14)

While this latter passage does not explicitly mention the *ger*, the conjunction of the two passages is a perfect illustration of the way in which the biblical legislation insisted on the fundamental equality of economic rights between citizens and immigrants.

The third element of economic vulnerability of the immigrant was in relation to the ability of the citizens to deny to strangers access to the common resources, as the citizens of Gerar denied water to both Abraham and Isaac.

---

34. Talmud, Bava Metzia, 59a and b.

The Torah created a set of distinctive common resources to which every poor citizen had access. In the context of agricultural productivity, the Torah had required that there be constant awareness of the needs of the poor, and regular sharing with them at each stage of the agricultural process. Thus, even prior to planting, a corner of the field (*pe'ah*) needed to be set aside from which only the poor would be permitted to eventually harvest. During harvest itself, both of grain and of grapes, individual stalks left behind (*leket* of grain and *olelot* of grapes), and whole sheaves left behind (*shikheḥa* of grain and *peret* of grapes) had to be left for the poor to collect. Neither the owner of the field, nor the harvesters working on his behalf, were permitted to circle back to collect the product left behind. We are most familiar with this set of biblical provisions due to the Book of Ruth in which Boaz insists that Ruth not go to any other fields, but remain within his fields to collect the produce needed to support herself and Naomi (Ruth 2:8–10).

The Torah was very detailed and explicit as to these requirements, and in each instance it insists that the common resource must be made available not only to the Jewish poor, but also to the stranger, the alien. As to *pe'ah, leket, peret,* and *olelot*:

> When you reap the harvest of your land, you shall not wholly reap the corners of your field, nor shall you gather the gleanings of your harvest. And you shall not glean your vineyard, nor shall you gather every grape of your vineyard; you shall leave them for the poor and the stranger: I am the Lord your God. (Lev. 19:9–10)

Additionally, as to *shikheḥa* and as to the olive harvest as well:

> When you reap your harvest in your field, and forget a sheaf in the field, you shall not go back to get it; it shall be for the stranger, the fatherless, and the widow, that the Lord your God may bless you in all the work of your hands. When you beat your olive trees, you shall not go over the boughs again; it shall be for the stranger, the fatherless, and the widow. When you gather the grapes of your vineyard, you shall not glean it afterward; it shall be for the

stranger, the fatherless, and the widow. And you shall remember
that you were a slave in the land of Egypt; therefore I command
you to do this thing. (Deut. 24:19–21)

Beyond these common resources, a segment of the tithes, ten percent
of the produce of years three and six of the seven-year Sabbatical cycle,
had to be set aside for the poor. Here too, the Torah specified that this
resource should be accessible also to the impoverished stranger in the
community:

> At the end of every third year you shall bring out the tithe of your
> produce of that year and store it up within your gates. And the
> Levite, because he has no portion nor inheritance with you, and
> the stranger and the fatherless and the widow who are within
> your gates, may come and eat and be satisfied, that the Lord
> your God may bless you in all the work of your hand which you
> do. (Deut. 14:28–29)

A further common resource was the produce of the Sabbatical year which
the owner of the field was not permitted to fully harvest for himself but
could only take what he needed while any person could enter onto his
property and take what he or she needed. Here too, the Torah explicitly
indicates that the stranger in the community was also fully entitled to
this common resource:

> And the Lord spoke to Moses on Mount Sinai, saying, "Speak to the
> children of Israel, and say to them: 'When you come into the land
> which I give you, then the land shall keep a sabbath to the Lord. Six
> years you shall sow your field, and six years you shall prune your
> vineyard, and gather its fruit; but in the seventh year there shall be
> a sabbath of solemn rest for the land, a sabbath to the Lord. You
> shall neither sow your field nor prune your vineyard. What grows
> of its own accord of your harvest you shall not reap, nor gather the
> grapes of your untended vine, for it is a year of rest for the land.
> And the sabbath produce of the land shall be food for you: for you,
> your male and female servants, your hired man, and the stranger

who dwells with you, for your livestock and the beasts that are in your land – all its produce shall be for food.'" (Lev. 25:1–7)

And finally, the interest-free loan has, throughout Jewish history, been a hallmark of charitable giving, second in importance only to providing someone with a job. The simple meaning of the text of the Torah extends also to the impoverished *ger* the entitlement to loans from other citizens without interest.

> If one of your brethren becomes poor, and falls into poverty among you, then you shall help him, like a stranger or a sojourner, that he may live with you. Take no usury or interest from him; but fear your God, that your brother may live with you. You shall not lend him your money for usury, nor lend him your food at a profit. I am the Lord your God, who brought you out of the land of Egypt, to give you the land of Canaan and to be your God. (Lev. 25:35–38)

Thus, the Torah attempted to assure the immigrant of his economic rights: firstly by granting security of ownership of his property from theft, and assuring his ability to trade with confidence of not being exploited; secondly the law attempted to assure that the immigrant would not be deceived in his transactions nor have payment of his rightful salary withheld or delayed; and finally, the Torah legislated that the *ger* had to be granted full rights, equal with any citizen, to the common resources assured to every impoverished person in the community, both to share in the society's productivity and to be entitled to loans without interest to provide for his or her basic needs.

4. Grant of Equal Legal Protection to the Immigrant

Underlying many of the vulnerabilities experienced by immigrants in the narratives of the Book of Genesis was the singular factor of the lack of legal protection for the stranger within the society. Thus, Abraham had no confidence that his wife or his life would be protected in his travels to Egypt, and if his wife would be taken by the locals, he would have no legal recourse and his resistance would result in his being killed. He experienced the same reservations about his travel to Gerar, as did his son Isaac later on. In each instance even an appeal directly to the king did not produce any legal protection. Likewise, Abraham expected no protection in regard to his purchase of land in Hebron, unless he took extreme steps to publicize the event and engage the local leadership in its negotiation. Jacob realized that his being defrauded by his uncle could not be remedied within the local legal structure because he was simply an outsider, as Laban kept reminding him. Nor did Jacob expect that justice would be done in regard to the rape of Dinah, neither by the king nor the townspeople of Shechem; and he feared that his resistance in an attempt to gain justice would result in the other local tribes uniting to exterminate his entire family. And Joseph clearly understood that as a slave he could have no expectation of even raising his voice in his own defense against a false accusation, nor any expectation of the simple performance of a reciprocal kindness.

How markedly different is the expectation legislated by the Torah as to the relationship of Israelite society to the resident alien, the stranger. The very first element of difference is that Moses, at the very moment at which he created the judiciary of the nation, instructed them to assume jurisdiction not only over conflicts between fellow citizens, but also conflicts between citizens and aliens. Thus,

> So I took the heads of your tribes, wise and knowledgeable men, and made them heads over you, leaders of thousands, leaders of hundreds, leaders of fifties, leaders of tens, and officers for your tribes. Then I commanded your judges at that time, saying, "Hear the cases between your brethren, and judge righteously between a man and his brother or the stranger who is with him." (Deut. 1:15–16)

It is striking that forty years earlier when Yitro was advising Moses about the establishment of the judiciary, he made no reference to the participation of aliens as litigants (Ex. 18:17–26). But now, at the start of the Book of Deuteronomy, as the Israelite nation is about to enter their land, where they will in fact be co-existing with other nations and tribes, Moses emphasizes that his charge to the judges is to keep the judicial process open to all who file claims before them, whether they are citizens or aliens.

A second element of significance in the biblical legislation is the repeated assertion that the laws to be applied to citizens and aliens alike by Israelite courts need to be the same. This is particularly emphasized in Leviticus chapter 24 which deals in sequence with elements of both criminal and civil liability – the death penalty for blasphemy and for homicide, monetary liability for damage to property and for bodily damage to a person. At the start and at the conclusion of that passage, the Torah emphasizes that these laws apply equally to the citizen and the stranger:

> Then you shall speak to the children of Israel, saying: "Whoever curses his God shall bear his sin. And whoever blasphemes the name of the Lord shall surely be put to death. All the congregation shall certainly stone him, the stranger as well as him who is born in the land. When he blasphemes the name of the Lord, he shall be put to death. Whoever kills any man shall surely be put to death. Whoever kills an animal shall make it good, animal for animal. If a man causes disfigurement of his neighbor, as he has done, so shall it be done to him – fracture for fracture, eye for eye, tooth for tooth; as he has caused disfigurement of a man, so shall it be done to him. And whoever kills an animal shall restore it; but whoever kills a man shall be put to death. You shall have the same law for the stranger and for one from your own country; for I am the Lord your God." (Lev. 24:15–22)

This teaching of the equal application of the laws to both citizens and to aliens is also legislated in a few other places in the Torah. For example, it is, as previously noted, specifically legislated as to sexual crimes:

> You shall therefore keep My statutes and My judgments, and shall not commit any of these abominations, either any of your own nation or any stranger who dwells among you. (Lev. 18:26)

Further, it is emphasized in regard to the equal application of the criminal laws in regard to accidental homicide:

> These six cities shall be for refuge for the children of Israel, for the stranger, and for the sojourner among them, that anyone who kills a person accidentally may flee there. (Num. 35:15)

It is also emphasized in the legislation regarding the sacrificial offerings required for the process of atonement for unintentional violation of the ritual laws:

> So the priest shall make atonement for the person who sins unintentionally, when he sins unintentionally before the Lord, to make atonement for him; and it shall be forgiven him. You shall have one law for him who sins unintentionally, for him who is native-born among the children of Israel and for the stranger who dwells among them. (Num. 15:28–29)

A third layer of judicial practice concerning the alien which was addressed and emphasized in the legislation of the Torah was the duty on the part of the judges to assure that in their application of the law to aliens there would be no bias due to the personal status of the litigant before them. In at least three instances this issue of eliminating prejudice against the stranger is addressed. One instance is:

> You shall not pervert justice due the stranger or the fatherless, nor take a widow's garment as a pledge. But you shall remember that you were a slave in Egypt, and the Lord your God redeemed you from there; therefore I command you to do this thing. (Deut. 24:17–18)

A second instance is in the restatement of the Covenant at Mount Ebal:

> Cursed is the one who perverts the justice due the stranger, the fatherless, and widow. And all the people shall say, "Amen!" (Deut. 27:19)

And the third instance is the continuation of the passage at the beginning of the Book of Deuteronomy in Moses' charge to the newly appointed judges:

> Then I commanded your judges at that time, saying, "Hear the cases between your brethren, and judge righteously between a man and his brother or the stranger who is with him. You shall not show partiality in judgment; you shall hear the small as well as the great; you shall not be afraid in any man's presence, for the judgment is God's. The case that is too hard for you, bring to me, and I will hear it." And I commanded you at that time all the things which you should do. (Deut. 1:16–18)

The "perversion of judgment" which is the focus of the first two texts above is identified in the third passage as the preferential treatment shown to the wealthy and the powerful at the expense of the weak and the stranger. The "righteous judgment" (*mishpat tzedek*) which is demanded in the first sentence of the third passage is precisely the assurance that the weak and the stranger will not be disadvantaged, not be biased against, in the application of the law in their cases. This is, of course, precisely the meaning also of the oft-quoted admonition of Deuteronomy 16:20, "Justice, justice shall you pursue," "*Tzedek, tzedek tirdof.*"

These then are the three components of justice in the legal process which the Torah guarantees to the immigrant. First, the assurance that jurisdiction will be accepted by the judiciary, so that the legal claims of the stranger will be heard. Second, that the laws to be applied to the alien will be substantially the same as those which would be applied to a citizen. And third, that in the actual adjudication of the case there will be no bias against the stranger as an outsider, but that he will be granted the same standard of "righteous justice" that is deserved by and administered to any citizen.

5. Protection of the Immigrant from Emotional Oppression

The experiences of an immigrant in the biblical narrative of Genesis often include being subjected to emotional abuse. Such abuse comes in many forms. In the case of Lot it was in the demeaning words of the citizens of Sodom saying of him, "This one came as a resident alien and he presumes now to judge us!" (Gen. 19:9). In the case of Abraham the emotional offense was twofold, first in his total defenselessness against the violent taking of the wells he had dug, and second in the dismissive denial of any responsibility by Avimelech for the actions of his own servants (Gen. 21:25–26). For Isaac the emotional offenses were in what the Torah describes as his own recognition of the intense jealousy of the citizens of Gerar which led them to stuff the wells dug by his father (Gen. 26:14–15); and then again in his realization that Avimelech's request for entry into a treaty with Isaac was not the result of love and respect, but was being grudgingly done in the interest of his nation despite his utter hatred of Isaac (Gen. 26:27). In the life of Jacob after his flight from Esau's hatred and threat to kill him (Gen. 27:41–45), in consequence of which he becomes an immigrant, there are repeated emotional assaults – from Laban's demotion of him within the family (Gen. 29:17), to his repeatedly being deceived and denigrated as a foreigner (Gen. 29:23–27), to his realization that his brothers-in-law were jealous of him and that their feelings had soured whatever respect Laban might have had for him (Gen. 31:1–2).

What legislative instruments does the Bible utilize in responding to these varied forms of emotional abuse and in attempting to reduce their presence in societies formed in the Abrahamic tradition?

A set of three verses in the Torah, two of them consisting of a law followed by a motive clause, set up a distinctive approach to the emotional protection of the stranger.

a. "You shall neither afflict (*toneh*) a stranger nor oppress him (*tilḥatzenu*), for you were strangers in the land of Egypt." (Ex. 22:20)[35]

b. "Also you shall not oppress (*tilḥatz*) a stranger, for you know the heart of a stranger, because you were strangers in the land of Egypt." (Ex. 23:9)

c. "And if a stranger dwells with you in your land, you shall not afflict (*tonu*) him." (Lev. 19:33)[36]

The legal content of these verses is clouded. What conduct is restricted by the word "afflict" – "*toneh*"? And how does that differ from the

---

35. Here, NKJV translates the word "*toneh*" as "mistreat."
36. Here, NKJV translates the word "*tonu*" as "mistreat." The motive clause follows in the next verse, which we shall see later.

meaning of the word "oppress" – "*tilḥatz*"? The earliest teachings in the rabbinic tradition already recognize that these two terms bear different but overlapping meanings in different contexts. The most general use of the term "*toneh*," or "*tonu*" – to "afflict," appears in the context of the laws of the Jubilee year:

> In this Year of Jubilee, each of you shall return to his possession. And if you sell anything to your neighbor or buy from your neighbor's hand, you shall not afflict (*tonu*) one another. According to the number of years after the Jubilee you shall buy from your neighbor, and according to the number of years of crops he shall sell to you. According to the multitude of years you shall increase its price, and according to the fewer number of years you shall diminish its price; for he sells to you according to the number of the years of the crops. Therefore you shall not afflict (*tonu*) one another, but you shall fear your God; for I am the Lord your God. (Lev. 25:13–17)

The *Midrash Halakha* to these verses recognizes two distinct legal meaning to the crimes referred to in verses 14 and 17. The context of verse 14 is the sale of property and therefore the Midrash asserts that the "affliction," the "*onaah*," in this instance is the economic exploitation of the ignorance of the purchaser, or of the vendor in the execution of the transaction by overpricing the property or by paying less than its fixed price.[37] This is referred to as "*onaat mamon*," financial affliction or exploitation. What then is the second crime of "*lo tonu*" – "you shall not afflict (*tonu*) one another" of verse 17? This, answers the *Midrash Halakha*,[38] is a separate crime of verbal affliction, illustrated there, and in the Mishna, as follows:

> Just as there is exploitation (*onaah*) in purchase and sale, so too there is exploitation through words (*onaat devarim*). One should not say [to a merchant], "How much is this object?" if he does

---

37. In either instance involving a loss in excess of one sixth of the value of the property. *Sifra, Behar*, Lev. 25:14 #3. See Maimonides, *Mishneh Torah, Laws of Sale* 11:1–2.
38. *Sifra, Behar*, Lev. 25:17 #4.

not want to buy. If someone was a penitent, one should not say to him, "Remember your former actions!" If someone is the child of converts, one should not say to him, "Remember the deeds of your ancestors." As it is written (Ex. 22:20), "You shall not afflict a stranger, nor oppress him."[39]

Now to return to our three verses related specifically to the *ger*, the stranger. The *Midrash Halakha* to the verse in Exodus[40] and the *Midrash Halakha* to the verse in Leviticus[41] both contend that the term *"toneh,"* or *"tonu"* – to "afflict," made criminal in regard to the stranger, relate specifically to making verbally offensive statements which cause emotional offense by exploiting the economic or social or psychological vulnerability of the victim. This approach is made explicit in the third case of the Mishna above, and is further elaborated in the lengthy passages of Gemara associated with that Mishna text.[42] The idea that these proscriptions are fundamentally addressed to the emotional state, to emotional abuse, is also powerfully reinforced by the motive clause associated with each of the verses, in its fullest form, "...for you know the heart of a stranger (*nefesh hager*), because you were strangers in the land of Egypt" (Ex. 23:9). The verse could just as accurately be translated as "for you know the feelings of a stranger (*nefesh hager*), because you were strangers in the land of Egypt."

What then is the content of the other term describing proscribed actions in relation to the stranger – the word *"tilhatz,"* translated usually as "oppress" (Ex. 22:20 and 23:9)? Here the early rabbinic literature, perhaps in order to sustain the parallel between the restrictions related to citizens and those related to strangers, insisted that the term *"tilhatz"* had reference to economic exploitation like that of the financial deception as to the value of property involved in *"onaat mamon"* – in monetary exploitation in purchase and sale.[43] Rashi in his commentary to

---

39. Mishna, Bava Metzia 4:10.
40. *Mekhilta DeRabbi Yishmael* to Ex. 22:20.
41. *Sifra, Kedoshim*, ch. 8, par. 2, to Lev. 19:33.
42. Bava Metzia 58b–59a. See Maimonides, *Mishneh Torah, Laws of Sale* 14:12–18.
43. *Mekhilkta DeRabbi Yishmael* to Ex. 22:20.

this verse, insists that the crime of "*tilḥatz*," of economic oppression of a stranger, is specifically related to robbery (*gezelat mamon*),[44] rather than to theft (*geneva*). What is distinctive about *gezela* (robbery) as opposed to *geneva* (theft) in Jewish law? Maimonides formulates the definition of *gezela* (robbery), as follows:

> What is meant by a robber? One who takes by force property belonging to a person. For example, a person who seizes movable property from another's hand, or who enters his domain and takes utensils against the owner's will, or who seizes his servants or livestock and makes use of them, or who enters his field and eats his produce. These and any similar acts are considered robbery.[45]

Why would Rashi insist that the crime of "*tilḥatz*" – of monetary oppression – is a reference to robbery rather than any kind of taking of property, including theft? Perhaps the distinctiveness of robbery as opposed to theft is precisely what makes such action similar to verbal oppression – the emotional level in both of them, in "*onaat devarim*" as in "*tilḥatz*," is the sense of helplessness as one directly confronts the oppressive action of the other. In the three cases of verbal affliction of the Mishna, the merchant, the penitent, and the child of converts have no control over the conditions which make them vulnerable to the exploitative speech of the one taunting them. The merchant cannot compel the shopper to purchase the goods, the penitent is already in that irreversible state, and the child of converts cannot control his own ancestry. They are therefore vulnerable to the taunting speech of the antagonist and are helpless to prevent their own hurt. Similarly, the victim of a robbery is in a state of helplessness to prevent the more powerful or better armed person from taking from him whatever he wants. Perhaps it is that very emotion of helplessness to which the Torah is referring when it calls upon the Jewish people to remember how they felt as slaves in Egypt. And precisely in consequence

---

44. Rashi to Ex. 22:20, s.v. *velo tilḥatzenu*.
45. Maimonides, *Mishneh Torah, Laws of Robbery and Lost Property* 1:3, translation slightly modified from that of Rabbi Eliyahu Touger available at https://www.chabad.org/library/article_cdo/aid/1088885/jewish/Gezelah-vaAvedah-Chapter-One.htm.

of their "knowing the feelings of the stranger," they should be motivated to refrain from engaging in similar actions against strangers in their own lives.

And how apt these descriptions are to capture the experiences laid out with such care in the Book of Genesis in which the ancestors of the Jewish people found themselves helpless against oppressors who either were able to taunt them verbally because they were immigrants, strangers, or who were able with impunity to take the property which rightfully belonged to them because of their lack of legal protection and lack of power to prevent the abuse. How better to protect future immigrants and strangers from such abuse than to criminalize both the verbal abuse and the robbery of property which would result in the same emotional offense, engendering in a vulnerable person the feeling of utter helplessness as against an emotional aggressor.

The capstone legal provision to this defensive protection of the emotional well-being of the immigrant is both most important and least enforceable. It is responsive to the feelings of jealousy and hatred which seem repeatedly to emerge in citizens as they become aware of the great success of the stranger, of the immigrant. Thus, in a few verses of Genesis chapter 26, the Torah describes a complex series of events, feelings, and responses related to Isaac in Gerar.

> Isaac becomes very successful. 26:13
> The Philistine citizens become jealous. 26:14
> They express their hatred by stuffing his wells. 26:15
> Avimelech expresses that hatred by telling Isaac that he should leave the country. 26:16
> As Isaac travels, the locals continue to harass him by stuffing his wells and challenging his right to own them. 26:18–21
> Isaac becomes frightened and God needs to appear to him to relieve his fear. 26:23
> As Isaac flees, Avimelech pursues and catches up with him. 26:26
> Isaac angrily rebukes Avimelech. 26:27
> Avimelech offers and Isaac agrees to enter into a treaty. 26:28–31

An almost precisely parallel set of feelings and actions by Laban and his sons and by Jacob, who remained a stranger in that home, are described as Jacob achieves success in the household of Laban, as in Genesis 30:43–31:54.

> Jacob becomes very successful. 30:43
> The sons of Laban become jealous and verbally express their feelings. 31:1
> Laban begins to hate Jacob. 31:2
> Laban expresses his feelings by repeatedly changing Jacob's salary. 31:7
> Jacob becomes frightened and God appears to assure him that He will be with him, but he needs to leave. 31:3, 5
> Jacob flees. 31:17–21
> Laban pursues and catches up with Jacob. 31:22–25
> Jacob responds with an angry rebuke. 31:36–42
> Laban offers a treaty which Jacob accepts. 31:44–53

It is obviously not accidental that the account of Jacob's entry into treaty with Laban concludes with a unique oath, "And Jacob swore by the Fear of his father Isaac."[46] The common elements of the emotional challenges experienced by Jacob and his father Isaac cannot but be recognized as a broader attempt to call attention to the commonality of these experiences in the lives of immigrants in ancient, and indeed as well in modern, times. Success of the immigrant engenders jealousy and hatred in the local citizens resulting in actions or speech which engender in the outsider intense fear of harm, and anger about the injustice of it, and may cause him to flee – if he has somewhere to escape to and the faith that things will be better for him elsewhere.

The Torah chooses to address this complex pattern of vulnerability to emotional abuse by imposing upon all citizens a duty to love the stranger.

> The stranger who dwells among you shall be to you as one born among you, and you shall love him as yourself; for you were strangers in the land of Egypt: I am the Lord your God. (Lev. 19:34)

---

46. Gen. 31:53; echoing Jacob's prior usage of that same phrase in Gen. 31:42.

The *Midrash Halakha* comments on the motive clause of this verse, "for you were strangers in the land of Egypt," by saying, "Know the feelings of strangers, for you yourselves were strangers in the land of Egypt."[47] This theme, that the motive clause is not just a command of maintaining historical memory, but is addressed to the deep emotional awareness which can generate true empathy, is here borrowed from the concluding element of the similar verse in Exodus which adds, "for you know the feelings of the stranger" (Ex. 23:9). Of course the implication of this point of emphasis suggests that the subject of this law is not the *ger* as convert, but is the *ger* as resident alien, since the Israelite people were clearly not converts in Egypt, but were resident aliens there.

The very existence of a legal duty to love the stranger bears with it layers of emotional meaning which are already explicated in prior verses in the very same chapter of Leviticus:

> You shall not hate your brother in your heart. You shall surely rebuke your neighbor, and not bear sin because of him. You shall not take vengeance, nor bear any grudge against the children of your people, but you shall love your neighbor as yourself: I am the Lord. (Lev. 19:17–18)

In this passage which mandates the love of neighbor, the achievement of such love is portrayed as the product of the elimination of a set of negative emotions, particularly the voiding from one's heart – of hatred, of vengefulness, and of grudges. It further implies that rebuke – the affirmative engagement in dialogue with the other as to the factors which have created these negative emotions to begin with – is the essential instrument through which the underlying negative feelings can be addressed, and can be hopefully overcome,[48] thereby making room for the affirmative emotion of love which needs to replace the negative emotions. All of this is manifested in the subsequent mandate in the same chapter extending the duty of love to strangers (Lev. 19:34).

---

47. *Sifra, Kedoshim*, ch. 8, par. 4, to Lev. 19:34.
48. Maimonides, *Mishneh Torah, Laws of Personal Development* 6:6.

This mandate of love of the stranger is further amplified and its spiritual significance is magnified in Deuteronomy.

> For the Lord your God is God of gods and Lord of lords, the great God, mighty and awesome, who shows no partiality nor takes a bribe. He administers justice for the fatherless and the widow, and loves the stranger, giving him food and clothing. Therefore love the stranger, for you were strangers in the land of Egypt. You shall fear the Lord your God; you shall serve Him, and to Him you shall cleave. (Deut. 10:17–20)

The amplification of the duty of love of the stranger is achieved in these verses by the assertion that God Himself loves the stranger. And further, that His divine love is manifest precisely in the absolute equality of all persons, in not granting any advantage to those who think they can bribe Him, in the administration of equal justice to the disadvantaged, and in manifestations of love by providing food and clothing. The fact that these are behaviors which are manifest by God Himself means that such conduct is to serve as a model for the way in which humans need to act. The spiritual magnification of the significance of such feelings of love and such loving conduct resides in the suggestion by the order of the verses, that the achievement of the mandate to love the stranger is a mandated mode of the fulfillment of the following verse, to fear the Lord, to serve Him, and to cleave to Him (Deut. 10:20).

The Torah clearly desired to prevent immigrants from having to suffer varied forms of emotional abuse such as those described in the biblical narratives of Genesis – being demeaned verbally, being made to feel helpless in the defense of their persons, their families, and their property, being subjected to jealousy, suspicion, and hatred. It achieved those goals by its legislation which criminalized such conduct and even forbade the underlying destructive feelings. The Torah attempted to achieve these goals not only by threat of punishment for criminal violation, but by generating a powerful awareness that upholding these protections was itself a profound spiritual value – that in some significant way it is precisely in the protection of the stranger that the most ultimate values of the divine will are achieved, that in the protection of the stranger one can best fulfill the essence of what the Lord our God desires and requires of us for our own benefit. As the Torah says at the start of that very paragraph which mandates love of the stranger:

> And now, Israel, what does the Lord your God require of you, but to fear the Lord your God, to walk in all His ways and to love Him, to serve the Lord your God with all your heart and with all your soul, and to keep the commandments of the Lord and His statutes which I command you today for your good? (Deut. 10:12–13)

C. THE RECIPROCAL CIVIC DUTIES OF IMMIGRANTS

In all of the instances in which the Torah protects immigrants by criminalizing evil conduct against them, the effect of creating duties on the part of citizens to abstain from what it deems to be inhumane behavior is to vest in the stranger the correlative rights not to be harmed by such cruel conduct. The starting point in the regulation of the conduct of citizens in Jewish law is usually the determination of duties, whether affirmative duties to act or prohibitions – that is, the duty to refrain from acting in a particular manner. This is the case in regard to what Maimonides considers to be all four of the dimensions of human choice-making, that is expressions of personal will, regulated by the 613 mitzvot of the Torah. They are the capacity to choose 1) what to believe, 2) how to act, 3) how to shape one's inner personality qualities, and 4) how to speak.[49] In each of these domains the mitzvot define the duties borne by each individual citizen, as well as those borne by particular classes of persons, or by persons of a particular status. Two of these regulated domains, what I believe, and how I shape my inner personality qualities, have their primary impact on the person him- or herself who makes the choice to act in accordance with the law, or to violate it. Therefore, in these domains, the mandate of a duty does not produce a correlative right on the part of any other individuals. By contrast, the other two domains, that of bodily action and that of speech, tend to have their primary impact on others, and only secondarily on the self. It is therefore primarily in these two areas of governance that the regulation of

---

49. Maimonides, *Book of Commandments*, *shoresh* 9.

conduct by the imposition of duties has the effect of vesting rights in others not to be injured by the way in which I act or speak. Thus, when the Torah prohibits homicide, it thereby grants a right to others not to be killed. The prohibition against theft yields a right not to have my property stolen. The prohibition against deception results in the existence of a right not to be deceived. The prohibition against inducing someone to commit a crime is correlatively a grant of a right not to be induced to commit a crime.[50]

The effect of this on our deliberation is that the Torah, by mandating the various forms of duties resting upon citizens to refrain from injuring fundamental life interests of strangers, is thereby vesting in those *gerim*, immigrants, five civic rights: to the protection of their lives, of their sexual safety, of their economic well-being, of their emotional security, and of their equal protection under the law. But these rights do not come without correlative duties on the part of the beneficiaries of the rights. As in the broader contours of the Jewish legal system, the bearer of rights is always also the bearer of duties.[51] What then are the civic duties which the immigrant bears as the correlatives of the rights which the Torah grants him?

The Torah does not contain an explicit listing or codification of the legal duties of strangers within Jewish society. Even the somewhat frequent reference to affirmative duties or prohibitions addressed to *gerim* remains difficult to allocate clearly as between non-Jewish resident aliens (*gerei toshav*) and converts to Judaism (*gerei tzedek*). But the Book of Genesis clearly refers to a set of commands issued by God to Noah and his children (Gen. 9:1–7), and early biblical narrative indicates the existence of crimes for which God punishes humans.[52] These texts gave rise to an unequivocal understanding within Jewish society that there existed a body of laws which were universal and to which even non-Jews were bound. Thus, the Book of Jubilees, usually dated as having been

---

50. Moshe Silberg, "Law and Morals in Jewish Jurisprudence," trans. Amihud I. Ben Porath, *Harvard Law Review* 75:2 (Dec. 1961): 306–331, especially 321–331.
51. Saul J. Berman, "The Status of Women in Halakhic Judaism," *Tradition* 14:2 (Fall 1973): 5–28, at p. 18 and related footnotes, nos. 57–63.
52. E.g. Genesis 4:10–11; 6:2; 6:11; 9:22–23; 12:17; 19:5–13; 20:3; and others.

composed in the middle of the second century BCE, reports Noah's instructions to his sons as to how they need to conduct themselves in the new world after the Flood.[53] That listing appears to include some seventeen laws which would regulate the conduct of all of humanity. While the tannaitic listing of the Noahide Laws lists only seven, it then adds minority opinions which might include five more.[54] Strikingly, all seven of the Noahide Laws in the talmudic text are amongst the seventeen found in the Book of Jubilees. Both of those lists explicitly include four of the five civic duties which are the correlatives of the rights granted to immigrants by biblical legislation, and both lists imply the fifth.

The four civic duties deemed to be universal by these two texts, which requires that they be observed even by the resident alien in the Land of Israel, are eventually codified by Maimonides as follows: the prohibitions against murder, against incest and adultery, and against robbery, and the duty to establish laws and courts of justice.[55] These are clearly the same as the duties imposed by biblical law upon Jews in their duties toward strangers,[56] and are themselves the correlatives of the rights which are vested in immigrants by those very laws. The fifth of the rights granted by biblical legislation to immigrants, which I denominated as the right of protection from emotional oppression, including the duty to love the stranger, is in fact also explicitly contained within the listing of the Book of Jubilees,[57] but is absent from the listing of Noahide Laws in the talmudic texts. Perhaps the expansive list of the Noahide Laws in the Book of Jubilees, which combines in a single verse, "to bless their creator, and honor father and mother, and love their neighbor," might be understood to at least intimate that the command "to bless their creator," which is included as another of the seven Noahide Laws in the talmudic list and in that of Maimonides, needs to be read as a duty of

---

53. *The Book of Jubilees*, trans. R. H. Charles (London: The Macmillan Co., 1927), 7:20–27, pp. 68–71, and Introduction, p. 30.

54. Sanhedrin 56a.

55. Maimonides, *Mishneh Torah, Laws of Kings* 9:1.

56. See above sections B, 1–4.

57. *The Book of Jubilees*, op. cit., at 7:20, p. 68.

love of God through expression of gratitude, which ought to serve as a basis of character formation leading to love of persons.[58]

The very existence of civic duties resting upon immigrants in the biblical perspective has the potential to undercut the claim that immigrants are exploiting their hosts by claiming rights without having to bear any responsibilities. It is likely that this very claim is one of the constant sources of resentment of and jealousy toward immigrants that the Torah is particularly concerned with reducing in its protection of strangers and immigrants.

	Cases	Genesis	Motive for Immigration	Vulnerabilities	Defensive Response
Abraham	1:1	12:1–5	vision of blessed life		
	1:2	12:10–20	famine → Egypt	threat of rape and murder	Abraham mad and asked Sarah to lie
	1:3	18:1–8		welcoming strangers as countercultural model	engaged his family
Lot	1:4	19:1–3		welcoming strangers at risk of rejection	negotiation
Messengers	1:5	19:4–26	on divine mission	homosexual rape and murder	violence and escape

---

58. It is worth noting that the somewhat enigmatic text in the Christian Bible, Acts 15:19–20 and 28–29, does seem to echo elements of the Noahide Laws in its resolution of the status of non-Jews who desired to become Christians. The passage does not require them to become Jews, but does require that they accept certain fundamental elements of Jewish law, possibly the avoidance of the three cardinal sins of idolatry, adultery, and murder (or possibly the more socially oriented restrictions against eating idolatrous sacrifices, or animals not properly slaughtered, or blood, in addition to a ban against fornication with sacred prostitutes). See Paul J. Achtemeier, "An Elusive Unity: Paul, Acts and the Early Church," *The Catholic Biblical Quarterly*, vol. 48, no. 1 (January 1986): 1–26.

	Cases	Genesis	Motive for Immigration	Vulnerabilities	Defensive Response
Abraham	1:6	20:1–15	economic success → Gerar	threat of rape and murder	Abraham and Sarah lie; chastisement
	1:7	21:22–32		theft of wells – no legal protection	rebuke and entry in treaty
		23:1–20	needs burial cave for wife → Hebron	deception – revocation of sale	public nego-tiation of contract; vigilance
	1:8	24:14	sends Eliezer to Haran for wife for Isaac	need to pre-serve welcom-ing strangers as countercul-tural model	search for wife with those qualities
Isaac	2:1	26:1–24	famine → Gerar	threat of rape and murder	Isaac lied
		26:14–23		jealousy of locals, stuffing of wells	persistence, pride
		26:26–29		hated by government	acknowl-edged hatred; rebuke; entry into treaty and flees
Jacob	3:1	27:41–45	threat to life → Haran		
		29:14–15		demotion in the family	marries a local woman
		29:16–28		deceived as to marriage	works harder
		30:25–43		deceived as to compensation	self-sacrifice, and plans for departure
		31:7–9, 38–42			

	Cases	Genesis	Motive for Immigration	Vulnerabilities	Defensive Response
		31:1–7		jealousy of Laban's sons and of Laban	flight
		31:20–21 31:36–42		false accusation of theft	righteous indignation, rebuke, and entry in treaty
	3:2	32:1–8, 13–21	returns to Canaan to find peaceful life	fear of Esau	verbal appeasement, offer of tribute, prayer, defensive action
	3:3	34:1–7 34:24–26		rape of Dinah by Shechem	negotiation, violence by sons
		34:30–31	sold as slave	sexual seduction; false accusation of rape; no legal rights	silence – his social position allowed him no response
Joseph		40:14–15		no debt or gratitude owed to him	
		41:9–14 41:39–45		pays the price of entry into the culture	shaves, changes clothes and jewelry, and signs of social status, marriage to an elite local woman

Cases	Genesis	Motive for Immigration	Vulnerabilities	Defensive Response
	4:2	42:1–24	famine – 1st trip to Egypt	false accusation – that they are enemies	persuasion, leave a hostage to save family
Jacob's sons and Jacob	4:3	43:1–14	famine – 2nd trip to Egypt	false accusation of theft	
		44:1–34		arrest of Benjamin	Judah endangers himself to rescue Benjamin
		45:26–28 46:1–7 48:1–11	family reunification (Jacob with Joseph)	does not recognize his grandchildren	blesses them

D. CONCLUSION

King Solomon in his wisdom said, "That which has been is that which shall be; and that which has been done is what shall be done; and there is nothing new under the sun" (Eccl. 1:9). We ought now to view the entire chart, outlining the narratives of the Book of Genesis in terms of the motives of people's immigration, the vulnerabilities they experience, and the responses they make in their own protection, as follows:

We can easily see the constancy of the human experience of immigrants. We emigrate because of famine, or to seek economic success, or because there is a threat to our lives, or because we are sold as slaves, or to be reunited with our families, or because we have a vision of a blessed life, or to serve as messengers on a divine mission, or just to be able to avoid hatred and violence in the country from which we flee. Our vulnerabilities as immigrants today are essentially the same as they were in biblical times, from Genesis to Ruth and beyond: we face the threat of murder or of rape; we may expect to meet with rejection, jealousy, or overt hatred; we may experience economic bias and false accusations and deception; and we expect to be denied equal legal rights.

And our defensive responses to those vulnerabilities remain limited. We may lie or deceive in order to gain the peace and safety of our intended new home; we will work harder than the locals, even self-sacrificially to demonstrate our good intentions; we will feel righteous indignation at the indignities heaped upon us, but will be reduced to silence out of fear of the enmity of our hosts; we will be persistent but tempted to be violent and to simply give up and leave; we will attempt to assimilate on the terms demanded by the local culture. Nothing new under the sun.

Yet, in the face of all that sameness, there is hope in the biblical legislation that promises protection and rights even to the most vulnerable. There can be security in the assurance that citizens will take pride in their Godly assumption of the responsibility to welcome the stranger and relieve her of her fear and her anxiety. There can be courage on the part of the new immigrant, understanding that he is not simply a beggar, but is a member of a community in which he, like all of his predecessors, have equal rights and opportunities, and the full range of civic duties to help build a safe and secure life for all residents of the country.

For Insiders or Outsiders? The Book of Ruth's American Jewish Reception

Rabbi Dr. Zev Eleff

I n May 1912, the editors of a Boston Jewish weekly published an article on "Ruth and Boaz." The writers gleaned a number of items from the Book of Ruth, but one lesson, they admitted, stood out: Ruth the Moabite foreigner excelled in the Land of Israelites. Therefore, the journalists surmised, "it makes no difference where a person is born or from what country he comes, if he is only good and noble. It is actions that tell and by our good actions we make ourselves pleasing to God and men."[1] That they contemporized the short biblical book in this way is not surprising. In that moment, the American Jewish community was deeply concerned over legislation that threatened to limit migration to the United States and a rising "Know-Nothing" attitude directed toward

---

1. "Bible Lesson: Ruth and Boaz," *Jewish Advocate* (May 24, 1912): 3.

newcomers and their American-born children. In fact, the same editors had just one week prior published an editorial on the contributions of migrant populations to the United States. Drawing on Mary Antin's recently published memoir, the New England journalists had claimed that it was the "immigrant who makes America 'The Promised Land.'"[2] The biblical figure of Ruth imparted the very same moral. Despite her background, Ruth settles in Judea and makes her home there, one that Scripture reports reared King David and his monarchical descendants.

Understanding the Book of Ruth like this was typical in the United States. In New York, for example, it was not uncommon for journalists to draw a parallel between Ruth and immigrants on Ellis Island.[3] Time and again, Jewish (and non-Jewish) writers and sermonizers looked to Ruth to explore the roles of "insiders" and "outsiders" in American life. Perhaps more than other sacred texts, Ruth is ripe for multiple interpretations. She is born an outsider, into a nation with whom the Torah, on the face of it, forbids from intermarrying (Deut. 23:4), even if the Moabite converts. Despite this, Ruth is transformed into an insider through her genuine conversion to Judaism, reinforced by her pledge to her mother-in-law Naomi: "Where you go I will go, and where you stay I will stay. Your people will be my people and your God my God. Where you die I will die, and there I will be buried. May the Lord deal with me, be it ever so severely, if even death separates you and me" (Ruth 1:16–17). Ruth's is an exceptional case – not just anyone can convert to Judaism. Her devotion to Naomi's family in the face of scrutiny from Israelite insiders and willingness to fulfill the levirate marriage requirements with her kinsman also betokens her commitment to become a member of an exclusive religious group. Then again, Boaz's final acceptance of Ruth despite her Moabite origins reflects a certain openness to incorporate outsiders and expands the possibility of whom we might consider a less exclusive breed of insiders. Aware of its utility for a so-called Nation of Immigrants, American readers seized on this story to tighten or loosen boundary lines between themselves and others around them. Paradoxically, Ruth can be interpreted as a narrative about the selectiveness of insiders or the imperative to reach out and convert outsiders.

---

2. "The Land of Promise," *Jewish Advocate* (May 17, 1912): 8.
3. See "Whither Thou Goest, I Will Go," *American Hebrew* (June 13, 1913): 192.

The persistent but oscillating image of Ruth is emblematic of how the Bible is discussed and remains forcefully present in the United States. Historians can never be certain whether the women and men quoted in this chapter first looked to the Bible to address cultural, political, and social questions or if they searched through Scripture to justify their point of view. However, this helps to prove that the Bible has always played a major role in American discourse and was utilized to persuade and mobilize others to reconfirm or adopt positions of significant importance.[4] For the Book of Ruth, the protagonist's legacy loomed large for all those considering or reconsidering religious and cultural identities in America's rapidly changing environment.

Ruth's reception in the New World and her transformation to an American insider was not at first a Jewish enterprise. The earliest and most visible Ruthian commentators were Protestants who considered Ruth a proto-Christian or the ancestor of their faith.[5] The Book of Ruth was – and continues to be – one of the most popular studied by women's Christian Bible groups. In the nineteenth century, Christian authors looked to Ruth as a model of refinement and "domesticated religion." This value, according to historian Richard Bushman, stood at the core of a religious enlightenment that looked to American women to maintain the prevailing religious sentiment in the home. They drew on Ruth's piety and loyalty to Naomi and the rest of Elimelech's household. Ruth's attachment to her mother-in-law struck a chord for American Christian writers who placed increasing value on devotion to mothers and the religious matriarchy that stewarded faith in the home. Like Ruth and her adopted mother, opined one author, "Washington revered his."[6]

Jews did not object to the adaptation of Ruth to American climes but sought to reclaim her as a Jewish insider.[7] Some took exception to

---

4. See Timothy Beal, *The Rise and Fall of the Bible: An Unexpected History of an Accidental Book* (New York: Mariner Books, 2011), 1–28.
5. Mary V. Spencer, "The Hebrew Convert," *Ladies' National Magazine* 11 (June 1847): 199.
6. "Be Kind to Your Mother," *Christian Observer* (June 1, 1850): 88.
7. See "To the Reader," *The Israelite* (July 15, 1854): 4. This editorial, penned by Rabbi Isaac Mayer Wise, appeared in the inaugural issue of his long-running and influential Jewish newspaper in Cincinnati.

the Christian usage, charging that Protestant preachers had "rob[bed] our finest characters from our Bible."[8] Yet, when Jewish writers did discuss her, they oftentimes depicted Ruth in similar light. The Jewish educator Herman Baar instructed youngsters that compared to Ruth there were no biblical books or passages "which impress the duties of children toward their parents more beautifully."[9] In her *Women of Israel*, the English novelist Grace Aguilar singled out Ruth as a symbol of domestic heroism, for her "filial devotion and individual goodness."[10] First printed in 1845 in London, Aguilar's well-read book was published in the United States six years later and soon after serialized in the New York Jewish press.[11] The educator and philanthropist Rebecca Gratz of Philadelphia welcomed Aguilar's work to refute the "impression so much insisted on that women were little considered for by the ancient people." Measuring Jewish teachings against their Protestant counterparts, wrote Gratz, "in the New Testament I do not know of a character so elevated as Deborah, or so lovely and loving as Ruth."[12] The same was the case for the composer Sir Fredric Hymen Cowen's oratorio featuring Ruth and its warm reception among Jews in the United States.[13]

Of course, the synagogue was also an important site for biblical interpretations. In a sermon delivered at B'nai El in St. Louis, Rabbi Morris Spitz preached that Ruth's commitment to the Jewish home was in complete concert with Jewish virtues. To him, Ruth was so "deeply impressed with the life and conduct of her husband, with the purity of the domestic happiness that she enjoyed during his lifetime, with the many virtues of his parents, and especially that equanimity and moral

---

8. See, for example, A. Benjamin, "Ruth and Modern Converts," *Jewish Messenger* (August 16, 1878): 6.

9. Herman Baar, *Addresses on Homely and Religious Subjects* (New York: H.O.A. Industrial School, 1880), 249. I thank Dr. Jonathan Sarna for alerting me to this source and furnishing a copy for me to review.

10. Grace Aguilar, *The Women of Israel*, vol. I (London: Groombridge and Sons, 1845), 353.

11. For the quoted section, see Grace Aguilar, "Naomi," *Jewish Messenger* (November 5, 1858): 89.

12. See Dianne Ashton, *Rebecca Gratz: Women and Judaism in Antebellum America* (Detroit: Wayne State University Press, 1997), 187.

13. "Ruth," *Jewish Messenger* (October 14, 1887): 5.

strength which the ancestral faith had imparted to Naomi amid the greatest vicissitudes and adversities." This version of Ruthian feminine heroics redounded to the Jewish cause in the United States. In the 1870s, a decade marked by declension and general religious disinterest among Jewish women and men, Spitz believed that this message would resonate with his listeners and propel them to "not merely confess Judaism but also profess it; not only believe in it but rather live in it."[14] In all these instances, Jews depicted Ruth with focused attention to attributes that conformed to American ideals. So doing they hoped would elevate Jews and Judaism to an insider status in the United States.

Ruth assumed an even more prominent place in American Jewish rhetoric as it became more essential to reinforce the Jewish foothold in the United States. This transpired around the turn of the twentieth century, as Jews figured more prominently in discussions over immigration and social justice. From 1880 to 1920, the Jewish population swelled from a quarter-million to more than three million women and men.[15] In this period, Jews were more visible and active in social welfare to support throngs of working-class Eastern European migrants and found the Book of Ruth a source of inspiration to better understand changing conditions of Jews and American identity.[16]

American Jews understood Ruth's quick-paced entrance into the Judean mainstream as an ancient model of democracy and fairness. That her descendant was King David proved the far-reaching open-mindedness of biblical Judaism. Some argued that the Book of Ruth anticipated the social and political activism that marked the Progressive Era of American life. In Joplin, Missouri, for example, an educator at the United Hebrew Congregation chose to produce a children's play of Ruth over other biblical dramas that did not sufficiently underscore

14. "Ruth, the Moabite," *American Israelite* (March 16, 1883): 309. On Jewish religious declension in the 1870s, see Zev Eleff, *Who Rules the Synagogue? Religious Authority and the Formation of American Judaism* (Oxford: Oxford University Press, 2016), 167–174.
15. For basic population figures of Jews in the United States, see Jonathan D. Sarna, *American Judaism: A History* (New Haven: Yale University Press, 2004), 375.
16. See Deborah Dash Moore, *At Home in America: Second Generation New York Jews* (New York: Columbia University Press, 1981), 61.

the Social Gospel sensibilities of the contemporaneous American religious scene. Other synagogues likewise featured an amalgamized Ruth-America themed pageants, especially during confirmation ceremonies scheduled for Shavuot, the holiday on which the biblical book was read in synagogue.[17] Owing to the sweeping republican spirit, Ruth appealed to the Missouri Jewish teacher because it was a "pastoral tract on tolerance," "monumental monograph on brotherhood," and "splendid preparation for democracy."[18] Another scholar told a rabbinical group that Ruth is "perhaps one of the earliest appeals ever made in behalf of religious and social equality."[19] All this helped Jews stake the claim that their faith rendered them earnest American insiders against those like industrialist Henry Ford who preferred to speak about a more exclusive Protestant America.[20]

Some reckoned that Ruth proved that Judaism could embrace even wider notions of religious choice and American inclusiveness.[21] In particular, Reform leaders were interested in changing non-Jewish outsiders to Jewish insiders. To them, Ruth's was a call for increased proselytizing – or at least vigorously welcoming, as the historian Heinrich Graetz had suggested – converts to Judaism.[22] Rabbi William Rosenau of Baltimore recognized a need to welcome gentiles into the Jewish fold in order to justify his faith's alignment with American pluralism.

17. See "Leavenworth, Kan.," *American Israelite* (May 13, 1915): 2; and "Children's Pageant on Temple Lawn," *American Israelite* (June 6, 1918): 6.

18. Joseph Leiser, "The Drama as a Means of Religious Instruction," *American Israelite* (April 20, 1916): 1.

19. See Sidney S. Tedesche, "Jewish Champions of Religious Liberty," *CCAR Year Book* 36 (1926): 202.

20. For one interesting use of Ruth to combat the vocal prejudices of Henry Ford by a US Senator, see Joseph S. Frelinghuysen, "The Jews and World Progress," *Jewish Advocate* (December 7, 1922): 12. For an brief overview of the history of tolerance and antisemitism in the United States, see Zev Eleff, "The Jewish Encounter with Discrimination, Tolerance and Pluralism in the United States," in *Interpreting American Jewish History at Museums and Historic Sites*, ed. Avi Decter (Lanham: Rowman & Littlefield, 2016), 161–178.

21. On this, see Lincoln A. Mullen, *The Chance of Salvation: A History of Conversion in America* (Cambridge: Harvard University Press, 2017), 9–11.

22. See Heinrich Graetz, *History of the Jews*, vol. I (Philadelphia: The Jewish Publication Society of America, 1891), 370–371.

Conversion proved the porousness of the insider-outsider dichotomy. Rosenau approvingly quoted the British thinker Claude Montefiore who had suggested about Ruth that the "book shows a fidelity wider than race."[23] And it was not just rabbis. A World War I veteran turned magazine publisher scolded the "old fogey Jews" who rejected loose conversion standards as a "terrible heresy," and provided Ruth and Boaz as a counterexample.[24] He would have likely, then, approved of the conversion of actress Elizabeth Taylor who switched religions from Christian Science to Judaism. Her Jewish education lasted nine months under the supervision of Reform Rabbi Max Nussbaum. Taylor converted shortly after her engagement to musician Eddie Fisher but made clear that her interest in Judaism had stemmed from her earlier marriage to Michael Todd (née Avrom Hirsch Goldbogen) and their conversations about the travails of Ruth.[25]

Some still understood the Book of Ruth as a tale of exclusiveness and the need for firm barriers between Jewish insiders and gentile outsiders. Tradition-minded Jews read about Ruth's singular determination to become a Jewess and surmised that the rank-and-file were undeserving of similar pathways to Judaism. Just the opposite, Ruth justified the claims to maintain stricter standards for conversion. In Philadelphia, the pseudonymous "Judaeus" expressed his disappointment that Reform Jews had adopted such openness when evaluating the merits of prospective converts. This writer was willing to accept choice candidates, to "welcome such proselytes as Ruth who, widowed and impoverished, still clung to her adopted nation and religion"[26] Others, however, were unworthy of Jewish insider status. Toward mid-century, Aaron Rosmarin

---

23. William Rosenau, "Illustrative Lesson on the 'Book of Ruth,'" *The Sentinel* (July 21, 1911): 12; and Claude G. Montefiore, *The Bible for Home Reading*, vol. I (London: Macmillan and Co., 1899), 184.

24. William B. Ziff, "Jewry Must About Face!" *The Sentinel* (November 8, 1934): 9.

25. Richard Mathison, "Liz Taylor's Conversion to Judaism Explained," *Los Angeles Times* (April 4, 1959): B2. Interestingly, Ruth's image was not much invoked in 1956 when Marilyn Monroe converted to Judaism. On this episode, see Lila Corwin Berman, *Speaking of Jews: Rabbis, Intellectuals, and the Creation of an American Public Identity* (Berkeley: University of California Press, 2009), 143–167.

26. Judaeus, "The Book of Ruth and Intermarriage," *Jewish Exponent* (May 20, 1904): 4.

of the Religious Zionist's Mizrachi Organization offered a similar point, contending that Ruth was better understood as a critique of individuals who ignored important distinctions between Jewish and Christian religious identities:

> The story of Ruth is an ancient tale with current implications that fit right into the contemporary American Jewish scene. There you have the full gallery of our contemporaries – the man who seeks to sever relations with his Jewish past and present, who seeks to escape his own people through the self-effacement of his national self and whose children go even farther, using intermarriage as a means for complete racial and religious self-denial. And there you have, too, Ruth – the perpetual symbol of the few and elite who, non-Jews at birth, find ties of human kinship with the Jew in the hour when some of his own kin desert him.[27]

But Rosmarin's assessment of Ruth stood in contrast with the prevailing American spirit of civil rights, pluralism, and tolerance. Consider Reform Rabbi Albert Goldstein of Boston who maintained that Boaz's generosity to Ruth and Naomi could be a model for political support of the "native Negro" or the "Puerto Rican fellow citizen."[28] Additionally, in the post-World War II period many Americans started to subscribe to a common set of "Judeo-Christian" values. This attitude changed Jewish feelings about insider-outsider dynamics, even for sensitive cases of conversion. In 1940, for instance, Orthodox Rabbi Samuel Rosenblatt cautioned that most conversions in Jewish history had resulted in "fiascos" because "would-be-converts to Judaism" rarely reached Ruth's pedestal.[29] By the late 1950s, Rosenblatt drew a far different lesson from Ruth: that "Jewish religion looks with favor upon newcomers to the Jewish fold."[30]

---

27. Aaron Rosmarin, "The Legends of Ruth," *Jewish Advocate* (May 25, 1944): 5; and *Jewish Exponent* (May 11, 1945): 16.
28. Albert S. Goldstein, "Conversion to Judaism in Bible Times," in *Conversion to Judaism: A History and Analysis*, ed. Max Eichhorn (New York: Ktav, 1965), 31.
29. Samuel Rosenblatt, *Our Heritage* (New York: Bloch, 1940), 161.
30. Samuel Rosenblatt, *Hear, Oh Israel* (New York: Philipp Feldheim, Inc., 1958), 351.

Nonetheless, the Book of Ruth remained useful to set apart outsiders from the establishment of insiders. The challenge was to identify an insider-outsider binary that resonated with American perspectives. Take, for instance, Twentieth Century Fox's 1960 movie, *The Story of Ruth*. Though Fox did not invest the same sort of resources that Universal International contributed to Kirk Douglas' *Spartacus* blockbuster which appeared the same year – $5 million in contrast to $12 million – the Ruth movie was a major production with clear political implications.[31] The widescreen rendition of Ruth was intended to reach a wide swath of viewers and to leverage the heroine as the ancestor of a "Tri-Faith America" of Protestants, Catholics, and Jews and to unite these groups against their common Cold War enemy: the Soviet Union.[32]

It was critical for producer Samuel Engel to cast someone who could appeal as an Israelite and appeared like the rank-and-file American woman. Engel selected the "Western-looking" nineteen-year-old Elana (née Cooper) Eden, an Israeli-born actress and daughter of Eastern European immigrants.[33] Not at all a household name, Eden still managed to win the role over 800 applicants, including Elizabeth Taylor and Sophia Loren.[34] Eden had trained at Tel Aviv's Habima Theatre and was the runner-up to Millie Perkins for the part of Anne Frank in the 1959 Fox film. The missed opportunity in the sure-to-be-acclaimed movie left Eden "fearfully depressed." But the audition serendipitously helped her edge out the competition for the Ruth movie.[35] Engel discovered Eden while reviewing the studio files in the recently completed Holocaust-themed film.[36]

---

31. See Herbert G. Luft, "Our Film Folk," *Jewish Advocate* (September 22, 1960): 15A.
32. See Kevin M. Schultz, *Tri-Faith America: How Catholics and Jews Held Postwar America to Its Protestant Promise* (Oxford: Oxford University Press, 2011), 15–42.
33. Thomas McDonald, "'Ruth' in Reality and on Screen," *New York Times* (January 31, 1960): X7.
34. See Arthur J. Berenson, "Like Ruth Amid the Alien Corn," *Jewish Post and Opinion* (May 27, 1960): 1; and Leonard Mendlowitz, "Star of 'Story of Ruth' an Israeli Sabra," *Jewish Criterion* (June 10, 1960): 5.
35. Hedda Hopper, "Elana Eden at 19 Captures Stardom in Her First Film," *Los Angeles Times* (May 8, 1960): H4.
36. See Philip K. Schneuer, "She Tested as Anne, Plays Ruth!" *Los Angeles Times* (December 23, 1959): 13.

In addition, Engel needed a script that would capture the attention of Jewish and Christian audiences. Screenwriter Norman Corwin therefore made sure to depict Ruth as a progenitor of both "insider" faiths. In one scene that liberally departed from Scripture, a town prophet tells Naomi that "through your daughter-in-law shall shoot forth many children and children's children, and a great king, and a prophet whom many shall worship as the messiah." One Jewish pundit took umbrage, decrying this use of creative license as "pitiful" and an altogether "objectionable scene."[37] But most let it slide. Instead, Jewish reviewers praised the film, dubbing it a "distinct tribute to the People of the Book."[38] American Jewish socialites welcomed Eden to Hollywood stardom, inviting her to major galas and fundraisers.[39] In the general press, a *New York Times* reviewer panned the movie as "rather stiff and pompous" but most other major critics in Boston and Los Angeles disagreed, offering praise for the newcomer Eden and the film.[40]

The Ruth film also resonated with the American public because of its portrayal of a familiar "outsider" enemy. Like the common impression of the Communist villains, Engel's movie depicted the Moabites as heartless with an "ideology so hostile to the Israelites."[41] Before her conversion, Ruth at first denounces Mahlon's "invisible God" and cannot understand how the Jewish Deity could disapprove of slaves and human sacrifices. Before his death – in this iteration, he is styled a martyred hero – Mahlon gives Ruth a miniature gold-plated Ten Commandments that symbolized a legal and moral code unknown to the religiously

---

37. Tim Boxer, "The Story of Ruth: Refreshing Diversion from Hollywood Formula," *The Sentinel* (June 23, 1960): 9.

38. Herbert G. Luft, "Story of Ruth Tribute to the Jewish People," *B'nai B'rith Messenger* (July 22, 1960): 8.

39. See, for example, "Stage Israel Salute Rally," *B'nai B'rith Messenger* (July 22, 1960): 1; and "'Ruth' Star, Deferred from Israel Army, Visits Atlanta," *Southern Israelite* (June 3, 1960): 4.

40. See Bosley Crowther, "Screen 'Story of Ruth,'" *New York Times* (June 18, 1960): 12; Marjory Adams, "Garden of Elana Eden Made Gay by Ruth Role," *Boston Globe* (June 13, 1960): 22; and Philip K. Scheuer, "Sincerity Marked in 'Story of Ruth,'" *Los Angeles Times* (July 1, 1960): 25.

41. See, for example, Herbert G. Luft, "Corwin Writes Biblical Scenario," *B'nai B'rith Messenger* (March 18, 1960): 25.

unscrupulous Moabites. Then, after accompanying Naomi back to Judea, Ruth encounters Boaz who laments the "long hard history between our countries." Ruth reminds Boaz and his Jewish brethren of their honorable and peace-loving religion. She is the once-outsider convert who counterintuitively restores the "Judeo-Christian" heritage to her new community of insiders and the American moviegoers who, Engel and Corwin would have had it, were due for a similar Bible lesson. Ruth's red, white, and blue outfits and the iconic image of the Ten Commandments then in vogue in American religious life do much to reinforce the issue.[42]

On the whole, Ruth persisted as a symbol of inclusion and "big-tent" insiderness to American Jews and non-Jews alike. For example, the Jewish children's writer Bea Stadtler's serialized and syndicated stories about "Debbie" often used the Book of Ruth to preach inclusion of neighbors, converts, and different varieties of Jews.[43] In an article published in the pages of *Conservative Judaism*, Rabbi Monford Harris wrote about the importance of togetherness, acceptance, and how Ruth supported "family cohesiveness spanning the generations."[44] Jewish feminists also seized on the image of Ruth, utilizing the biblical figure in inclusive-minded liturgies designed to make space for those who claimed feelings of marginalization.[45] The Ruth story also inspired creative conjurings of how the multifaceted and all-embracing Jewish infrastructure handles all different kinds of Jews. In 1975, New York's Board of Jewish Education reimaged the biblical tale in "today's world"; how the well-heeled

---

42. See Jenna Weissman Joselit, *Set in Stone: America's Embrace of the Ten Commandments* (Oxford: Oxford University Press, 2017), 101–126.

43. See Bea Stadtler, "Debbie and the Book of Ruth," *Jewish Advocate* (May 27, 1982): 2; and Bea Stadtler, "Debbie 'Gleans' Her Closet," *Jewish Advocate* (May 23, 1985): 17.

44. Monford Harris, "'The Way of Man with a Maid' – Romantic or Leal Love," *Conservative Judaism* 14 (Winter 1960): 36. See also Joel Rembaum, "Dealing with Strangers: Relations with Gentiles at Home and Abroad," in *Etz Hayim: Torah and Commentary*, ed. David L. Lieber (New York: Rabbinical Assembly, 2001), 1379–1380.

45. See Norma Baumel Joseph, "Letters," *Women's Tefillah Newsletter* 1 (August, 1985): 4; Penina V. Adelman, *Miriam's Well: Rituals for Jewish Women Around the Year* (New York: Biblio Press, 1990), 84–93; and Annette Daum, "Language and Liturgy," in *Daughters of the King: Women and the Synagogue*, ed. Susan Grossman and Rivka Haut (Philadelphia: The Jewish Publication Society, 1992), 201.

and robust Jewish social welfare organizations might have partnered to solve the plight of Naomi and Ruth:

> They would have turned to the Joint Distribution Committee (JDC) in Moab for assistance. Through the Jewish Agency they would have been flown to Israel, put up in the absorption center for new *olim* where they would have stayed for months, being processed, learning Hebrew and adjusting to their new surroundings. The Jewish Agency also would have sought housing for them and Naomi, an elderly woman, might have entered a Malben institution for necessary care. Ruth, after marrying Boaz and bearing a son, might enroll him either in an ORT (Organization for Rehabilitation through Training) school to learn a trade or in a UJA academic high school.[46]

Then again, perhaps Ruth would have looked to resettle elsewhere. Once again, the Board of Education indulged a self-described "fantasy" of biblical proportions. In a second retelling, Ruth and Naomi would have fared just fine in New York:

> Had they elected to settle in the United States, they would have been aided by the United HIAS Service (HIAS) and the New York Association for New Americans (NYANA). Upon arrival on these shores, Ruth might have availed herself of one of Federation's 130 social service, health, educational and recreational agencies. Naomi might have been placed in one of Federation's six

---

46. *Tzedakah Guidelines: A Discussion and Program Guide for Pupils and Teachers, Shavuoth 5735* (New York: Board of Jewish Education, Inc., 1975), 3. All of the listed organizations are familiar to general readers with the exception of Malben. Founded in 1949 by the Joint Distribution Committee, Malben aimed to assist "handicapped immigrants" in Israel. I thank my colleague Menachem Butler for obtaining a copy of this pamphlet for my research. Much earlier, in 1926, the Hebrew writer Hayim Nahman Bialik, influenced by midrashic literature, authored his own alternate-history of Ruth titled *Megillat Orpah*. This was translated and summarized in the American Jewish press. See, for instance, Bea Stadtler, "Of Ruth and Orpah," *Jewish Advocate* (May 23, 1974): A11.

homes for the aged and/or sought health care in one of the eleven hospitals and medical care facilities supported by Federation.

Ruth might have turned to the New York Board of Rabbis for spiritual guidance and clarification of her religious status. After marrying Boaz and giving birth to a son, she could have turned to the Board of Jewish Education for information on the religious schools available in her neighborhood. For recreational activities, her children would attend the local "Y."[47]

The exception to Ruthian inclusiveness was the Orthodox. For the so-called Yeshiva World sector of this religious group, Ruth's was a message of merit, authenticity, and, most of all, exclusiveness. Rabbi Avrohom Chaim Feuer put forward the Book of Ruth as a stark counter-example to the ever-changing "situational ethics" of American life. In his reading of the sacred text, Ruth served as a hallmark of steadfast devotion to a timeless set of principles and people that could not be widened or reoriented.[48] Likewise, Rabbi Nosson Scherman admonished readers in the earliest years of the ArtScroll publishing enterprise that even in the turbulent years in which Ruth lived, "Israel was far, far above the moral, ethical, scholarly, and religious standards of the twentieth century which so enjoys basking in the self-anointed status of occupant of civilization's highest rung."[49] This same circle also took issue with the Board of Education's Ruthian counter-history. Rabbi Nisson Wolpin shuddered to consider the outcome of Ruth's experiences with the myriad of modern-day Federation-led aid institutions. In Israel's absorption center, "would she have learned the 613 mitzvos?" Had Naomi moved into an old-age

47. Ibid.
48. Avrohom Chaim Feuer, "To Kiss – Or to Embrace? The Book of Ruth and Kabolas Ha'Torah," *Jewish Observer* 5 (May 1969): 18–19.
49. Nosson Scherman, "An Overview – Ruth and the Seeds of Mashiach," in *Megillas Ruth: A New Translation with a Commentary*, ed. Meir Zlotowitz (New York: ArtScroll Studios, 1976), xxvii. For a trenchant critique of this volume, see Isaac Boaz Gottlieb, "The Book of Ruth," *Tradition* 21 (Spring 1983): 75–83. Other Ruth commentaries appeared around this time in English but do not seem to have offered similar contemporary critiques. See "Books in Review," *Jewish Observer* 11 (May 1976): 29–30.

facility, "who would have directed Ruth to Boaz?" On the prospect of Ruth's encounter with the New York Board of Rabbis, Wolpin lambasted, "Imagine the liberating experience for Ruth if Board-member Rabbi Sally Priesand is her counselor or any other Reform member, for that matter, when she petitions for 'clarification of her religious status': Would they require her to accept the authority of a personal-and-universal Deity and His mitzvos, when they themselves do not?"[50]

The Modern Orthodox rabbinate also tended to read the Book of Ruth as establishing borderlines when it came to conversion, even if its rhetoric was mild compared to the Orthodox Right. To be sure, there were some like Rabbi Shlomo Riskin who drew upon Ruth to urge against stricter conversion standards in the State of Israel, and to "accept the sincere proselyte with sensitivity and compassion."[51] But Rabbi Walter Wurzburger seems to have spoken for more of his Orthodox-affiliated Rabbinical Council of America colleagues who highlighted Ruth as a narrow example of someone who punctiliously abided by "all the conditions governing Jews."[52] Wurzburger criticized Reform leaders who used Ruth to extend the borders of Jewish identity without recalling that she was also the prototype for unimpeachable faith and sincere conversion. Similarly, Rabbi Basil Herring advocated an "approach that carefully screens potential converts, that does not accept them for conversion until it becomes quite clear after study and practice that they will subscribe in deed to the laws of the Torah and the tradition, in the faithful pattern of Ruth the daughter-in-law of Naomi."[53]

Similar sentiments can be found in less obvious venues and among less typical Orthodox personalities. One writer felt compelled to remind the readers of an Orthodox women's magazine that the process

---

50. "'Borrowed' Symbols," *Jewish Observer* 10 (May 1975): 25–26. In June 1972, Rabbi Sally Priesand became the first woman ordained at the Reform-affiliated Hebrew Union College.

51. Steven Riskin, "Conversion in Jewish Law," *Tradition* 14 (Fall 1973): 39.

52. Walter S. Wurzburger, "Patrilineal Descent and the Jewish Identity Crisis," *Judaism* 34 (Winter 1985): 122.

53. Basil F. Herring, "To Convert or Not to Convert," *RCA Sermon Manual* 39 (1981): 193. See also Bernard L. Berzon, "The Symptoms of a World Gone Mad," *RCA Sermon Manual* 44 (1986): 25.

for conversion was long and not every prospective proselyte completes the training or is in the end accepted like Ruth. His intention was to warn "those eager beavers who can't wait to propose a match for this bright new kid on the block even before he or she has completed the formal requirements" for conversion.[54] As well, the popular and progressive Israeli thinker, Rabbi Adin Steinsaltz, submitted that Ruth "require[s] us to welcome the proselyte in our midst" specifically because she was "unique in the Scriptures in that she is described as being wholly pure" – among the Moabites she was viewed as an "exception, as an outsider."[55]

Then again, in a more recent formulation, the leading Orthodox scholar Rabbi Hershel Schachter offered that the Book of Ruth is traditionally read on Shavuot because it is emblematic of the source of all *"kedushat Yisrael,"* Jewish sanctity. Even the Israelites at Sinai stood along the foothills as outsiders before "converting" to Judaism.[56] This, then, is the dual and oft-competing American legacy of Ruth. The biblical heroine is at once a principled convert who set a formidable standard for anyone else seeking to become a Jewish insider and a reminder to include the outsider, a theme of tolerance that touches upon a longstanding tension in the United States. Like other biblical figures, the malleable image of Ruth mattered much to Jews and other religious people looking to anchor themselves and their experiences in the swift-changing currents of American culture.

---

54. Ira Axelrod, "The Strangers Among Us," *Jewish Homemaker* (June 1993): 29.
55. See Adin Steinsaltz, *Biblical Images: Men and Women of the Book*, trans. Yehuda Hanegbi and Yehudit Keshet (New York: Basic Books, 1989), 117–123. On the reception and controversy surrounding this book, see "Right-Wing Rabbis Ban Scholars' Books," *Jewish Week* (August 25, 1989): 9.
56. Zvi Schachter, "BeGeder Kedushat Yisrael," in *Rav Chesed: Essays in Honor of Rabbi Dr. Haskel Lookstein*, vol. II, ed. Rafael Medoff (Jersey City: Ktav, 2009), 208.

Ruth's Journey: What Social Work Can Teach Us about Immigration, Loss, Trauma, and the Shaping of Identity Texts

Dr. Danielle Wozniak

INTRODUCTION

Social workers are called to accompany people through shattering pain that we know will leave indelible marks on their lives. And we are called to be that voice for social justice even when it is inconvenient or offensive. This is in our code of ethics. This is our work. It is complex work that involves intervention at the micro level with individuals, couples, and families while simultaneously intervening at the macro level by changing social policies and by calling attention to and de-normalizing cultural beliefs and practices that create the harsh landscapes upon which people try to survive. To do our job, we must understand the impact of loss, trauma, and change on the human psyche, understand human behavior and reactions, and, above all, understand what can help heal these indelible wounds. We must also understand the impact of our formal policies and laws, and what policies mean to those who follow, implement, and contest them. We must understand the unintended consequences of policy and be able to decipher the cultural beliefs and myths upon which our policies rest. This is work that helps individuals find a place in a cultural identity narrative. It is also work that shapes the narrative and pushes, through advocacy, for change.

In this chapter I suggest that the Book of Ruth, when understood from the macro and micro social work perspectives, holds salience for us today both as a guide for our own response to immigrants and asylum seekers and as a book that can help us build deeper understanding for those who come to our borders. Ruth is the quintessential immigrant and foreigner. And it is the meaning of her foreignness to which we should pay close attention. As Bonnie Honig suggests, "the foreignness of Ruth is what enables her to supply the Israelites with a refurbishment. [S]he chooses them in a way that only a foreigner can ... and thereby re-marks them as the Chosen People."[1]

Ruth's story points to our own struggle with a national identity text vis-à-vis our response to immigration and asylum seekers. Currently the radically different ideas of what is "right" or "good" relative to immigration policies point to a fractured nation in need of re-making and redemption as national identity hangs in the balance and, I argue, democracy itself is at stake. It is upon this contested landscape that asylum seekers plead their cases and hope to find a home as they flee violence, death threats, and trauma in their native lands.

Because the macro and micro perspectives must always be understood in juxtaposition, an analysis from the micro perspective suggests we consider what we know about Ruth's life and experiences through the lens of social work theory on trauma and loss. I examine the ways in which intersecting micro dynamics shaped her experiences and her choices much like it shapes the life course of contemporary asylum seekers who are undeniably damaged and further traumatized by the current policy, practice, and anti-immigration vigilantism. While we consider Ruth's story, we keep in mind that while "not every migration story is filled with trauma, migration is always a disruption, a period

---

1. *Democracy and the Foreigner* (Princeton: Princeton University Press, 2003), 7.

of disequilibrium, that necessitates the seeking of a new equilibrium, and a new balance."[2] When migration is coupled with loss, mourning, food scarcity, and fear emanating from the social and cultural context, then the outcomes are significantly altered and finding equilibrium and healing from loss is prevented. This is where Ruth's story diverges from that of contemporary immigrants. In the end, Ruth thrives. She is recognized and embraced. She remarries and starts a new life as an accepted member of her new community. Current immigrants are not so fortunate. They enter a landscape where they are regarded as a threat, thus precluding the possibility of their inclusion. On this landscape, individuals traumatized by their flight face arrest, separation from their children, and deportation. It is this landscape that leaves *us* wanting redemption.

THE IMMIGRATION EXPERIENCE AND THE SOCIO-CULTURAL CONTEXT: THE MACRO PERSPECTIVE

As I write this chapter, men, women, and children escaping lives of pain and desperation in Central Latin America are marching through Mexico toward the US in hope of finding a home that will not just welcome them, but will provide them with the rights and resources they need to survive and ultimately thrive. They are coming to the United States because our traditional identity narrative has included welcoming the immigrant and providing this experience. Our cultural stories tell of people who arrived "with nothing" and who ended up millionaires through their own hard work. These stories also set a standard. Inherent in this message is an accepted definition of what it means to be a "successful" and "good" immigrant. However, nowadays, the rhetoric used by nationalist politicians to describe immigrants has become a lightning rod for the woes of working-class Americans. Immigrants are described in pejorative terms. They are dirty, unintelligent, leeches on the system, to be feared when they cannot be stopped. These stories have been embraced by those who feel cheated of opportunities and robbed of their chance for success. "Successful" immigrants work hard, are industrious and do well.

---

2. Robert A. Neimeyer, *Techniques of Grief Therapy: Assessment and Intervention*, Series in Death, Dying, and Bereavement (New York: Taylor and Francis, 2015), 4.

During the current presidential administration, anti-immigration rhetoric and nativist policies have intensified. Immigrants have been criminalized, totalized as rapists, drug dealers, thugs, and gang leaders, They have been detained in stark detention centers, devoid of comfort and, in a horrifying policy, mothers have been separated from children with little hope of reunification. On the eve of national elections, *The New York Times* wrote, "President Trump's closing argument is now clear: Build tent cities for migrants. End birthright citizenship. Fear the caravan. Send active-duty troops to the border. Refuse asylum."[3]

Rhetoric, and the beliefs it inspires, is not innocuous. The image created is that there is something significantly different about immigrants. They are less than human, physically threatening, and therefore *a priori* incapable of being "good." It is thus legitimate to reject them. By accepting this narrative, we can on one level retain our identity as a nation that welcomes the "tired, poor huddled masses yearning to breathe free" *and* assert a racist discourse by qualifying the message of acceptance to, if they look like "us" and act like "us" and can be a "good" immigrant.

Our nation needs immigrants, not just in our economy, or in our universities, but to affirm our basic democratic way of life. Thus, what is at stake in the acceptance or rejection of this vision is our national identity and the democratic principles upon which that identity rests. Our origin story (reenacted every Thanksgiving) is that our country was founded by people escaping religious persecution. Our identity is built on the belief that we are a safe and welcoming haven for those on a similar trajectory because we *empathically* know and understand this journey. Bonnie Honig also suggests that American democracy *depends* on the presence of the immigrant to reaffirm our values. We must be chosen by immigrants because we are choice-worthy; we must be able to see our country through their eyes as full of hope, promise, and prosperity in order to affirm our values and national ideals. "In short, exceptionalist

---

3. Michael D. Shear and Julie Hirschfeld Davis, "As Midterm Vote Nears, Trump Reprises a Favorite Message: Fear Immigrants," *The New York Times*, November 1, 2018, https://www.nytimes.com/2018/11/01/us/politics/trump-immigration.html.

accounts of American democracy are inextricably intertwined with the myth of an immigrant America."[4]

The very idea that *foreignness* is *required* to affirm and redeem a national identity is a theme central to the Book of Ruth. Ruth, a Moabite and a widow, travels with her mother-in-law to Bethlehem. Unlike Abraham, the only other biblical figure in whose story the doubling of the Hebrew word for "go" (*lekh*) appears, Ruth is not commanded by God to undertake this journey – she is not told "*lekh lekha*, go for yourself"; rather, she tells Naomi, "wherever you go, I will go." She decides to go of her own free will and we are told that when she is implored by her mother-in-law to return to her natal home, she does not. Instead, she professes her selfless dedication to Naomi and her willingness to adopt her mother-in-law's customs and lifeways. Unlike Abraham's journey, Naomi and Ruth travel with nothing and are promised nothing upon their arrival.[5] Ruth knows that as a Moabite, she will be regarded as a foreigner from a people who are abhorrent to the Israelites. She arrives in Bethlehem, marries a relative of her dead husband, and there starts the line of King David. She maintains her commitment to her new people with integrity and fidelity and, in so doing, transforms the Israelite character, corrupted under the rule of the Judges. According to Honig, Ruth's foreignness, her status as an immigrant, is central to the intensity of meaning in the story. Not only is her story embraced as a testament to her integrity and selflessness, but her choices reaffirm for the Israelites that their Abrahamic values are the *right* ones – they were chosen by God, and through Ruth's choosing them, she affirms their status as the chosen people.[6]

It is important to ask, if Ruth is the quintessential immigrant who helps the Israelites redefine themselves, what does it say about who we are as a people and a nation, when we reject the idea that we can, should, or need to be chosen? What is at stake when we no longer empathically

---

4. Honig, 73–75.
5. For these and other differences between Abraham and Ruth's journeys, see Yair Zakovitch, "Through the Looking Glass: Reflections/Inversions of Genesis Stories in the Bible," *Biblical Interpretation* 1, 2 (1993): 146–147.
6. Honig, 42, 45.

see the person of the asylum seeker and instead make human beings (vs. their actions) illegal? When we assert totalizing images of marauding bandits? When we reduce groups of diverse human beings to voiceless cultural categories? What happens when we fail to acknowledge our own journeys to a new world full of hope and promise by failing to see the journey and the pain of another?

In semiotic terms, the rhetoric used to describe current immigrants changes the myth about America and alters our identity narrative. Immigrants are no longer coming to America in search of a better way of life or democratic freedom. Unlike our ancestors who trudged through Ellis Island, who were disadvantaged and who brought labor or knowledge or both to contribute to our country, in a new dystopian myth, immigrants and asylum seekers are criminals who are coming to take our resources, rape our women, and live off the spoils of our hard work. They are coming to pollute our country and in so doing, to take our identity; to make "us" no longer "us." In this narrative, we are victimized by immigrant attacks on our national identity which we must defend. Those who oppose immigration are thus the defenders of America. What is also asserted is that because this is such a significant threat, and because we are in such jeopardy, protecting our national identity takes precedence over the preservation of democracy.

Immigrants in this myth no longer signify the value and superiority of democracy, capitalism, representational government, or freedom. Instead they signify the need for protectionism, nationalism, and swift authoritarian response. Consumers of the myth are absolved from identifying with the journey of these asylum seekers because the new myth asserts that these people are *different* from "us" and different from our ancestors. This is a myth of exclusion, divided into insiders and outsiders; it is intended to divide. Because these immigrants have been defined as outsiders who are "not like us," real Americans are everything they are not. *Real* Americans have white, not brown skin; *real* Americans speak English not Spanish; *real* Americans are already here, not trying to come into the country. This myth signifies the superiority of a very delimited group of people and is easily nurtured by white nationalism and neo-Nazis. This is the battle that currently rages in the US. It is a battle for a definitional story about ourselves through our story of others.

THE IMMIGRANT EXPERIENCE AND THE FACE
OF TRAUMA: THE MICRO PERSPECTIVE

New asylum seekers will attempt to enter a nation that takes an openly hostile policy stance toward them. The pain they bring with them on their journey to our borders will be intensified and exacerbated by our response. Many of these people are seeking refuge from gangs, threats of death, domestic violence, and grinding poverty. They are referred to as "rapists," "criminals," and "drug dealers" but not as "mothers," "husbands," "brothers," or "widows." We don't hear about the human pain that impels people to leave their home, their families, and all that they know, and risk their lives to find safety.

Not long ago the former Director of Immigrations and Customs Enforcement, Thomas Homan, invoked this criminalizing rhetoric. "If you're in this country illegally and you committed a crime by being in this country, you should be uncomfortable; you should look over your shoulder. You need to be worried. No population is off the table."[7] Not only have deportation efforts sharply increased under our current administration, but ICE is waging a broad campaign of fear designed to alienate, criminalize, and make immigrants feel as though they are unilaterally not wanted.[8] In 2017, the agency showed a 42 percent increase in arrests from the previous year. Most of these arrests were for people who had overstayed their visas but who had no criminal record.

Into this social landscape, Gloria, a 43-year-old woman from El Salvador crossed the border in 2010 with her children after her husband was violently murdered. Her children are doing well in school and she supports them as a babysitter to a family who is very happy with her. She comes to a mental health clinic asking for help. She has seen those in her neighborhood taken and deported by the government. She says in a whisper, "We're not documented." Gloria expresses extreme fear and anxiety that her family will be found and deported to El Salvador

---

7. Stephan Dinan, "No Apologies: ICE Chief Says Illegal Immigrants Should Live in Fear of Deportation," *Washington Post*, June 13, 2017, https://www.washingtontimes.com/news/2017/jun/13/thomas-homan-ice-chief-says-illegal-immigrants-sho/.
8. Nancy Beckerman, "Immigration and ICE: The Cost of Deportation Trauma Outweighs the Risk" (2017), unpublished manuscript.

where they will surely be killed. As she explains, she begins to cry, "Please, please help me. I am so scared for my children. I am afraid I will be found out and separated from them, or my children and I will have to go back. We left because we weren't safe. My children are watching the news and the neighborhood and now they are afraid that I'll be taken away from them. Please help me."[9]

Gloria is anxious and afraid. Her presentation of trauma at the clinic is an artifact not just of this murder and a harrowing flight years earlier, but the result of policies and practices that outlaw her presence. To her identity of widow, mother, victim of violence, and refugee, she must now add criminal, resulting in cognitive dissonance, as this socially imposed label diverges from her own reality. She must also fear that the tenuous existence she has built in the hopes of leading a violence-free life may come crashing down on her. That stress rarely sits with one person. Families are systems and thus anxiety and trauma are shared by her children who fear going outside or who are taunted at school or harassed on their way home.[10]

Marisol Garcia[11] crossed the border recently with her young daughter from Guatemala. To support her family after her husband's death, Ms. Garcia bought a taco stand, not realizing that the previous owner was paying an extortion fee to the gang, Mara 18. They demanded she pay and threatened to kill her and her family. To prove their point, they murdered the owner of the store next to hers. She paid the extortion fee for seventeen months until she got sick. When she had no money,

---

9. Gloria's real name has been changed to protect her identity. This is a case shared with me by my colleague Dr. Nancy Beckerman. Gloria presented her story at a mental health clinic in the Bronx.

10. The Southern Poverty Law Center has documented the way in which children of immigrants, or sometimes simply children who are non-white, are approached and told to "get out of the country" or told that they "should be made to wear shock collars." Examples can be found at https://www.splcenter.org/20161129/ten-days-after-harassment-and-intimidation-aftermath-election.

11. The name of this woman has been changed to protect her identity as have certain details about her experience. She is a woman Dr. Katherine Mitchell of Yeshiva University's Wurzweiler School of Social Work met while volunteering in Dilley, Texas, at an immigration detention center. This woman was seeking asylum. I thank Dr. Mitchell for sharing this case with me for this chapter.

they shot her young daughter in the ankle. She closed the taco stand but the gang continued the extortion. She cleaned houses to be able to pay them, and then the gang demanded more. Afraid and angry, she made a police report. Once she had done that, she knew she could not stay. She and her daughter hid temporarily in the local Catholic church. Then they took a bus to the Mexican border and crossed by way of the river. Wet and cold, they walked for days before they were detained and brought to the detention center in Dilley, Texas, where they waited to tell their story.[12]

The painful stories Gloria and Marisol tell, though they are separated by more than 2,000 years and thousands of miles, have elements of the one Ruth may have told. There is a significant body of literature that helps us understand how humans react to loss, widowhood, economic uncertainty, trauma, and pain inherent in immigration. What can we learn when all three stories are examined together/side by side?

All three women had to mourn their losses. After the death of Mahlon, Ruth, like her contemporary counterparts, would have entered a time of active mourning conceptually delineated by stages and tasks to accomplish to move toward successful resolution. Early grief is marked by a period of reacting to the loss. The unimaginable has happened, causing a wound that feels like a part of us is being ripped away.[13] Mourners in this stage grapple with a state of disbelief. Then slowly, as the full weight of what has happened bears down, the bereaved begin to understand that this wound is not something they will get over; there is no remedy, no way to fix or to undo it. It is irrevocable. Ruth's wound would have been compounded by the fact that her husband's death signaled not only the end of their life together, but the end of her chance to be a mother with her husband, the end of *their* visions for a family. For Marisol and Gloria, their mourning is compounded by the terror of witnessing their husbands' brutal murder and abject panic that they and their children could suffer

---

12. Law students from Yeshiva University's Cardozo School of Law interviewed her for a credible fear statement and Dr. Katherine Mitchell helped her tell her painful story. You can read all of Dr. Mitchell's notes on her blog, https://blogs.yu.edu/wssw-news/tag/katherine-mitchell/.

13. Neimeyer, 5.

the same fate. Danger signals a fight-or-flight response, causing both women to flee. But flight, even with the hope of safety or a better life, also brings more losses. All three women lost what was familiar, left their homes, their routines, and the lives they had envisioned for themselves.

Early-stage mourning gives way to reconstructing as the bereaved accepts that the loss is permanent and begins to search for a way to "find" and reconnect with the loved one. This might include introducing the loved one in conversation or remembering with others what the deceased was like. Staying with Naomi would have been critical to Ruth at this time. Ruth would not only be free to reminisce with Naomi but would *need* to, to restore a sense of attachment to her husband while adjusting to life without him. As Ruth holds onto Naomi, she simultaneously holds onto her husband's memory. In Naomi's reflection of Mahlon, Ruth is able to locate him and hold onto a piece of him, thus steadily working through her bereavement.

Marisol and Gloria have fled in terror, taking only what they can carry. They each have children to help locate the memories of their dead husbands but these memories, unlike Ruth's, always end with traumatic loss. Memories of their husbands always point to the fact that they were and are not safe. Additionally, Gloria must monitor her speech and that of her children and only present a very superficial view of who they are and what they have been through so as not to reveal they are here illegally and be deported back to their deaths. Because fear of detection and deportation and memories that highlight the violence and traumatic loss are superimposed on and coupled with their reminiscences, these women's mourning is neither simple nor easy. It is confounded and compounded by the heavy weight of trauma and anxiety.

Perhaps the most salient feature of Gloria and Marisol's journeys is that they are not free to move past the high anxiety and fear required to propel them out of their countries toward what they hoped would be safety.[14] Fight-or-flight allows us to mobilize energy quickly to deal with the danger at hand. But because they fear detection and deportation,

---

14. Paul Cilia La Corte and Angelina Jalonen, *A Practical Guide to Therapeutic Work with Asylum Seekers and Refugees*, Practical Guides (London: Jessica Kingsley Publishers, 2017), 23.

they must stay in a state of hyperarousal. Staying in flight mode where fear and anxiety become chronic conditions may allow us to survive the dangers in our environment, but it takes its toll in terms of mental health issues like depression and insomnia, and physical issues like high blood pressure and obesity.[15]

Grieving takes place when we have the psychic energy to grieve. When energy is syphoned into maintaining a hypervigilant state, mourning cannot progress successfully. Consequently, both women are stranded in the first stage of mourning, feeling constantly like the loss is fresh. Gloria and Marisol are also stuck in their immigration journey. The goal of immigration is to successfully resolve the sense of utter disruption caused by leaving one's home and to begin to adjust to a new life while holding onto the memories and knowledge of the old life. But they cannot feel safe because they are being hunted as illegal people. They cannot find or make a home.

This is not what happened to Ruth. After Ruth journeys to Bethlehem and meets Boaz, he sees her as a foreigner, but he also recognizes her character and worth. Their marriage marks the beginning of a new life based on the integration of her dead husband's legacy. This signals that she has entered the final stage of mourning, reorienting. This stage brings with it the need to revise the self-narrative. It is the work of tying pieces of a life together for a future. Ruth must become Boaz's wife even as she remembers Mahlon. In chapter 4 verse 10, Boaz proclaims to the community, "Moreover Ruth the Moabitess, the wife of Mahlon, have I acquired to be my wife, to raise up the name of the dead upon his inheritance, that the name of the dead be not cut off from among his brethren, and from the gate of his place; ye are witnesses this day."

Thus, Ruth's story is one of resolve. She is redeemed by the Israelites and the Israelites are redeemed by her because they allowed themselves to *see* her as a person, to recognize the ḥesed in her words and actions. Through that recognition, they claim her for their own as she claims them. She does not remain an Other or foreigner. The last

---

15. "Understanding the Stress Response: Chronic Activation of this Survival Mechanism Impairs Health," *Harvard Mental Health Letter* (March 2011, updated May 1, 2018), https://www.health.harvard.edu/staying-healthy/understanding-the-stress-response.

time she is named, mentioned in 4:12, she is no longer referred to as a Moabite. She is simply, Ruth.[16]

CONCLUSION

What lies ahead for those who are granted asylum is not easy. Like all immigrants before them, women like Gloria and Marisol, if they are permitted to stay, must learn the language, figure out how to support themselves, learn the rules of the society they will, hopefully, call home, and acculturate to create a new identity. They must heal from the traumas they have experienced and they must resolve their grief. Healing from trauma is the work of creating new meaning and a new sense of self. It is the work of moving from the identity of victim, to survivor, to someone who can thrive in spite of the terror and losses they have experienced. Healing from loss also means finding ways of integrating their old lives into new ones. For Marisol and Gloria, this work is stymied. When one lives in a constant state of fear and anxiety, when flight might be once again imminent, or when the world around them is deaf to their pain or worse, hostile, moving through trauma toward healing becomes impossible.

Much of twentieth-century anthropologist Ernesto de Martino's work is to examine our place as human beings within society. His idea of the "crisis of presence" occurs when we are overwhelmed by loss and alienation caused because the world we inhabit can no longer reflect our internal world, because we have lost what is familiar, lost our community. For de Martino, at the core of this crisis is the anxiety that "underlines the threat of losing the distinction between subject and object, between thoughts and action, between representation and judgment, between vitality and morality: it is the cry of one who is wobbling on the edge of the abyss."[17] This is the place where Gloria and Marisol find themselves. They are alone, separated from all that is familiar. Their trauma makes it

---

16. Tamara Cohn Eskenazi and Tikva Frymer-Kensky, *The JPS Bible Commentary: Ruth* (Philadelphia: Jewish Publication Society, 2011), xliv–xlv.
17. Ernesto de Martino, "Crisi della presenza e reintegrazione religiosa," *Aut Aut* 31 (1956): 17–38, cited in Cristiana Giordano, *Migrants in Translation* (University of California Press, 2014), 82.

impossible to return to, connect with, or perhaps even remember their old lives. As R. K. Papadopoulos suggests, "[t]he adversity experiences are so overwhelming that they tend to erase most previous experiences. This erasing is likely to create a sense of disorientation which may... throw them off balance with detrimental effects."[18] They thus exist in a painful liminality, unable to move forward, unable to claim much from the past. They live with the knowledge that they are socially reviled and with the terror that they may be deported. At the same time, they are seen as criminals and social leeches though they are trying to raise healthy children who are becoming a part of American society.

Those who work with immigrants know that we have to work on both the micro and macro levels together to "be a bridge to foster the internal process of an individual's reorganization of his or her personal identity"[19] while simultaneously calling our attention to the implications of social policy on the mental health of refugees, and the moral health of our nation. The story of Ruth calls us to consider redemption through Abrahamic moral virtues. It also chronicles a story where the presence of an outsider is to some degree problematized and requires a response, first from Boaz, then community members, then God. There is only one response that is acceptable if the Israelites are true to who they are.

I suggest that we are in need of redemption now as much as the Israelites in the time of the Judges. Boaz had accepted his obligation to marry Ruth. What of our moral and humanitarian obligation to refugees and asylum seekers established through the United Nations International Bill of Human Rights? By defining our response to Others, we simultaneously define ourselves. Or put another way, our view of the Other, our willingness to understand who the other is, may help us decipher who we are and who we are becoming. We can choose the cultural myths we create and those to which we ascribe. *We* are the authors. We, as a community, are at a point of decision and at that point of response.

---

18. Renos K. Papadopoulos, "Refugees, Trauma and Adversity-Activated Development," *European Journal of Psychotherapy and Counselling* (2007): 9:3, 304.

19. Susan Ligabue, "Forced Migration and Refugees: Trauma Experience and Participatory Care," *Transactional Analysis Journal* (2018): 48:2, pp. 166–180.

A Brief Overview of Asylum for Noncitizens in the United States

Lindsay Nash, Esq.

In the era of the Trump administration, immigration has come to the fore like few times in recent memory. It is a front-page issue more often than not, ever-trending on social media, and a topic that has generated a groundswell of activity in the courts and the streets. Terms such as "immigration detention," "unaccompanied minor," and "removal proceedings" have suddenly been heard at cocktail hours and family dinner. As a result, immigration is no longer a niche issue or one relegated to our nation's borders – and, if this era has any silver lining for those who care about immigrant rights, it is that Americans across the spectrum and the country are being forced to consider the critical place and role that affording refuge to those persecuted has played in our nation's past. In considering the biblical Book of Ruth and the role immigration plays in that narrative, it is worthwhile to review the history of persecution-based immigration in America.

Our nation's complicated and conflicted relationship with immigration did not, by any means, begin with the Trump administration.

On the contrary, distrust of and animus toward "foreigners" – citizens of other nations – is as old as America itself. For example, in 1798, the still relatively new federal government enacted a series of laws which, among other things, allowed for the detention and deportation of non-citizens who were deemed dangerous or simply from a hostile nation.[1] In another example infamous for its blatant discrimination, Congress passed legislation that, among other things, dramatically restricted immigration by Chinese citizens based on widespread bias against this group.[2]

But, despite these xenophobic eras, America has also been considered a place of protection, particularly in the era following World War II. In keeping with a deep nationwide skepticism and bias in and after the 1930s, the United States was notable for its low rates of offering asylum to those in need, even as Nazism – and therefore the crisis of European refugees – worsened in the 1940s.[3] This restrictionism was widely attributed to paranoia and "downright bigotry."[4] This low point, however, also ushered in a turning point: America began accepting larger numbers of Jewish refugees and ultimately began offering protection to larger and larger numbers of people seeking protection from persecution,[5] culminating in the Refugee Act of 1980, which formally brought protections for "refugees," as defined by international agreements, into domestic US law.[6]

---

1. See, e.g.: An Act Respecting Alien Enemies, 1 Stat. 577 (1798); An Act Concerning Aliens § 1, 1 Stat. 570 (1978).
2. See: An act to Prohibit the Coming of Chinese Persons into the United States, 27 Stat. 25 (1892); An Act to Execute Certain Treaty Stipulations Relating to Chinese ("Chinese Exclusion Act"), 22 Stat. 58 (1882).
3. Daniel Gross, "The U.S. Government Turned Away Thousands of Jewish Refugees, Fearing That They Were Nazi Spies," *Smithsonian Mag.* (Nov. 18, 2015), https://www.smithsonianmag.com/history/us-government-turned-away-thousands-jewish-refugees-fearing-they-were-nazi-spies-180957324/.
4. Ibid.
5. See, e.g.: An Act for the Relief of Certain Refugees, and Orphans, and for Other Purposes, 67 Stat. 400 (1953); An Act to Authorize for a Limited Period of Time the Admission into the United States of Certain European Displaced Persons for Permanent Residence, and for Other Purposes, 62 Stat. 1009 (1948).
6. An Act to Amend the Immigration and Nationality Act to Revise the Procedures

Thus, while the basis for much of the United States' law regarding protection from persecution or torture comes from its agreements with other nations, the specific protections it offers and the mechanisms for obtaining protection are found in our domestic laws and regulations. Among the number of types of persecution-based protections that can be found in US law, asylum is the most commonly known and, in many ways, strongest type of protection.

To be eligible for a grant of asylum, it is not enough that noncitizens face very real danger in their country of origin. Rather, he or she must show that they are a "refugee" as defined under the Immigration and Nationality Act.[7] That definition includes the requirement that a noncitizen have "a well-founded fear of persecution on account of" one of five protected grounds: race, religion, nationality, membership in a particular social group, or political opinion.[8]

As such, our asylum laws offer protection for those who have a fear of persecution, but only if that persecution is (1) well-founded – meaning subjectively and objectively reasonable; (2) on account of a protected ground; and (3) committed by the home country government or an entity that government cannot or will not control.[9] Accordingly, while our protection regime sets forth a clear structure for affording protection from persecution, that extension of protection is limited in important ways.

In addition, as recent events have illustrated all too clearly, the barriers to obtaining protection are even higher for individuals who come to our nation's borders to seek protection. While individuals who apply for asylum from the interior of the United States are generally entitled to a number of procedural protections – including the right to present evidence in support of their claim and the right to representation by a lawyer at their own expense – those who come to the border seeking

---

for the Admission of Refugees, to Amend the Migration and Refugee Assistance Act of 1962 to Establish a More Uniform Basis for the Provision of Assistance to Refugees, and for Other Purposes, 94 Stat. 102 (1980).

7. 8 U.S.C. § 1101(a)(42)(A).
8. Ibid.
9. See ibid.; 8 C.F.R. § 1208.13; *Matter of Acosta*, 19 I&N Dec. 211, 233 (BIA 1985), *modified on other grounds by Matter of Mogharrabi*, 19 I&N Dec. 439 (BIA 1987).

permission to apply for asylum face even more difficult hurdles. Those individuals, who are often at the end of an arduous journey and still in the throes of trauma, must immediately demonstrate their claim for asylum without any of those procedural safeguards. Specifically, they are typically arrested, held in detention, and required to articulate their claim for protection to a trained government officer.[10] If they prove to the government officer that they have met a threshold level of likelihood that they will ultimately be able to make out a claim for protection, they are permitted to proceed to a full hearing during which they can present evidence and be represented by a lawyer.[11] If, however, these individuals, who often are traumatized and lack any formal legal knowledge, cannot demonstrate their ability to meet each of the requirements for protection, they are denied the opportunity for an asylum hearing and, in most cases, rapidly deported to the very danger from which they fled.[12] Thus, given the summary process and difficulties that these individuals face, it is often the case that those who have fled quickly and are most in need of aid are the ones who face the most difficulties in obtaining help, and even fall through the cracks.

Given the continued importance of persecution-based protections in our immigration law, it will be critical to remember the sobering historical reminders of instances in which we have opted for restriction as we are confronted with and respond to new challenges to the nation's asylum system in the years ahead.

---

10. 8 U.S.C. § 1225(1)(B)(iii)(IV).
11. 8 U.S.C. § 1225(1)(B)(ii).
12. 8 U.S.C. § 1225(1)(B)(iii)(I), (V).

Biblical, Midrashic, and Talmudic Meanings

The Roots of the Book of Ruth: Lot and Abraham

Dr. Yael Ziegler

As an independent book, the Book of Ruth is remarkably well crafted, offering many opportunities for extracting meaning from its literary construction.[1] The book can obtain additional meaning when one examines it within the broader canonical context, noting parallels between biblical characters and plotlines outside of the book.[2] Considering the thematic and linguistic similarities and differences can yield

---

1. Many articles and commentaries have noted the rich literary artistry of this short book. See, e.g., Stephen Bertman, "Symmetrical Design in the Book of Ruth," *JBL* 84 (1965): 165–168; D. F. Rauber, "Literary Values in the Bible: The Book of Ruth," *JBL* (1970): 27–37; Edward Campbell, Jr., "The Hebrew Short Story: A Study of Ruth," in *A Light Unto My Path: Old Testament Studies in Honor of Jacob M. Myers*, ed. H. N. Bream and R. D. Heim (Philadelphia: Temple University Press, 1974), 83–101; Jack M. Sasson, "Ruth," in *A Literary Guide to the Bible*, ed. Robert Alter and Frank Kermode (London: Fontana, 1987), 320–327.
2. Rabbinic sources tend to view individual biblical books within their broader canonical context. For more on this idea, see Yonah Frankel, "Aḥdut HaMikra," in *Darkhei HaAggada VeHaMidrash* (Givatayim: Yad LaTalmud, 1991), 161–196 (Hebrew).

otherwise unnoticed ideas and draw the reader's attention to some of the broader themes of the Bible.

The present analysis focuses on the intertextual allusions between the Book of Ruth and the story of Abraham and Lot in the Book of Genesis. Both Ruth and her sister-in-law, Orpah, are Moabites, descendants of Lot. While Lot seems initially attached to his uncle Abraham, acting as a willing partner in Abraham's journey, Lot's pivotal decision to live among the evil people of Sodom ultimately shapes his destiny, that of his family, and that of his disreputable descendants, Ammon and Moab. That fateful decision returns full circle in the Book of Ruth, as Ruth the Moabite, a descendant of Lot, returns to the path of Abraham.

LOT AND ABRAHAM

Positioned initially as a central figure in Abraham's narrative, Lot willingly accompanies Abraham on his journey, clinging to Abraham even as he makes his way from Canaan to Egypt and back again.[3] This cooperative journey comes to an abrupt end when a disputation arises between the shepherds of Lot and Abraham and Abraham suggests that they part ways. Lot agrees and, veering from Abraham's proposed suggestion that he go left (north) or right (south), instead heads straight for the fertile cities of the Plain, namely Sodom (Gen. 13:10–12).[4] Implicitly casting doubt upon Lot's decision, the following verse describes the inhabitants of Sodom as "evil and very sinful to the Lord" (Gen. 13:13). According to some commentators, the dual description of Sodom's wickedness points to two distinct sins: social wrongdoing and sexual immorality.[5] These sins emerge as Sodom's trademark vices in Genesis 19, where the

---

3. Radak (Gen. 12:5) maintains that Lot is an enthusiastic participant in Abraham's mission, commenting that the plural form of the verbs that describe Abraham's actions in Genesis 13:5 (*rakhashu* and *asu*) points to a joint effort between Abraham and Lot. He also points out that the fact that Lot leaves his grandfather to accompany his uncle indicates that Lot particularly wants to be with Abraham. This, explains Radak, is because Lot has learned belief in God from Abraham.

4. The notion that left and right refers to the north and south is also indicated in Ezekiel 4:4–6. For a twist on this, see Ezekiel 16:46.

5. Y. Sanhedrin 10:3. Targum Pseudo Jonathan (Gen. 13:13) maintains a similar approach.

story of the Sodomites' collective demand to rape Lot's guests depicts them as both sexually depraved and socially deviant. Ezekiel 16:49 directs attention to the miserly behavior of the Sodomites, who had plenty of bread and the tranquility of satiation, yet did not support the poor and the needy.

Biblical interpreters treat Lot's choice to live with the people of Sodom in various ways. Some of the midrashim, cited by Rashi, view Lot's move as an indication of his sinful persona, and maintain that he chose to go to Sodom because he desired to live among lewd people.[6] These midrashim regard Lot's decision to leave Abraham as a rejection of Abraham and of God.[7] Radak consistently regards Lot's actions in a positive manner, pointing to Lot's confidence that the evil Sodomites will not sway him from his faith and integrity.[8] As the story unfolds, it seems that Lot does in fact maintain his commitment to the ideals embodied by Abraham. The story of Lot generously hosting the strangers who arrive in Sodom (Gen. 19) echoes the narrative from the previous chapter, in which Abraham generously hosted the same strangers (Gen. 18).[9] While some exegetes focus on the slight differences between these consecutive narratives,[10] the similarities outweigh the differences. Both Rashi and Radak cite a midrash that asserts that the narrative indicates that Lot learned how to treat guests from Abraham. Nahmanides also mentions Lot's behavior with approval. The proximity of these stories, their linguistic similarities, and the peculiar fact that Abraham and Lot host

---

6. *Tanḥuma Vayera* 12; Rashi, Gen. 13:10.
7. Genesis Rabba 40.
8. Radak, Gen. 13:11.
9. Abraham is an exemplary host, sitting at the entrance to his tent, seemingly waiting for guests to arrive (Gen. 18:1). He runs to greet his guests, bows to the ground (Gen. 18:2) and is deferential, referring to himself as "your servant" and to the guests as "my masters" (Gen. 18:3). Abraham then offers the guests water to wash their feet and gives them food (Gen. 18:4–5). Lot acts in a similar, if not identical, manner. In Genesis 19, we find Lot sitting at the entrance to the gate of Sodom, presumably waiting for guests (Gen. 19:1). When Lot sees the angels, he rises to greet them and bows his face to the ground (Gen. 19:2). Lot is likewise deferential, referring to himself as "your servant" and to his guests as "my masters" (Gen. 19:2). Lot also offers the angels water to wash their feet and gives them food (Gen. 19:2–3).
10. See, for example, Sforno, Gen. 19:3; *Or HaḤayim*, Gen. 19:1, 3.

the very same guests reinforce the sense that Lot has not strayed far from Abraham's path when it comes to the treatment of strangers. Lot retains his generosity, despite the fact that he lives in the city of Sodom, where callous treatment and violence toward strangers appear to be the cultural norm.

In spite of his personal integrity, Lot's decision to live among the people of Sodom links his fate to that of the depraved city. The chapter that follows Lot's decision to dwell in Sodom vividly illustrates this point by describing Lot's capture during a war waged against Sodom (Gen. 14). Lot becomes a victim of the environment that he chose. Later, when God decides to annihilate Sodom's inhabitants, God only saves Lot from Sodom's divine annihilation because of his relationship to Abraham:[11]

> And it was when God destroyed the cities of the plain, *and God remembered Abraham* and He delivered Lot from the upheaval, when God overturned the cities in which Lot lived. (Gen. 19:29)

If the people of Sodom are slated for destruction, then Lot, who cast his lot with theirs, should rightly perish alongside them. God saves Lot because of Abraham's merit.

Abraham makes the opposite choice of Lot, consistently maintaining a discreet distance from the inhabitants of Canaan. Each time that the text informs us that there are Canaanites in the vicinity, Abraham pulls up his tent and moves away (Gen. 12:6–8; 13:7, 9, 18). Moreover, when Abraham buys land from the Hittites to bury Sarah, he insists on paying for it, and during the course of their dialogue famously informs them, "I am a stranger and a sojourner among you" (Gen. 23:4). Abraham wants to owe no debts and have no intimate ties with the people of Canaan. To this end, Abraham refuses to take spoils of war from the king of Sodom (Gen. 14:22–24) and adamantly insists that his son not marry the daughters of Canaan (Gen. 24:3). Throughout his life,

---

11. The narrative trajectory implies that Lot's favorable actions contribute to his salvation. Nevertheless, the verse explicitly credits Abraham with Lot's salvation.

Abraham strives to maintain his independence and separateness from the inhabitants of Canaan.[12]

THE CONSEQUENCES OF LOT'S BEHAVIOR

What are the consequences of Lot's decision? Despite his virtuous act of hosting the strangers, Lot fails to live a life of integrity in Sodom. As we will see, Lot pays a high price for his choice to live alongside its people's wickedness. The consequences of Lot's behavior manifest themselves in the two areas of Sodom's failings: proper social interactions and sexual morality.

Social Integrity

Lot's attempt to wield kindness in Sodom spins out of control, forcing him to commit an inestimable act of cruelty. The people of the city surround Lot's home, demanding that he surrender his guests so that they can rape them. Searching for a solution, Lot offers his daughters to the townspeople as a replacement for his guests, telling the voracious mob that they can "do with the [girls] what is good in your eyes." By this scandalous proposal, Lot perverts the very trait of kindness that motivated him to save the men. Nahmanides notes the ironic pivot taken by the story of Lot's generosity:

> From the praise of this man, we arrive at his condemnation, for he labored hard to be a host and to save [his guests], because they came under his protection. But to pacify the inhabitants of the city by relinquishing his daughters – this is nothing if not evil-hearted.[13]

Lot finds himself in a situation in which he behaves in an evil manner commensurate with the cruelty of the people of Sodom. This act of surrendering his daughters does not seem in consonance with Lot's personal

---

12. This does not contradict the designation of Abraham by God as "father of many nations" (Gen. 17:5). Abraham's universal role does not mean integration into the surrounding culture of Canaan, whose sinfulness has sealed their fate (Gen. 15:16).
13. Nahmanides, Gen. 19:8.

decency. Accordingly, the story leads us to a stunning conclusion: Lot's personal righteousness has been compromised by the corrupt environment that he chose.

Perhaps unsurprisingly, Lot's descendants emerge as the cultural and ethical heirs of Sodom. Known for their lack of generosity, the Torah forbids Ammon and Moab from joining the nation of Israel:

> No Ammonite or Moabite shall come into the community of God…because of the matter in which they did not greet you with bread and water on your journey out of Egypt. (Deut. 23:4–5)

Lot's decision to live in Sodom takes a long-term toll on his family. In spite of his bid to maintain his generous character, his descendants become the diametrical opposite of charitable hosts. The cultural norms of Sodom penetrate deeply into Lot's family.

Sexual Morality

Lot's choice to integrate into the culture of Sodom likewise results in a violation of sexual morality that is not of his own making.[14] After the destruction, Lot and his daughters flee to the mountains, where Lot's daughters get their father drunk and commit incest with him.[15] The verses explicitly state that Lot has no knowledge of the act (Gen. 19:33, 35).[16] Once again, Lot does not intentionally behave like the people of Sodom. Instead, Lot becomes the victim of circumstances that do not reflect on his personal virtue, but are a direct result of his fateful choice to live in Sodom.

---

14. Lot's decision to throw his daughters to the townspeople was also a violation of sexual morality. Some rabbinic interpreters conclude that this behavior is evidence of Lot's sexual deviance (e.g. *Tanḥuma Vayera* 12; Nahmanides, Gen. 19:8). In any case, Lot's behavior begins to resemble that of the Sodomites.
15. Their stated reason for this behavior is that they believe that the human race has been destroyed and that it is up to them to repopulate the world (Gen. 19:31). However, it should not escape the reader's attention that Lot's willingness to surrender his daughters to the lascivious mob returns to haunt him in this episode, where his daughters violate him without his consent.
16. Rabbinic interpreters tend to regard Lot as partially culpable, in spite of the textual disclaimer (Horayot 10b, Numbers Rabba 3:13).

Lot's choice also affects the sexual morality of his descendants in the long term. In a brief (but perhaps representative) episode, women of the Moabite nation engage with Israel in licentious behavior (Num. 25:1), an incident that recalls their ignominious lineage.

THE CONSEQUENCES OF ABRAHAM'S BEHAVIOR

Having chosen to maintain his separateness from the inhabitants of Canaan, Abraham, in contrast to Lot, maintains these two qualities of generosity and sexual morality. These become two of the cornerstones of Israel's national character.

The trait of *hesed* is central to the definition of the nation of Israel. As noted previously, the Torah bars the Moabites and Ammonites from membership in Israel due in part to their lack of charity (Deut. 23:4–5). Maimonides asserts that if one meets a member of Israel who lacks compassion or is cruel, one should be suspicious of his ancestry.[17]

Had Abraham chosen to integrate with the people of Canaan, it almost certainly would have compromised the nation's adherence to proper sexual conduct. Leviticus 18:3 explicitly prohibits the nation of Israel from adopting the sexual mores of the Canaanite former inhabitants of the land, indicating that only if Israel practices moral sexual conduct will God permit the nation to remain in the Land of Israel.

Due to the corrupt cultural norms of the indigenous Canaanites, God instructs the nation of Israel to dispossess them of the land. Israel's aim is to create a new society, rooted in righteousness alongside sexual morality. Had Abraham integrated with the Canaanites, he would not have the ability to create a nation based on these distinctive values, which are diametrically opposed to the values held by the Canaanites.

SUMMARY

The result of Lot's choice is that his descendants perpetuate Sodom's culture, becoming the spiritual heirs of that doomed society.[18] This process begins even in Lot's own lifetime and affects his own behavior as well, no matter how well-intentioned it may be. The corrupt societal norms of

---

17. See *Laws of Gifts to the Poor* 10:2.
18. Zephaniah (2:9) likens the fate of Moab and Ammon to that of Sodom and

Sodom infringe upon the integrity of Lot's social interactions and sexual morality. Sodom's moral bankruptcy also manifests in Lot's descendants, Moab and Ammon. Abraham, in contrast, remains distinct from the inhabitants of Canaan, allowing him to preserve his unique qualities, which lay at the heart of the value system of the future nation of Israel.

THE BOOK OF JUDGES AND LOT AND ABRAHAM

As a preface to understanding Ruth's role in reversing Lot's trajectory, I will offer several brief observations about the era of the Judges, when the Book of Ruth takes place. The Book of Judges records a period of progressive deterioration in Israel's history. It opens with Israel's failure to complete the conquest of the land, affecting their ability to create a society based on its own distinctive values. Instead, the Israelite tribes continue to live amongst the Canaanites, assimilating their culture and values.[19] One anticipated consequence of this decision is that Israel begins to intermarry with the Canaanites (Judges 3:5–6) and worship their idolatry (Judges 2:2; 6:10; 10:6). More to the point, Israel has made the Lot choice, that of integration instead of separation. Consequently, Israel drifts away from the path of Abraham during the period of the Judges.[20] Their choice to integrate with the Canaanites takes them onto

---

Gomorrah: "Therefore I swear, says God, Moab will be like Sodom and the children of Ammon shall be like Gomorrah: clumps of weeds and patches of salt, and desolation forever."

19. Note the description of Israel living amongst the Canaanites in the first chapter of the Book of Judges (e.g. 1:27, 29, 30). See especially the formulation in 1:32, which describes the tribe of Asher dwelling "in the midst of the Canaanites, the inhabitants of the land."

20. Numerous references to Abraham in the Book of Judges seem to allude to Israel's desertion of Abraham's values at this time. Parallels between Gideon and Abraham that hint that Gideon has veered from Abraham's path include the linguistic similarity between Judges 6:39 and Genesis 18:32. Similarly, Jephthah seems to model himself after Abraham in his sacrifice of his daughter (compare Judges 11:34 to Gen. 22:2), an endeavor that only draws attention to the ironic contrast between them (see *Midrash Aggada* [Buber], Lev. 27). The distortion of Abraham reaches its zenith in the story of the concubine and her husband, who takes a *maakhelet* to dismember her (Judges 19:29). The only other place where this word appears is in the story of Abraham and the *Akeida* (Gen. 22:10), where it is used to fulfill God's command. A full examination of this topic is beyond the scope of the present analysis.

Lot's path, which leads to the abandonment of societal responsibility and sexual morality.

As the book progresses, the nation of Israel begins to resemble Ammon and Moab, Lot's descendants and the spiritual heirs of Sodom. Consider, for example, the following incident: As Gideon's war against Midian begins to draw to its conclusion, Gideon continues to pursue the Midianite kings across the Jordan River. Exhausted and hungry, Gideon's troops pass through two Israelite towns, Sukkot and Penuel.[21] Gideon's request for food is met with cynical refusal (Judges 8:6): "Are [the Midianite kings] Zevach and Zalmunah in your hands that we should give your army bread?!" The people of Sukkot and Penuel deny food to their own brethren, who are fighting on the nation's behalf! The miserly behavior of these Israelite towns resembles that of Sodom, as well as Ammon and Moab.

The shocking conclusion of the book (Judges 19) is a story of moral and sexual corruption, linguistically and thematically modeled upon the narrative of Sodom and Gomorrah. Here more than anywhere, we see how the nation has veered perilously far from the path of Abraham and is instead treading upon the path of Lot.[22] Israel has abandoned the values of social and sexual morality that formerly lay at its core. The erosion of these values calls into question the nation's continued existence in the land. Israel displaces the Canaanites in order to uproot their

---

21. Rashi explicitly notes that the inhabitants of Sukkot are Israelite; see also Joshua 13:27. Penuel seems to be the place named by Jacob after his encounter with the angel in Genesis 32:30–31. See also I Kings 12:25.

22. In addition to shared word *maakhelet* and the comparisons to the story of Lot in Sodom, there are many indications that suggest that this story in particular represents the perversion of Abraham. Consider the cluster of parallels at the opening of the story that recall Abraham: the concubine's father's offer to feed the Levite, *se'ad libekha pat leḥem* (Judges 19:5), recalling Abraham's nearly identical generosity to his angelic guests (Gen. 18:5); the Levite's early waking, *vayashkem baboker* (Judges 19:8), recalling Abraham (Gen.19:27; 20:8; 21:14); the duration of three days, the two saddled donkeys, and the altered phrase, *vayokhlu sheneihem yaḥdav* (Judges 19:6), which recalls the similar, *vayeilekhu sheneihem yaḥdav* (Gen. 22:6) with regard to Abraham. This cluster of parallels invites the reader to recall Abraham, only to perceive the profound difference between the behavior of the characters in Judges and Abraham.

corruptions – if Israel returns to those abominable practices, they will suffer the same fate as the expelled Canaanites.[23]

THE BOOK OF RUTH

The Book of Ruth (which takes place during the time of the Judges) depicts Bethlehem as a society with degenerate values that mirror those in the Book of Judges. Its inhabitants are miserly[24] and sexually immoral.[25] Nevertheless, as the solution to the disastrous situation, the Book of Ruth presents two characters who tender a new direction: generosity instead of miserly behavior, and morality in place of indecency. While I will not examine Boaz's character in the present analysis,[26] I would like to suggest one way in which Ruth guides the nation from the path of Lot to the path of Abraham.

The Path of Lot and the Path of Abraham

In the opening chapter of the Book of Ruth, Ruth and Orpah, Moabite descendants of Lot, stand together with Naomi at a crossroad between Moab and Bethlehem. These Moabite women are poised to decide whether to return to Moab or accompany their mother-in-law, Naomi, to Bethlehem.

Orpah

Initially, Orpah and Ruth speak in one voice, insisting that they will both accompany Naomi to Bethlehem. Eventually, however, Naomi's arguments prevail over Orpah, and she returns to Moab. Orpah's decision, following Naomi's persistent bid to convince her to return, appears

---

23. Many biblical passages emphasize this point. See, for example, Leviticus 18:1–4, 24–28; 20:22–24. II Kings 17:7–8 attributes Israel's eventual expulsion to her return to the practices of the former inhabitants of the land.
24. No one offers food to Naomi when she returns to Bethlehem, despite the fact that she returns during the harvest. In chapter 2, Ruth must glean like a pauper in the fields due to the disinclination of the townspeople to act with generosity toward Naomi.
25. Note Boaz's explicit instruction to the young men not to grope Ruth in the fields (Ruth 2:9).
26. For more on Boaz's role, see Yael Ziegler, *Ruth: From Alienation to Monarchy*, Maggid Studies in Tanakh (Jerusalem: Maggid, 2015), 27–58 and *passim*.

to be reasonable. Orpah has been kind and compassionate toward her mother-in-law. Naomi blesses her effusively in God's name, appreciatively describing her (alongside Ruth) as one who deserves God's kindness (Ruth 1:8–9).

Surprisingly, rabbinic sources sharply criticize Orpah for her actions. A midrash (Ruth Rabba 2:9) offers the following homiletic etymology for Orpah's name:[27]

> The name of one was Orpah, for she turned the nape of her neck (*hafkha oref*) to her mother-in-law.

The phrase "*hafakh oref*" suggests that Orpah's action is both cowardly,[28] and callous. While this depiction seems excessively harsh, it does not actually misrepresent Orpah's actions. This critical approach is likely rooted in the evident contrast between Orpah's desertion of Naomi and Ruth's unswerving loyalty. In the final analysis, Ruth assumes responsibility for Naomi, while Orpah abdicates. Moreover, technically, this is a first-rate etymology: the name Orpah links easily with the word "*oref*," the nape of one's neck. This midrashic etymology, then, offers a viable portrayal of Orpah, even if it is somewhat unjust.

It is startling, therefore, that a gemara (Sota 42b) offers an even harsher etymology for Orpah's name:

> Why was she called Orpah? For everyone sodomized her (*orpin ota*) from behind.

This scathing critique of Orpah's character is very difficult to sustain. In fact, the Book of Ruth offers no hint whatsoever of Orpah's promiscuity. Why does the midrash offer an etymology that does not cohere with the textual portrayal, when the first etymology is linguistically and thematically fitting?

---

27. Rabbinic literature often uses etymological explanations of names as a homiletical tool to offer insights into the essence of a person's character.
28. Joshua 7:8 employs this phrase to describe Israel running away from a battle.

Despite its textual baselessness, the portrait of Orpah as a licentious woman emerges as the dominant portrait of her in the Midrash. She is described in several midrashim as a promiscuous woman whose exploits include bestiality, sodomy, and indiscriminate, copious sexual activity.[29]

The rabbinic portrayal of Orpah is profoundly different from the biblical one. According to the text, Orpah is a compassionate and moral woman. There is no hint of promiscuity and no censure of her character. Why do rabbinic sources roundly defame Orpah?

In creating this image of Orpah, these rabbinic sources may not be commenting on Orpah's persona, but rather on the predictable consequences of her choice. Orpah's decision to return to live in Moab, the spiritual heir of Sodom, sets her on the path of her ancestor Lot. Like Lot, Orpah's choice to return to a depraved surrounding, a society steeped in cruelty and immorality, will invariably determine her future and that of her descendants. By portraying Orpah as a person who willfully deserts her unfortunate mother-in-law and lives a life of shameless immorality, the midrashim draw a parallel between Orpah and Lot. Even if these figures display personal behavior that is above reproach, their assimilation into a cruel and promiscuous society has far-reaching ramifications; they and their descendants are doomed to perpetuate the values of the society in which they reside.

Ruth

Rabbinic sources depict Ruth, who remains with Naomi, as the paradigm of kindness. This portrayal coheres well with the biblical portrayal of Ruth, who regularly goes beyond the call of duty in her altruistic treatment of Naomi. A more peculiar phenomenon is the common rabbinic representation of Ruth as the exemplar of modesty. Ruth's modesty emerges in the midrashim in several different forms. She is depicted modestly bending down to glean up the sheaves of wheat in the field (Shabbat 113a). In another midrash, Ruth refrains from flirtation with the young men (Ruth Rabba 4:9). According to a midrash cited by Rashi (Ruth 3:5), Ruth chooses to amend Naomi's instructions to go to Boaz's

---

29. See, for example, Ruth Rabba 2:20; Ruth Zuta 1; Rashi's commentary on I Sam. 17:23.

field dressed up and perfumed, lest someone suspect her of promiscuity. She prefers instead to dress and perfume herself only once she has arrived at the field (*Tanḥuma Behar* 3).

This modest representation of Ruth is not indicated anywhere in the narrative.[30] It hardly seems coincidental that rabbinic sources sketch a portrait of Ruth that is the polar opposite of their portrait of Orpah! In this schema, Ruth is both kind and modest, while Orpah lacks generosity and sexual morals. The rabbinic portrait of Ruth appears based less on her textual persona and more on her decision to abandon Moab. By choosing to join the nation of Abraham, Ruth positions herself to become a paradigm of *ḥesed* and morality. Her choice indicates her intent to adopt the traits of Abraham and enable her descendants to do the same.

Ruth: The *Tikkun* for Lot

In choosing to continue with Naomi to Bethlehem, Ruth is choosing the path of Abraham. Boaz's words of admiration for Ruth's deeds implicitly recognize the deeper significance of her decision:

> And Boaz answered and he said to her, "It has surely been told to me all that you have done with your mother-in-law after your husband died, and you left your father (*avikh*) and your mother and the land of your birthplace (*eretz moladteikh*)." (Ruth 2:11)

By using words reminiscent of God's command to Abraham in Genesis 12:1, "Go (*lekh lekha*) from your land (*artzekha*), your birthplace (*moladetkha*) and the house of your father (*beit avikha*)," Boaz directs attention to the similarity between Ruth's act and that of Abraham. Ruth's later declaration that she will follow Naomi at all cost (*baasher teilekhi eileikh*) – away from the familiar and into the unknown – also evokes the language of God's command to Abraham (*lekh lekha*).

---

30. It seems that the opposite is the case. The narrative portrays Ruth as a woman who has arrived from a promiscuous culture and only gradually learns to integrate and adopt the modest norms of the Israelite culture. See Ziegler, 259–263.

In addition to the ramifications that Ruth's Abraham-like choice has for herself and her descendants, Ruth's choice represents a historic correction, or *tikkun,* of Lot's fateful separation from Abraham. The narrative that recounts Lot's decision to *separate* from Abraham uses the verb *"parad"* several times: [31]

And each man separated (*vayiparedu*) from his brother. (Gen. 13:11)

Ruth's speech of loyalty to Naomi concludes with her declaration that only death will *separate* her from Naomi:

I swear by God that only death will separate (*yafrid*) between you and me. (Ruth 1:17)

Ruth's decision to cleave to Naomi returns her to a path that her ancestor Lot had relinquished, at great personal cost to himself and his descendants. Lot's descendant, Ruth, returns to the path of Abraham and becomes a model of *ḥesed* and modesty.[32]

RUTH: A ROLE MODEL FOR ISRAEL

Ruth's choice to journey to Bethlehem leads her to a very different Israel than the one envisioned by Abraham. At this time, the nation has strayed perilously far from the path of Abraham, veering precipitously toward the Lot path. As noted, the Book of Judges opens with the nation making the

---

31. Abraham's initial suggestion in response to the friction between the shepherds likewise employs this root: "Separate, please, from me (*hipared na me'alai*)" (Gen. 13:9). See Genesis 13:14 for a third usage of this word.
32. The keyword of the first chapter in Ruth is the verb "to return" (*shuv*), which appears twelve times (six times to refer to a return to Moab and six to a return to Judah). This verb is appropriate when it refers to Naomi on her return to Bethlehem and Orpah on her return to Moab. It is odd, however, that the word *"shuv"* appears to refer to Ruth's journey to Bethlehem in Ruth 1:22. Ruth's return makes little sense within the narrow context of the Book of Ruth (although some interpreters regard this as Ruth's repentance [*teshuva*] – see, e.g., Y. Yevamot 8:3; F. Bush, *Ruth, Word Biblical Commentary* 9 [Dallas: Word Books, 1996], 96). Nevertheless, when viewed in a broader biblical context, Ruth's journey to Bethlehem is indeed a "return"; it represents the closing of the circle begun with Lot's abandonment of Abraham in Genesis 13.

Lot choice to integrate into its Canaanite surroundings and concludes with an incident that replicates the depravity of Sodom. Disaster looms ominously on the horizon, as Israel's fate hangs in the balance.

Thus, Ruth is not the only one who must choose whether she wishes to remain on the path of Moab or return to the path of Abraham. This is the very choice facing the people during the period of the Judges. Will they continue on the doomed path of Moab or return to the ways of Abraham?

Ruth's choice to return to Bethlehem enables her to become a role model who can direct the nation back to the path of Abraham during the period of the Judges. In this way, the Book of Ruth guides the nation who has drifted away from the path of Abraham back to its original path, facilitating the restoration of *hesed* and morality to the nation of Israel.[33]

---

33. Ruth's descendant, David, appears to be the ostensible solution for the era of the Judges. In its ideal state, the Davidic monarchy is designated to create a just and moral society. The ultimate failure of the monarchy notwithstanding, the monarchy initially presents a solution for the chaotic period in which Israel has deteriorated and stands on the brink of societal and moral collapse. For more on this topic, see Ziegler, 15–26 and *passim*.

David's Ancestry and the Meaning of Ruth

Rabbi Shalom Carmy

C an the book of Ruth be identified with one theme? Should it? R. Zeira says: "This scroll contains neither impurity nor purity, neither stringency nor leniency, and why was it written? It is to teach you the reward of those who act with loving-kindness" (Ruth Rabba 2:15). Immediately before this statement R. Ḥanina b. Ada mentions that Naomi's daughters-in-law, Ruth and Orpah, had devoted themselves to the burial of their spouses and had given up their right to the *ketuba*.

Offhand, there seems to be no compelling reason to reduce a biblical book to one idea. It is almost as if R. Zeira is attempting to forestall attempts to harness Ruth to some other overarching idea. No doubt other candidates are available. The introduction to *Daat Mikra* on Ruth lists no fewer than five ideas taught by the Scroll: These include the value of the Land of Israel, the value of faithful conversion, submission to fate and diligent work, the desire to depict an episode from the period of the Judges, and to record a story illustrating the vitality of certain halakhot. The editor insists that all these themes are intended by the text "without a doubt." With all due respect, although all these ideas can be found and can, if required, be made the topic of a sermon, they do not appear self-evidently prominent for the ordinary reader.

One theme, however, is impossible not to notice. The book ends with the genealogy of Boaz extending to David. It would not have been surprising had one of the midrashic rabbis proposed that the purpose of Ruth was to supply the lineage of David. Some later writers have gone further and concentrated on the paradoxical elements in David's family history, namely his being descended from Ruth the Moabite convert, whereby the greatest sanctity emerges, in a mystical fashion, from the blending of the aristocratic house of Judah and the seed of Moab. From the sixteenth-century commentator Rabbi Moshe Alshekh this occult notion migrated into the ArtScroll Ruth intended for lay readers.[1] R. Zeira's stress on the everyday morality of the book sounds almost like a counterpoint to the mystical, royal-centered alternative.

The genealogy of David might be remarkable for two significantly different reasons. On the one hand, David is descended from Judah via Perez. The birth of Perez, and his preeminence over his twin brother Zerach, is already announced in Genesis 38. Jacob's blessing to his children (Gen. 49:10 – "the staff shall not veer away from Judah") assigns unique distinction to the tribe of Judah. Ibn Ezra, for example, takes this to mean that Judah is intended to be the leader of the tribes from the beginning, which is why the banner of Judah is in the vanguard in the desert (Num. 1) and elsewhere. Rashi holds that beginning with the emergence of David the tribe of Judah fulfills this destiny as the foremost among the tribes.

On the other hand, David's being the progeny of Ruth attaches potential stigma to his name. From certain hostile perspectives his ancestry is inferior, perhaps even unworthy. Deuteronomy 24:5 rules that Moabites may not enter the "congregation of God"; that is, they may not intermarry with Jews of standard genealogy. The Halakha, to be sure, limits the prohibition to male Moabite descendants: women

---

1. The paradoxical nature of David, and hence the messianic line, coming from the incestuous acts of Lot and his daughters (Gen. 19) also appears in Maharal, *Netzah Yisrael*, chapter 32. For elaboration on this theme, see the opening chapter by Halpern in this volume.

may enter the congregation and the marriage of Boaz and Ruth exemplifies the law. All the same, the biblical text, read without the Oral Law interpretation, invites prejudice against all Moabite converts, male and female. Whatever else the story of Ruth signifies, to recount approvingly the story of Boaz and Ruth would then serve as a counterweight to such potential disparagement. As we noted, some Jewish thinkers even came to regard David's irregular background as a mystical virtue rather than a deficiency, though this tendency is not pertinent to our discussion. The rabbinic discourse about "Moabite males but not Moabite females" clearly implies that the lenient ruling, which legitimized David's status, was not self-evident at the time. In theory that interpretation could have been reversed later on, in which case legitimacy would be retroactively withdrawn from the descendants of Boaz and Ruth.

Nevertheless, I submit that both the genealogical prestige of David as the king to be and the possible objection to him on genealogical grounds are underplayed rather than overplayed in the biblical corpus overall and in Ruth particularly.

As to kingship, the leadership of Judah among the sons of Jacob is promoted in the last chapters of Genesis where he negotiates with his father about the brothers' second journey to Egypt and where he confronts the still-disguised Joseph in the hour of peril. As noted, Jacob's blessing singles him out as leader and potential sovereign. We have seen the alternative explanations of Rashi and Ibn Ezra about the content of the blessing: does it mean that Judah will stand at the head of Israel from the beginning of Jewish history (even before the rise of David) or that he will succeed to kingship at a particular stage of the story (at the time of David)?

Despite these factors, Jacob's blessing/prophecy is not explicitly cited in the early biblical narrative. At the beginning of Judges, for example, Judah is selected to lead the offensive against those Canaanites who remained after the campaigns of Joshua. Ibn Ezra indeed regards this as evidence for his interpretation of Jacob's blessing. But this reading is not stated in Judges – one may adopt Rashi's view that Jacob's words apply to the later period and maintain that Judah's preeminence in Judges 1 is a one-time divine election not grounded in Jacob's blessing. The rest of the Book of Judges, in which Judah does not play a particularly distinguished role, unfolds with no reference or allusion to Jacob's deathbed blessing. Only in the last episode – the concubine of Gibeah – is Judah again selected to lead the other tribes, this time in civil war against Benjamin. The result is disastrous. In Judges the blessing of Jacob is not at all set up as a deterministic "roadmap" played out in the later narrative.

When the time comes for Samuel to appoint a king, the biblical text says nothing about a presumed right or precedence of Judah to the crown. Saul of Benjamin is chosen. When Saul's kingship is rejected and he must be replaced, the prophet goes to Bethlehem where he eventually anoints David, thus bringing Jacob's blessing to fruition, according to Rashi. Yet nothing in the text implies that Samuel's choice of David's family and of David is programmed, so to speak, as such a fulfillment. The inevitability of these happenings is known to us, but only in retrospect. The prospective reading is open-ended; it depends on the choices of the protagonists rather than on the fulfillment of an ancient prophecy.

Throughout his career David faces rivals and enemies. In rabbinic literature, David's detractors refer to his dubious lineage to impeach his public standing. "Whose son is the young man?" asks Doeg the Edomite, when David smites Goliath, and the Talmud takes the remark as a snide comment about his parentage, implying that he is not only unworthy to join royalty, but perhaps unworthy to marry within the Jewish congregation. Doeg insinuates that the lenient decision may not be the final word on David.[2] In the biblical text, however, it seems that Doeg is merely asking a question, albeit perhaps an unfriendly one, about the young champion's family. In the Bible, neither Doeg nor any of David's other adversaries explicitly denigrates him because of his controversial genealogy.

Let me draw an analogy to the way that the consequences of David's sin with Bathsheba are portrayed in II Samuel and in the Talmud. The prophet Nathan tells David that he will be punished severely for the sin, primarily through his children – the death of Bathsheba's firstborn infant, Absalom's rebellion and so forth. At the same time, the rebellion, which almost costs David his throne, is presented in terms of natural psychological-political causation rather than as the execution of

---

2. Yevamot 76b.

divine punishment for David's sin. The divine role is evident to the reader even if it is not made explicit in the long narrative. The Talmud, however, makes David quite self-conscious about the opprobrium attached to him due to his guilt: he imagines himself harassed by sly questions about the penalty for adulterers.[3] His penance and his sense of unworthiness loom large in Psalm 51 and in rabbinic interpretations of other verses though they are absent from the political conflict portrayed in Samuel.[4] What may be prominent in the drama of David's private religious life and his connection to God is not in the foreground of his political biography.

In a word, there is no contradiction between the explicit biblical account and the rabbinic elaboration. If David was disparaged on the grounds of his ancestry, as the Talmud tells us, the slurs are nevertheless discernible only between the lines of the biblical text, so to speak, rather than stated openly. Likewise, the insinuations about David's private behavior do not overtly spill over into the politically centered story line. Anyone familiar with contemporary political abuse can easily think of parallels. This distinction between what is openly alleged and what is merely hinted at is a significant one, both in politics and in human intercourse.

The upshot of our discussion to this point may appear confusing. On the one hand, in the light of the prohibition against Moabite intermarriage in Deuteronomy and the attention it gets in rabbinic literature, the problem of David's ancestry is too important to ignore. The genealogy that ends the Book of Ruth attests to the importance of the royal lineage. At the same time, I argued that neither Samuel nor Ruth confront this problem openly. How then does the Book of Ruth help us think about David and his origins?

My response is that Ruth comments on David's line, going back to Ruth, precisely by presenting her marriage within the framework of an idyllic, decidedly non-polemic story. The reader cannot avoid the negative connotations of Elimelech's abandonment of the Land of Israel for

---

3. Sanhedrin 107a.
4. See my discussion in "Personal Ethics, Public Virtue and Political Legitimacy in Biblical Kings and American Presidents," *Presidential Studies Quarterly* (March 2010): 40:1.

Moab. The reader is made very much aware of Ruth's sacrifice in cleaving to her mother-in-law and embracing a new national and religious identity, and we are told about the economic hardships that meet her as an isolated newcomer in Bethlehem. Once Boaz becomes committed to Ruth's welfare, we are reminded of the various difficulties that may block her marriage to him. As noted, these impediments could have been spelled out in halakhic language and the social stigma attendant upon them might have been confronted directly and even polemically. Instead, while these hurdles are alluded to, they do not become the main subject of the narrative but instead serve as the vaguely sketched background to the story. The result may not be especially useful to the halakhist who wants to evaluate the precise halakhic issues under debate: although the external similarities between what Boaz proposes and the institution of *yibum* are inescapable, the Bible does nothing to formulate clearly what has to be done and why. All the same the biblical account may be of great significance in appreciating the human sensitivities at stake.

Let me illustrate this idea with one exegetical example: In Ruth 3:18 Naomi assures her daughter-in-law that Boaz will not rest until he settles the matter this very day. The reader has every reason to expect prompt action from Boaz. In chapter 4, however, we are told that Boaz repairs to the city gate; there he encounters the "redeemer," the relative of Ruth's family who apparently had precedence over Boaz in taking over Elimelech's property and marrying Ruth. Malbim, who noticed and was puzzled by Boaz's leisurely conduct, explains that had the redeemer not happened to come by, Boaz would have summoned him to the court. One could equally well suggest that Boaz knew that the redeemer would inevitably turn up, perhaps on his way to or from his fields. Whatever the reason, the exposition in the text does not reinforce our anticipation of Boaz's desire for quick action.

Why did Boaz take his time? It is possible that Boaz preferred to approach him in a public forum, rather than privately, in order to ensure that the redeemer felt obliged to take action immediately; otherwise he could have deferred his decision for another day. It is also possible that Boaz did not want to pressure the redeemer. The evidence for this is that Boaz initiates a conversation with him, first about redeeming the property and only afterwards about marrying Ruth. In this way Boaz gives the redeemer opportunities to back out of the deal without embarrassing Ruth. The redeemer might have declined to take over the property, in which case the question of marriage would never have come up. If Boaz indeed wanted to marry Ruth, the perception of alacrity in moving the matter along might have created the appearance, in the eyes of the community, that Boaz was overly eager to marry her himself. The redeemer's final withdrawal remains ambiguous: he fears "destroying [his] inheritance." These words avoid spelling out the exact nature of his worries: he may be referring to social or halakhic problems – Ruth's inferior status as a Moabite convert or concern that the halakhic dispensation "male Moabite and not female Moabite" might turn out to be impermanent;[5] or there might have been unspecified difficulties of an economic nature, perhaps tied to the redeemer's children or wives.

And so, we arrive at a conclusion. On the one hand, the last verses, taking us from Judah through Boaz and Ruth to David, are too significant and climactic to be marginalized. On the other hand, as noted, the text carefully avoids addressing the genealogical issues in a polemical context, or even making their exact nature explicit. This is precisely what we would expect if the purpose was to recognize the unusual nature of David's origins without in any way making them the subject of overt gossip and scandalmongering. Hence the delicacy with which the dialogue is carried on underlines the mood of loving-kindness that R. Zeira found characteristic of this biblical book.

---

5. Rashi to Ruth 4:6 alludes to his uncertainty or ignorance about Ruth's halakhic status.

Ruth, the Rabbis, and Jewish Peoplehood

Dr. Malka Z. Simkovich

J ewish scholarship on the Book of Ruth often presumes the eponymous heroine to be a prototype for Jewish converts. Willingly leaving her homeland to follow her mother-in-law Naomi into a foreign Israelite community, Ruth enthusiastically abandons her former life and embraces her role as a surrogate progenitor for the family of Avimelech. The last verses of the book, which list Ruth's descendants, imply that Ruth's reward for sacrificing her gentile identity is that she becomes the foremother of King David. The tension established at the beginning of the story when Ruth leaves her homeland and gives up her familial ties is thus resolved with Ruth's establishment as foremother of the Davidic dynasty, which conveys the sense that Ruth has fully assimilated into the fabric of her Israelite community.

While this reading of the book of Ruth is prevalent today, early rabbinic interpreters take a different approach when it comes to the book and to the figure of Ruth. A number of rabbinic passages which discuss Ruth call her "Ruth the Moabite," implying that she is not a fully assimilated Israelite. Some midrashic texts go so far as to contrast Ruth with "legitimate" Israelites. Ruth's non-Israelite ancestry comes to the fore in many of these sources, which cite legends regarding Ruth's ascendants, who were said to be terrible antagonists of the Israelites.

In this chapter, I will briefly consider why early rabbinic sources preserve Ruth's status as a perpetual outsider rather than as an assimilated convert, and I will argue that the rabbinic insistence that Ruth remain a Moabite likely reflects a universalist outlook on the part of the Rabbis. By keeping Ruth a Moabite and yet upholding her position as a pious convert, the Rabbis portray David as descending from both an Israelite and a non-Israelite, which in turn may justify the Rabbis' vision of a universal messianic rule overseen by the descendants of David's family. Rabbinic authors of legends about Ruth may have also been aware of her prominent role in early Christian sources, which portray her as either a progenitor of Jesus or as a symbol of the Church. Rather than insisting on Ruth's Jewishness to counter Christian interpretations, as one might expect, the Rabbis affirm Ruth's status as a gentile in order to conscientiously paint gentiles into the rabbinic portrait of Israelite tradition and to promote a universalist worldview that presumes an interactive dynamic in which the fate of Israel affects and interacts with the fate of all of humankind. Finally, the rabbinic acclamation of a pious Moabite woman would have served to combat accusations of Jewish insularity that were circulating in the Greco-Roman world.

RABBINIC IMAGES OF RUTH

Rabbinic interpretations of the Book of Ruth show acute interest in the origins of Ruth and her family. Instead of arguing that Ruth and her family descended from Israelites or righteous gentiles, however, these legends insist that not only was Ruth a Moabite, but that she descended from the most ignoble of Moabites who were infamously antagonistic to the Israelites. One legend, for example, asserts that Ruth is the daughter of the Moabite king Eglon, who is the grandson of the Moabite king Balak:

> R. Yehuda said in the name of Rav: "A person should always engage in Torah and in the performance of commandments, even if his intention is not pure, because [actions done] with ulterior

intention lead to [actions done with] with pure intention. For as a reward for the forty-two sacrifices which Balak the wicked offered, he merited to have Ruth descend from him, as R. Yose son of R. Ḥanina said: 'Ruth was the daughter of the son of Eglon, who was the son of the son of Balak the king of Moab.'"[6]

This talmudic passage claims that Ruth is the descendant of Eglon and Balak, the two most notorious Moabite rulers in the Hebrew Bible. Balak is the king of Moab who is fearful that the Israelites will defeat his people and asks the prophet Balaam to curse the Israelites in Numbers 22–23. Despite Balaam's efforts, God prevents him from cursing the Israelites, causing Balak to become furious with humiliation. In Judges 3, likewise, the Moabite king Eglon allies with the Ammonites and Amalekites to attack Israel and force them into subjugation for eighteen years. Eglon serves as the leader of a triad comprising Israel's worst enemies. In addition to being portrayed as a menacing and dangerous antagonist, Eglon is also portrayed as an overweight fool. Tricked into dismissing his officials when the Israelite judge Ehud tells him that he has a secret to share with him, Eglon is killed in a surprise attack when Ehud leans toward him and unsheathes a two-edged sword on his right rather than left side, and stabs Eglon in the stomach. Both Balak and Eglon are thus depicted as enemies of Israel, and fools who stand helpless in the face of a divine plan.

The Talmud notes that despite his myriad sins, Balak merited to become an ancestor of the pious Ruth because he offered forty-two sacrifices to God.[7] It would have been perhaps simpler and more intuitive for the Rabbis to paint Balak as completely evil, and Ruth as descending from a pious family. But because the rabbinic authors are interested in linking Ruth with Balak, the question of how Balak came to merit being her forebear had to be addressed. The motivating factors which led to the legend that Ruth descended from the two most notorious Moabite leaders are also unclear. Perhaps her connection to these kings amplifies her extreme piety, since as a Moabite princess, she would have been

---

6. Horayot 10b (translation mine).
7. Num. 22:40, 23:1, 23:14, 23:29.

enmeshed in Moabite culture and would have stood to lose not only her family, but also her wealth and status. The benefits that Ruth stood to gain had she remained attached to her Moabite pedigree were clearly substantial. On the other hand, some talmudic passages describe Ruth as a Moabite without focusing on her extreme piety. One such passage reads:

> R. Eleazar also stated: "What is meant by the phrase, 'And in you the families of the earth will be blessed'? The Holy One, blessed be He, said to Abraham, 'I have two good shoots to engraft onto you: Ruth the Moabite and Naamah the Ammonite.'"[8]

This Midrash reads the phrase "and the families of the earth will be blessed (ונברכו) in you" as "the families of the earth will be ingrafted (ונרכבו) in you." In order to make this reading work, the rabbinic author had to switch the כ and the ב in the word ונברכו, which is a strange maneuver, since the original reading seems more intuitive than the revised reading. By reading the phrase as a prediction that gentiles will become engrafted onto the Abrahamic family, Ruth becomes part of the original divine plan for the Israelites' destiny, rather than a fortuitous surprise that God must accommodate. That Ruth's entry into the Israelite family is inherent to God's plan in turn suggests that David was always meant to descend from a Moabite. In this sense, Ruth is a permanent part of the Abrahamic family whose role precedes her own birth, and yet she remains forever a Moabite, even after her death.

The process of grafting requires an outside branch to be bound with an implanted branch. While the grafted branch never becomes completely connected to the implanted root, its offshoots derive from both the graft and the branch that is connected to the implanted root. If Ruth is the grafted branch in this midrashic legend, then she never becomes fully assimilated into the "tree" of Judaism, but remains "Ruth the Moabite," that is, identifiably different from the organic Israelites among whom she lives. Her descendants, however, are indistinguishable from other Israelites.

---

8. Yevamot 63a (translation mine). Naamah was the mother of Rehoboam, who was the ascendant of Hezekiah (I Kings 14:31).

Perhaps the most explicit depiction of Ruth as a permanent Moabite in rabbinic literature appears in the midrashic collection of the *Sifre*. The presentation of Ruth as a Moabite in this passage is particularly perplexing, since Ruth's identity as a Moabite is not mentioned as a way to praise her extreme piety and devotion to Judaism. The passage reads:

> How do you know that Ruth the Moabite did not die before she saw Solomon, her grandson, as a judge in session and judging the case of the whores? As it is said, "The records are ancient. They were the potters, and those who lived at Netaim and Gederah were there on the king's service" (I Chr. 4:23). Now it is an argument *a fortiori*: Now, if this one, who derived from the people concerning whom it is said, "You shall not marry among them and they shall not marry among you" (I Kings 11:2), because she brought herself near, the Omnipresent drew her still nearer, if an Israelite carries out the Torah, all the more so.[9]

The *Sifre* proves that Ruth lived to watch her descendant Solomon adjudicate court cases by citing an obscure verse in I Chronicles that refers to people, presumably gentiles, who attended to King Solomon in his court. To understand how the *Sifre* is using this verse as a source to refer to Ruth's longevity, the reader must be familiar with the context in which this verse appears. The passage in Chronicles reads:

> The sons of Judah: Perez, Hezron, Carmi, Hur, and Shobal.... The sons of Shelah son of Judah: Er father of Lecah, Laadah father of Mareshah, and the families of the guild of linen workers at Bethashbea; and Jokim, and the men of Cozeba, and Joash, and Saraph, who married into Moab but returned to Lehem (now the records are ancient). These were the potters and inhabitants of Netaim and Gederah; they lived there with the king in his service.[10]

9. *Sifre Numbers* to Num. 10:29–36; #78; trans. Jacob Neusner in Neusner, *Sifre to Numbers: An American Translation and Explanation, Volume 1: Sifre to Numbers 1–58* (Tampa Bay: University of South Florida, 1986).
10. I Chr. 4:1, 21–23 (NRSV).

According to I Chronicles 4, a descendant of Judah named Saraph married a Moabite woman and returned to Lehem. This clearly parallels the story of Ruth, who travels to Bet Lehem to live with her mother-in-law, and conceives a child with Boaz, a descendant of Judah. In Chronicles, members of Saraph's family become the "potters and inhabitants of Netaim and Gederah." The author of the midrash preserved in *Sifre*, then, believed that the gentile members of Solomon's court were kin of Ruth, which would suggest that she was alive during his reign and was responsible for bringing them into his household. Remarkably, this midrash presents Ruth as being closely associated with her gentile family, even while being present in Solomon's court, four generations after she joined the family of Avimelech and later Boaz.

That Ruth and her Moabite family never assimilated into the Davidic family is confirmed by the closing *a fortiori* argument of the midrash: If God draws close Ruth the Moabite, who came from a nation whose women were forbidden to marry Israelites, how much more will God draw close pious Israelites. This statement is shocking in that it presumes that Ruth is not an Israelite. Like the legend preserved in Yevamot which views Ruth as a foreign graft but her children as deriving from the original root of Abraham, this text keeps Ruth at genealogical bay, even as she is described as the foremother of King Solomon.

RUTH IN EARLY CHRISTIAN SOURCES

The Gospel of Matthew, generally thought to be a mid- to late-first-century work strongly impacted by the writer's Jewish identity, opens with a genealogy of Jesus which includes Ruth as one of his ancestors. This genealogy consists of three sets of fourteen generations, with one set extending from Abraham to David, another set extending from David to the Babylonian exile in 586 BCE, and a final set extending from the beginning of the exilic period to Jesus. Ruth is one of just four women, all outsiders to the Israelite community, who are mentioned as part of Jesus' ancestry. The genealogy reads as follows:

> An account of the genealogy of Jesus the Messiah, the son of David, the son of Abraham. Abraham was the father of Isaac, and Isaac the father of Jacob, and Jacob the father of Judah and

his brothers, and Judah the father of Perez and Zerah by Tamar, and Perez the father of Hezron, and Hezron the father of Aram, and Aram the father of Aminadab, and Aminadab the father of Nahshon, and Nahshon the father of Salmon, and Salmon the father of Boaz by Rahab, and Boaz the father of Obed by Ruth, and Obed the father of Jesse, and Jesse the father of King David.

And David was the father of Solomon by the wife of Uriah, and Solomon the father of Rehoboam, and Rehoboam the father of Abijah, and Abijah the father of Asaph, and Asaph the father of Jehoshaphat, and Jehoshaphat the father of Joram, and Joram the father of Uzziah, and Uzziah the father of Jotham, and Jotham the father of Ahaz, and Ahaz the father of Hezekiah, and Hezekiah the father of Manasseh, and Manasseh the father of Amos, and Amos the father of Josiah, and Josiah the father of Jechoniah and his brothers, at the time of the deportation to Babylon.

And after the deportation to Babylon: Jechoniah was the father of Salathiel, and Salathiel the father of Zerubbabel, and Zerubbabel the father of Abiud, and Abiud the father of Eliakim, and Eliakim the father of Azor, and Azor the father of Zadok, and Zadok the father of Achim, and Achim the father of Eliud, and Eliud the father of Eleazar, and Eleazar the father of Matthan, and Matthan the father of Jacob, and Jacob the father of Joseph the husband of Mary, of whom Jesus was born, who is called the Messiah. So all the generations from Abraham to David are fourteen generations; and from David to the deportation to Babylon, fourteen generations; and from the deportation to Babylon to the Messiah, fourteen generations.[11]

The presence of gentile women in Matthew's genealogy led some early Christian interpreters to argue that the covenantal community which centered on the teachings of Jesus was open to gentiles who had faith in Jesus, as evidenced by Jesus' own line featuring pious gentile women who were connected to the Israelite family only through marriage. By

---

11. Matthew 1:1–17 (NRSV).

the second century, however, some Church Fathers treated Ruth not simply as a biological ancestor of Jesus, but as a symbol of the Church who represents a system in which one can achieve salvation through faith in Christ.

One of the earliest examples of such typological interpretation can be found in the writings of Hippolytus of Rome (170–235 CE). Hippolytus focuses on Boaz's invitation to Ruth to eat bread, dip it into wine, and to drink water drawn by the young reapers (Ruth 2:9–14). Hippolytus concludes that the reapers in this passage represent the Apostles, who offer Ruth the gift of baptism. Along with the prophets, the Apostles draw water from the everlasting fount of immortality and quench the thirst of the spiritually deprived by offering them grace through Jesus.[12] According to this reading, Boaz represents Christ, and Ruth represents the people of the Church.

Origen of Alexandria (c. 184–253) likewise specifies that Ruth symbolizes the Church. Whereas for Hippolytus, Ruth is a *typus Ecclesiae* (a typology of the Church), for Origen, Ruth is a *typus Gentium* (a typology of the Gentiles), who models ideal gentile behavior by embracing Christianity.[13] Building on the fact that Ruth is an outsider to the Israelite community, Origen believes that the message of Ruth's book is that gentiles will be embraced by Jesus, should they follow the teachings of the Church. Origen's focus on Ruth's gentile identity makes sense when considering the fact that the Romans of his city were deeply antagonistic to Christianity in the early third century, when Christianity was not yet a legalized religion. Origen's message is that gentiles need not be antagonistic toward Christianity, for they stand to enjoy the benefits of salvation that faith in Jesus will bring.

Later Christian interpreters built on the notion that Ruth is a symbol of the Church. According to Ambrose (c. 340–397), for instance, Ruth enters not the Israelite community, but the Church, and the fact

---

12. Ruth 2:9, in Hippolytus of Rome, *Hippolytus Werke. Kleiners Exegetische und Homiletische Schriften*, trans. Hans Achelis (Gottingen: Forgotten Books, 1987), 120. Cited in Elena Giannarelli, "Ruth in the Church Fathers," *SIDIC* 23 (1990): 12–15.

13. Origen, *Fragmenta e catenis in Ruth*, PG 12 989D; *Fragmenta e catenis in Mattheum*, ed. Klostermann-Benz, GCS 41:1 fr 6 1. Cited in Giannarelli, 13.

that she enters as a Moabite, and as someone whom the Israelites were forbidden to marry, is significant. Ambrose writes:

> For this woman who was an alien, a Moabitess, a nation with whom the Mosaic law forbade all intermarriage, and shut them totally out of the Church, how did she enter into the Church, unless she were holy and unstained in her life above the law? Therefore, she was exempt from this restriction of the Law, and deserved to be numbered in the Lord's lineage, chosen from the kindred of her mind, not her body. To us she is a great example, for that in her was prefigured the entrance into the Lord's Church of all of us who are gathered out of the Gentiles.[14]

Like other Church Fathers, Ambrose reverses symbolic norms by presenting Christians as embodying the true People of Israel. By entering the Church through pious faith rather than through works, Ruth becomes an example to all gentiles who want to enter the Christian covenantal community through their faith in Jesus rather than through conversion to Judaism. The notion that gentiles could convert to the new covenantal community of Jesus followers through faith rather than through "works," that is, through Jewish law, is first argued by Paul, and this argument is taken up by Church Fathers who believed that the best way to establish the borders of the Christian community was to differentiate themselves from Judaism by articulating a binary of Christian faith versus Judaism legality. For these Church Fathers, Ruth embodies not Jewish legality, but Christian faith.

The Antiochan bishop John Chrysostom (c. 349–407) also presents the Israelite community that Ruth enters as typologically symbolic. But Chrysostom's portrayal of Ruth diverges from Ambrose's portrayal. According to Chrysostom:

---

14. Ambrose, *Exposition on Luke*, 3, in *Exposition of the Holy Gospel According to Saint Luke*, trans. Theodosia Tomkinson (Etna: Center for Traditionalist Orthodox Studies, 1998).

See, for instance, what befell Ruth, how like it is to the things which belong to us. For she was born of a strange race, and reduced to the utmost poverty, yet Boaz when he saw her neither despised her poverty not abhorred her mean birth, as Christ having received the Church, being both an alien and in much poverty, took her to be partaker of much blessings. But even as Ruth, if she had not left her father, and renounced household and race, country and kindred, would not have attained unto this alliance; so the Church too, having forsaken the customs which men had received from their fathers, then, and not before, became lovely to the Bridegroom.[15]

Whereas for Ambrose, Ruth represents gentile converts who are welcomed into the Church, for Chrysostom, Ruth represents the Church in toto, and Boaz represents Jesus, who welcomes all congregants into the Church. And just as Ruth had to abandon her homeland and family in order to fully bond herself to Boaz, so too all Christians must abandon their pagan ways in order to fully bond themselves to Jesus. The story of Ruth has no symbolic significance for Jews according to this reading: it is instead a reminder to Christians that, regardless of one's background, all people are welcomed by Jesus, provided that they fully abandon their sinful past and the families who reared them in a life of paganism.

CONCLUSION: THE MOABITE RUTH
AND THE CHRISTIAN RUTH

Early Church Fathers retrojected Christian theology onto the Israelite period by reading biblical passages as predictors of the coming of Jesus, or as symbols representing aspects of his life. That early Christians applied such methods to obscure biblical texts such as the Psalms and Isaiah is unsurprising, since passages in these books require interpretation to be understood. It is more striking, however, that Christians also interpreted the figure of Ruth, whose eponymous book is a straightforward narrative which poses no obvious interpretive or exegetical difficulties,

---

15. John Chrysostom, "Homilies," 17, in *The Homilies of St. John Chrysostom* (Oxford: Library of the Fathers of the Holy Catholic Church, Oxford University Press, 1842).

as a prefigure of Jesus and the Church. The rabbinic portrayal of Ruth as a beloved outsider who never quite sheds her Moabite identity may be a response to Christian presentations of Ruth, which portray her as a symbol of the Church which is open to all, and which opposes the closed and insular Synagogue. By persistently calling Ruth a Moabite and depicting her as a righteous heroine, the Rabbis manage to reincorporate Ruth into their religious tradition while presenting rabbinic Judaism as open to all those who embrace their God and way of life.

Bread, Vinegar, and Destiny

Simi Peters

"Come here, and eat of the bread, and dip your morsel in the vinegar."

(Ruth 2:14)

W ith these prosaic words, Boaz invites Ruth to join his reapers at the communal meal he has provided for them. Ruth is one of many paupers making use of the laws of the harvest season to provide for her mother-in-law and herself by gleaning in the wake of the reapers. Ruth Rabba, a midrashic commentary on the Book of Ruth, derives a lengthy, complex set of readings from this fleeting interaction, carrying the reader off on a journey through Jewish history, and then back again to a workaday moment in the field.

In exploring how the midrashic authors manage to find Jewish history in the account of a meal, we need to bear in mind that they view the Book of Ruth as significant not only because of its intrinsic religious content, but primarily because it records the foundational narrative of the Davidic dynasty; from their perspective, allusions to Jewish history are to be expected. More broadly, though, in every encounter with Midrash, we should be aware that the Rabbis are acutely sensitive to the nuances of biblical style and language. On a first reading, the verse that follows seems straightforward. As the commentary in Ruth Rabba will demonstrate, it is anything but:

> And Boaz said to her at mealtime, "Come here (*goshi halom*), and eat of the bread, and dip your morsel in the vinegar"; and she sat at the side (*mitzad*) of the reapers, and he held out (*vayitzbat*) to her parched grain; and she ate, and was satisfied, and she left over. (Ruth 2:14)

RUTH RABBA 5:6: THE FIRST OF SIX INTERPRETATIONS

And Boaz said to her at mealtime, "Come here" (Ruth 2:14). R. Yoḥanan interpreted this [verse] six ways:

[The first is that] it is speaking of David.

Come here: Approach royalty, for *halom* is none other than royalty. That is what is written, *that You have brought me to this place (halom)* (II Sam. 7:18).

and eat of the bread: This is the bread of royalty;

and dip your morsel in the vinegar: These are the sufferings, as it is said, *God, do not rebuke me in Your anger* (Ps. 6:2);

and she sat at the side of the reapers: The kingdom was hunted away from him temporarily, as R. Huna said, "All those six months that David was fleeing from Absalom, were not counted in the reckoning [of his years of reign] ...";

and he held out to her parched grain: That his kingdom returned to him as it is said, *now I know that God has saved His anointed one* (Ps. 20:7);

and she ate, and was satisfied, and left over: He eats in this world, he eats in the messianic days, and he eats in the Future to Come.

Mapping the Life of King David onto a Verse from Ruth
Context as a clue to meaning

Part of what drives R. Yoḥanan's interpretation is his sense that this verse doesn't really fit its context. Chapter 2 opens with Ruth "happening" upon Boaz's field (Ruth 2:3). As a Moabite convert, she is fully conscious of being a social pariah. Although the harvest laws permit her to glean in any field, Ruth anticipates being barred entry from places where her new status might be questioned. She intimates as much to her mother-in-law before setting out: "I will go now to the field, and glean among the sheaves, *after those whom I will find favor in their eyes*" (Ruth 2:2).

Discovering that Ruth is Naomi's daughter-in-law, Boaz engages her in conversation, taking pains to convey his recognition of her conversion and his admiration for her kindness to Naomi. He urges her to glean exclusively in his field because he has instructed his servants not to harass her, implying that she might not be equally well treated elsewhere. Boaz also invites her to help herself to the water provided for his own servants, a courtesy not offered to other gleaners (Ruth 2:5–13). Ruth responds with almost excessive gratitude to Boaz's kindness, although he has done no more than would be expected from a kinsman. Her overreaction is testimony to her profound sense of isolation. Ruth knows that in this social setting, her status is well below that of Boaz's servants (Ruth 2:13).

In the context of this high-flown dialogue, the wording of Boaz's invitation to the meal – down to the suggestion that she dip her bit of bread in vinegar – seems odd, as does the mention of seemingly extraneous details such as where Ruth sits, how Boaz serves her, and that she has some leftovers from the portion she receives. Biblical style is generally terse, with little description of this kind; we would expect Boaz's invitation to Ruth to be recorded in a brief third-person statement. From a midrashic perspective, then, we need to account for all this detail.

Language
Come here or approach hither?

Another element motivating R. Yoḥanan to look at the verse more closely is that the language used here is not what we would expect. Boaz's invitation to Ruth opens with the words "*Goshi halom*," translated above as "Come here." While this gloss is accurate, it fails to convey the connotation of either word. The root N-G-SH, from which the word *goshi* is derived, is perhaps better translated as "approach" or "draw near," and has a more weighty undertone than the simple "*bo*" (come). Usually, the root N-G-SH is used in depictions of battle or confrontation,[16] in situations demanding a special effort,[17] in summonses to holy places,[18] or in the performance of ritual acts.[19] The tone of this verb seems too loaded for such a commonplace situation.

The same can be said of the word "*halom*," translated in this verse as "here." There are two similar adverbs of place in biblical Hebrew: "*hena*" and "*halom*." "*Hena*," the more common of the two, appears forty-five times in Tanakh, while "*halom*" appears only eleven times. The flavor of this word is probably better conveyed by the archaic "hither" which means "to (or toward) this place." "*Halom*" appears in very specific kinds of contexts, such as depictions of revelatory encounters, or moments of historic significance.[20]

On the face of it, Boaz is simply inviting Ruth to eat with his servants. Or is he? The word choices in this invitation seem more befitting of a momentous occasion. As R. Yoḥanan sees it, this verse portends much more than either Boaz or Ruth can imagine.

Halom as royalty

Picking up on these nuances of language, R. Yoḥanan opens his commentary with "*Come here*: Approach royalty, for *halom* is none other than royalty. That is what is written, *that You have brought me to this place* (halom)." This proof-text depicts a pivotal moment in the life of King David. Having brought the Ark of the Covenant to Jerusalem, he hopes to fulfill his

---

16. For example, Gen. 44:18, I Sam. 17:10, 16, 40.
17. For example, Gen. 29:10.
18. For example, Ex. 28:43.
19. For example, Deut. 21:5.
20. For example, Gen. 16:13, Ex. 3:5.

dream of building the Temple. Initially, the prophet Nathan approves David's plan, but God instructs him to tell David that he cannot do as he wishes. In submission to God's will, David prays before Him, expressing gratitude and humility for all that God has given him: "Who am I, God, my Lord, and who is my household, that You have brought me to this place (*halom*)?" (II Sam. 7:18). "This place" is David's exalted royal status, a position that extends to all his descendants, down to the Messiah.

Finding a pattern

R. Yoḥanan might have ended his commentary by showing us the connection between the word "*halom*" in Samuel and Ruth; the subtle allusion is illuminating in itself. Instead, he goes much further. First, he maps the entire verse onto the life-story of David as king. Then, taking off from David's life, R. Yoḥanan frames Boaz's invitation to Ruth as a foreshadowing of the entire Judean royal history, moving on to Solomon, Hezekiah, and Manasseh, and culminating with the Messiah. Parsing each phrase of the verse in turn, he imposes the same pattern on each king's life, finding symbolic significance at every point.

THE SECOND OF SIX INTERPRETATIONS

Another explanation:
Come here is speaking of Solomon.

Come here: Approach royalty;

and eat of the bread: This is the bread of royalty, as it is said, *And the bread of Solomon for one day was sixty kor of flour and thirty kor of fine flour* (I Kings 5:2);

and dip your morsel in the vinegar: This is the soil of [his] deeds;

and she sat at the side of the reapers: The kingdom was hunted away from him temporarily, as R. Yoḥai bar Ḥanina said, "An angel descended in the image of Solomon and sat on his throne, and Solomon went around the entrances of Israel, saying, *I am Kohelet; I was king over Israel in Jerusalem* (Eccl. 1:12). What would one of them do? She would put before him a plate of beans and strike him with a reed on his head and say to him, "Is not Solomon sitting on his throne, and you say, 'I am Solomon king of Israel'?!"

and he held out to her parched grain: That his kingdom returned to him;

and she ate, and was satisfied, and left over: He eats in this world, he eats in the messianic days, and he eats in the World to Come.

Similarities and Differences

Comparing the two readings, we can see that they share the same general structure, following the order of the verse to impose a pattern: royalty, "bread," "vinegar," temporary loss of the kingdom, the restoring of the kingdom, and "eating" in this world, in the messianic days, and in the World to Come.

The bread of royalty

There are, however, some significant differences. First, the connection between bread and royalty, mentioned without elaboration in the David reading, features prominently with Solomon. "*And eat of the bread*: This is the bread of royalty, as it is said, *And the bread of Solomon for one day was sixty kor of flour and thirty kor of fine flour*" (I Kings 5:2). This passage is part of a long description of the magnificence of Solomon's reign in I Kings 5. The provisions consumed daily in the royal household are listed in detail. By any measure, the food is costly and the quantities staggering, an indication – among others – that Solomon has an extensive government structure. With so many eating at the king's table, his court is truly a seat of power. No other Israelite king is described this way.

"Bread" is necessary to sovereignty, because "bread" symbolizes sustenance. For a king, it represents dominion over his subjects as well as his obligation to provide for them. The king's economic power is acquired through conquest and taxation, and his stewardship is critical to the financial welfare of his people. In the history of the Davidic dynasty, Solomon's reign is the most striking example of a king exercising this power for the benefit of his kingdom as well as for himself. Solomon's judicious use of resources grants his subjects a prosperity and security unprecedented up to his time, and never again achieved after it: "Judah and Israel were as numerous as the sand that is on the sea, *eating, and drinking*, and happy" (I Kings 4:20).

Vinegar: suffering or sin?

Another difference between R. Yoḥanan's first and second readings is that for David, vinegar symbolizes suffering, while for Solomon it represents sinfulness. As we will see, "vinegar" is a complex symbol for R. Yoḥanan. The five kings of the Davidic dynasty listed in this midrash, including the future Messiah, all experience "vinegar" in their lives – David, Hezekiah, and the Messiah as sufferers, Solomon and Manasseh as sinners. This too is a definitive aspect of monarchy as R. Yoḥanan understands it. Power comes with a heightened potential for pain as well as a larger arena for moral success or failure.

Vinegar, son of wine

R. Yoḥanan's appropriation of vinegar as a symbol for suffering is easily accounted for since this imagery appears in both Psalms and Proverbs.[21] Explaining his use of the same symbol to represent sinfulness is more difficult, although the key to this problem may lie in finding the answer to a different question: Why does R. Yoḥanan focus on these four kings of Judah – David, Solomon, Hezekiah, and Manasseh – rather than others?

Vinegar is wine that has soured, hence the rabbinic term for wine vinegar, "vinegar son of wine" (*ḥometz ben yayin*). Although vinegar has its uses, it is the less valued by-product of a more valuable substance, giving rise to the expression "vinegar son of wine" as a metaphor for the wicked child of a righteous father.[22]

R. Yoḥanan presents us with two father-and-son pairings in which the son is less righteous than his father, choosing kings who span the timeline of Judean sovereignty: David and Solomon rule early in the dynasty; Hezekiah and Manasseh rule close to its disastrous end. Each in his own way exemplifies the best or the worst of royal power and, in the case of Solomon, perhaps both the best *and* the worst. To be

---

21. See Psalms 69:22, Proverbs 10:26, and Proverbs 25:20.
22. Bava Metzia 83b.

sure, Solomon's sins, however much they are condemned in Kings and Chronicles, do not approach the evils perpetrated by Manasseh. His misdeeds are also partially mitigated by his personal devotion to God and the building of the Temple. Still, in detailing Solomon's sins, I Kings 11:4 and 6 compare him negatively to his father. Might Solomon have been judged differently had he not been the "son of wine"?

In focusing on father-and-son pairings, R. Yoḥanan highlights the hereditary nature of monarchy. The advantage of a hereditary position is that it virtually guarantees dynastic continuity. Inevitably, though, some heirs to the throne will be unworthy because their succession is based on birth, not merit. The ultimate exemplar of this is Manasseh, the most morally corrupt king of the Davidic dynasty. So egregious is his damage to the realm, that the destruction of the Judean kingdom is attributed directly to him, although it takes place long after his reign. Even the unremitting righteous activism of his grandson Josiah is unable to reverse the fatal consequences of his actions: "And like [Josiah] there was no king before him who returned to God with all his heart and all his soul and all his strength according to the whole Torah of Moses; and after him there did not arise one like him. *But God did not return from His great wrath which He was angered by Judah, because of all the provocations that Manasseh provoked Him*" (II Kings 23:25–26). When kings inherit the throne, they benefit from their predecessors' good choices and suffer from their mistakes as a condition of their position.

Sitting at the side of the reapers:
R. Yoḥanan contradicts the biblical account
In both the David and Solomon readings, and later, in referring to Hezekiah, Manasseh, and the Messiah, R. Yoḥanan glosses the phrase "and she sat at the side of the reapers" as "the kingdom was hunted away from him temporarily." Playing on the word "*mitzad*" (at the side of), R. Yoḥanan turns it into "*notzda*" (was hunted), a verb which shares two letters of the same root.[23] In Samuel, Kings, and Chronicles, four of the

---

23. Although it differs in meaning. Some commentators interpret "*notzda*" as "his kingdom was sidelined from him," which is closer in meaning to "*mitzad*." I have opted for the "hunted" gloss because it fits better with the syntax of the sentence in the source.

five kings mentioned by R. Yoḥanan have their kingdoms "hunted away from [them] temporarily": David by his son Absalom, Hezekiah and Manasseh by the Assyrians. Even the Messiah will suffer a temporary loss of power, according to R. Yoḥanan.

As a statement about the realities of sovereignty, the comment is true to life. Power is indeed an uncertain state. Kings have enemies, and no real control over circumstances leading to their usurpation. The problem is that R. Yoḥanan's claim of Solomon's loss of power completely contradicts the biblical accounts of his life. Solomon, alone of the kings alluded to in the midrash, appears to rule in complete security, unlike his father David who does suffer having his kingdom "hunted away from him temporarily."

To sketch Solomon's loss of power, R. Yoḥanan draws from a midrashic tradition based on a verse in Ecclesiastes: "I am Kohelet;[24] I *was* king over Israel in Jerusalem" (Eccl. 1:12). Reading the verse as though it means that Kohelet had been king and was no longer, the midrash portrays Solomon being displaced from his throne by an angel, to wander anonymously among his subjects. Since this midrash is impossible to reconcile with the accounts of Solomon's reign in Kings and Chronicles, it cannot be taken literally. What, then, does R. Yoḥanan mean to convey by introducing it here?

Solomon is the mightiest Judean king, presiding over a golden age of peace and prosperity; he is also the most cognizant of how fleeting his success will be. Even as Solomon records his own greatness in Ecclesiastes 2, he foregrounds his awareness that nothing he has created is permanent. Indeed, toward the end of Solomon's reign, his hard-won peace begins to unravel (I Kings 11:14–25). Worse, God tells him that in punishment for his sins, he will lose dominion over most of Israel, with his son retaining only the tribe of Judah (I Kings 11:11–13).

Although Solomon never experiences the humiliation of being deposed, the midrash cited by R. Yoḥanan is in keeping with the mindset of the man who writes, "And I hated all the labors that I labored under the sun, for I would leave them to a man who would come after me. And who knows if he would be wise or foolish, and he would rule over all that I toiled and did with wisdom under the sun" (Eccl. 2:18–19). The angel

---

24. Another name for Solomon, based on textual clues and oral tradition.

sitting on Solomon's throne in his place – a divine messenger sent to humble a prideful king – is a fitting metaphor for Solomon's consciousness that his kingdom will be "hunted away from him" after his death.

Power Restored

In his commentary on the phrase "and he held out to her parched grain," R. Yoḥanan asserts that the kings who lose their thrones are restored to power: "his kingdom returned to him." At first glance, imposing this meaning on a description of Boaz serving some food seems arbitrary. A closer look shows us that it has some grounding in the language of the verse.

In describing how Boaz serves Ruth a portion of parched grain, the verse employs a verb appearing nowhere else in Tanakh – *vayitzbat* – translated here as "and he held out."[25] Once again, the translation fails to capture the full sense of the word. As Rashi points out, the Mishna[26] uses the same root (TZ-B-T) in the word for "handle" (*bet hatzvita*), an object grasped with a pinching or contraction of the fingers.[27]

On the basis of the word "*vayitzbat*," R. Yoḥanan pictures Boaz serving Ruth "a little bit [using] his two fingers," rather than pouring out a generous amount. By analogy, a throne lost and then restored is a meager portion. The king who never faces a challenge to his dominion may feel secure, imagining that his might will protect him. The king who has experienced the loss of his throne, however temporarily, can never again feel that certainty; a sword always dangles over his head, even if the rest of his reign passes peacefully.

THE THIRD, FOURTH, AND FIFTH OF SIX READINGS

> **Another explanation:**
> *Come here* is speaking of Hezekiah…[28]

---

25. Following Rashi's commentary based on *Targum Yonatan* (*oshit*).
26. Ḥagiga 3:1.
27. In Modern Hebrew, "*litzbot*" means "to pinch."
28. I have omitted this relatively short section because it repeats the basic template of the David reading. The main difference is in the verses quoted to illustrate the different states of "royalty," "bread," "vinegar," etc. As with David, "vinegar" signifies suffering, rather than sinfulness.

Another explanation:

Come here is speaking of Manasseh.

Come here: Approach royalty;

and eat of the bread: This is the bread of royalty;

and dip your morsel in the vinegar: that he soiled his deeds like vinegar, from evil deeds;

and she sat at the side of the reapers: that his kingdom was hunted away from him temporarily, as it is written, *And God spoke to Manasseh and to his people and they did not listen; and God brought upon them the army generals of the king of Assyria and they bound Manasseh with fetters* (II Chr. 33:10–11).

R. Abba bar Kahana said "shackles." R. Levi bar Ḥayata said, They made him a copper barrel and stoked the flame beneath him, and he was crying out, "This idol [save me]! That idol save me!" When he saw that the [idols] had no effect at all, he said, I remember that Father made me read [the verses] *When you are in your distress and [all these things] find you [at the end of days and you will return to God, your Lord and listen to His voice] for your Lord is a merciful God [He will not abandon you and will not destroy you]* (Deut. 4:30–31). I will cry out to Him. If He answers, good. If He does not answer, it is all one and the same – all the faces are equal. At that hour, the ministering angels rose up and blocked all the heavenly windows, and said before Him, Master of the Universe, a man who set up an idol in the Sanctuary, You will accept him in repentance?! He said to them, If I do not accept him in repentance, I will be locking the opening before all penitents. What did the Holy One blessed be He do? He dug an opening under His Throne of Honor, from a place where no angel can have dominion. That is what is written, *And he prayed to Him, and He was petitioned by him, and He heard his plea* (II Chr. 33:13)...

and he held out to her parched grain: that his kingdom returned to him, as it is said, *And He returned him to Jerusalem, to his kingdom* (II Chr. 33:13)...

and she ate, and was satisfied, and left over: He eats in this world, he eats in the messianic days, and he eats in the World to Come.

Another explanation:
It is speaking of the messianic king (*melekh hamashiah*)... [29]

Royalty as Eternity

Throughout his projection of the verse from Ruth onto the lives of the Judean kings, R. Yoḥanan's reading of the last phrase makes the greatest leap from the physical to the spiritual. He maps Ruth's ordinary act of eating onto her descendants' lives in the most profound way: "*and she ate, and was satisfied, and left over*: He eats in this world, he eats in the messianic days, and he eats in the Future to Come." As in some of the other commentary, R. Yoḥanan appears to be imposing a predetermined template onto the verse without any regard for its actual meaning. It is also strange that R. Yoḥanan includes Manasseh among the kings who "eat in the messianic days and the World to Come," given his evil deeds and a repentance not worthy of being received by God. To understand what R. Yoḥanan is doing here, we need to explore his sixth interpretation, in which he goes back to the Book of Ruth to explain the plain sense of the verse.

THE FINAL READING

Another explanation:
Come here is speaking of Boaz: Draw near to here;

and eat of the bread: This is the food of the reapers;

---

29. As with the Hezekiah reading, I have omitted most of this relatively short section because it repeats the basic template of the David reading, only with verses that apply specifically to the Messiah. One other notable difference is that the phrase "and she ate, and was satisfied, and left over" is omitted from the Messiah reading since it need not be stated that the Messiah "eats in this world, eats in the messianic days, and eats in the World to Come."

I have also omitted a section of the midrash which follows the fifth reading – a comparison of the first redeemer (Moses) and the last redeemer (the Messiah) – because it is tangential to the rest of the midrash.

and dip your morsel in the vinegar: It is the way of reapers to dip their bit of bread in vinegar. R. Yoḥanan said: "From here [we learn] that they bring out different types of pickles to the threshing floors."

and she sat at the side of the reapers: She sat at the side of the reapers certainly;

and he held out to her parched grain: A little bit [using] his two fingers. R. Yitzḥak said, "We can hear two things from this. Either a blessing rested in the fingers of that righteous man, or a blessing rested in the intestines of that righteous woman. *From that which it says, and she ate, and was satisfied, and left over, it seems that the blessing rested in the intestines of that righteous woman.*"

R. Yitzḥak bar Maryon said, "Scripture comes to teach us that if a man does a mitzva, he should do it with a whole heart. For if Reuben had known the Holy One blessed be He was writing about him, *And Reuben heard and he saved him from their hand* (Gen. 37:21), he would have carried him on his shoulders to his father. And if Aaron had known the Holy One blessed be He was writing about him, *and here, he is coming out to greet you* (Ex. 4:14), he would have come with drums and dancing to greet him. *And if Boaz had known the Holy One blessed be He was writing about him,* and he held out to her parched grain and she ate, and was satisfied, and left over, *he would have fed her fatted heifers…"*

Back to the Field

In this final section, R. Yoḥanan sees the verse as a straightforward description of what takes place in the field on the day that Boaz invites Ruth to eat with his reapers. He summons her to sit down and tells her to help herself to the reapers' food, including the garnishes that are served as a matter of course in a harvest meal. For her part, Ruth places herself at the side of the table, not pushing toward the front where Boaz sits, in a sign of modesty and common sense. Boaz makes the gesture of serving her himself, "a little bit using his two fingers," yet Ruth is satiated even from this, and is able to take what is left back to Naomi, along with her gleanings from the field (Ruth 2:18). How is that possible? Because, as R. Yitzḥak tells us, there is a blessing within "that righteous woman" which transforms a few pinches of parched grain into a filling meal.

The road from Ruth and Boaz in the field to the ultimate messianic redemption of the world is not smooth. With dominion come greatness and responsibility, but also suffering, corruption, and loss. Significantly, even an evil king like Manasseh is a necessary part of the process that leads to the Messianic Age. He attains a place in history as part of the chain of succession, but he also gains eternal life, despite his flawed repentance, so that others will learn that the door is always open to return to God. This too is a necessary part of the redemptive process.

On one level, the only thing that happens in this narrative is that Boaz makes a kind gesture to a kinswoman ignored by everyone else. In his meditation on the history and meaning of the monarchy, R. Yoḥanan shows us that this small deed contains the seeds of eternity. The midrash ends with a gentle criticism of Boaz and a call to perform our good deeds generously in the recognition that we cannot know the impact of our actions.

Unbeknownst to him, when Boaz invites Ruth to eat with his servants, he is actually calling their shared descendants to a transformative destiny, irrevocably changing the entire world with a simple act. This alone is not sufficient to create a redemptive dynasty, however. That can only be accomplished by the courage and loving-kindness of Ruth who "ate, and was satisfied, and left over." She alone could take something so small and make it so great.

Understanding Malbim's Dispassionate Scripture: The Case of Naomi's Lament Turned Lecture

Rabbi Dov Lerner

Apenniless Naomi stands on the threshold of Bethlehem, and, reacting to the shock of old neighbors, she offers us what is ostensibly one of the rawest moments in Scripture. And yet, Malbim[1] – with

---

1. Meir Leibush ben Yehiel Michel Weisser was born in Volochysk in 1809 and passed away on Rosh HaShana 1879, in Kiev. Over his lifetime, he held seven rabbinic posts spanning Eastern Europe, including six years as chief rabbi of Romania, a post from which he was expelled. He published a halakhic commentary and anthology, a compendium of nine sermonic homilies, a near-comprehensive biblical commentary, autobiographic poetry, and a morality play. The most complete academic biographies can be found in Noah Rosenbloom's *Malbim: Exegesis, Philosophy, Science, and Mysticism in the Writings of Rabbi Meir Leibush Malbim*, and, with a deeper focus on the events surrounding his expulsion from Bucharest, in Jacob Geller's *HaMalbim: Maavako BaHaskala UVaReforma BeBukarest (1858–1864)*.

highly intricate and deeply original interpretive mechanics – neuters her emotive force and contorts her poetic but visceral grief into an act of deliberate and calm teaching. As we shall soon see, he turns what others have read as blistering lamentation into a placid lecture. And this evasion, even erasure, of natural feeling, forms a broader pattern across the biblical commentaries of this exegetical master.[2]

In fact, for this very reason – Malbim's seemingly unfeeling exegesis – Moshe Segal singles him out as the prototypical commentator of the Ghetto period, spanning from roughly the end of the fifteenth century until the end of the eighteenth century.[3] In every age, in every place, in every culture, Segal claims – from Babylonian midrashists to Alexandrian allegorists to Spanish philosophers, Provençal mystics, and French literalists – biblical exegesis has served as the channel through which Scripture's static semiotics resonate; and in each of those ages, places, and cultures, that production of biblical meaning is powered and bound by the realities of Jewish life. Thus, as the three centuries separating Isaac Abravanel and Moses Mendelssohn were host to some of the most despicable living conditions in the history of diasporic Jewish life, majestic scriptural interpretation is inconceivable. In this "Age of the Ghetto," Segal argues, the biblical text was, by necessity, passed through the prism of a grim and grisly reality, generating what he considers an exegetical desecration of Scripture. For him, Ghetto-inflected biblical commentators disfigured the text with sophistic dialectics and perverted biblical figures with the imposition of a piteous paradigm – turning kings and captains and prophets and preachers into bland indigents and bookish pedants, more likely to repulse than inspire us – and as an exemplar of the work produced in this squalid exegetical period, Segal proffers Malbim's commentary.

He catalogues his evidence as a sequence of instances where Malbim misses the presence of human sentimentality, culminating in what

---

2. This pattern across Malbim's biblical commentary is the subject of my current doctoral thesis undertaken at the Divinity School of the University of Chicago, under the prospective title, "Dark Matter: Malbim's Exegetical Pedagogy."

3. M. H. (Moses Hirsch) Segal, *Parshanut HaMikra: Sekira al Toldoteha VeHitpatḥuta* (Jerusalem: Kiryat Sefer, 1952), 111–113.

he considers to be the most flagrant illustration of Malbim's "emotional numbness," *"kehut haregesh"* (p. 111) – his treatment of Jephthah's need to slaughter his daughter (Judges 11). Malbim, in Segal's presentation, is blind to the power of the pair's dramatic and emotive posture, reducing their final exchange to an emotionally hollow debate about the possibilities of annulling a religious vow. Malbim, in Segal's overtly derisive reading, is charged with dragging biblical grandeur into the weeds of bland legalese, hollowing Scripture of passion, and profaning its natural profundity. In his words:

> This sophistic commentator does not appreciate nor feel that his bandying about the laws of vows violates the sanctity inherent in the sublime sorrow of this suffering father and blameless yet brave daughter. (p. 113)[4]

Over the coming pages I hope to show that Malbim's pattern of interpretive work emerges not from a historically suppressed exegetical imagination or an oppression-induced emotive deficiency, but as a deliberate choice designed to mitigate the sentimentalization of Scripture – a choice stemming from a larger spiritual vision. Within this context, Malbim's inimitable treatment of Naomi's aforementioned grief – which we shall read in more detail – achieves a deeper significance; it no longer serves as a mere exegetical curiosity but contributes to a broader philosophy of both interpretive and spiritual ethics. Malbim's transformation of Naomi's pain into a moment of composed pedagogy, we shall see, functions as a signal for how he intends the biblical text to be read writ large, and how he believes the righteous should live their lives.

* * *

It is in the second of Malbim's published sermons that we most clearly see his attitude toward visceral feeling:

---

4. Translation mine.

With wisdom, faith, and acts of virtue and justice…the core of all these things, is to do them purely for the goodness contained with themselves alone…only for the sake of God who commanded them all, which is the fundamental goodness and true bliss, not fusing in his soul any other intent or incentive, from pleasure to profit…. However, it is not so in cases where he sees instantaneously and presently, with his external senses, the temporal benefits of wealth or glory and so on, which he will attain with wisdom and acts of justice; all the more so, if he feels with them the satisfaction of corporal urges, such as with ritual obligations involving eating or other pleasures…then it is incredibly difficult, by human nature, to drive these from his mind, and not allow them to forge any impression on his soul, and perform these goods purely for their inherent goodness…for these servants – impulse and imagination – have already learned to take their share first, and the external senses become active before the inner senses get a chance to implant the goodness and bliss of the act itself on the soul.[5]

For Malbim, the pinnacle of spiritual life is the riddance of self-interest – the saint must subdue every sense of fiscal, physical, or psychological pleasure. Even when directed toward a virtuous cause, visceral instinct is a distraction from the equanimity that pure service requires – it cannot contribute toward a redeemed existence as it drags the soul into a narcissistic state, a state when the self begins to eclipse divinity. Thus, for Malbim, life is best spent pruning impulse to improve the soul. In perhaps its pithiest form, this time in his biblical commentary, Malbim puts it as follows:

> The core of living is the life of the intellect and of service, which is called "Human Living," not the life of feelings, which is mere animal living. (Gen. 23:1)

In fact, in that second sermon, Malbim offers two stark examples of how the fate of biblical figures was shaped by feeling. In one instance

---

5. Malbim, *Artzot HaShalom* (Bnei Berak: Mishor, 1994), 31.

he offers a radical reading of a well-known piece of Davidic history – the reason behind God's denial of David's wish to build His Temple. The biblical Chronicler reports that Nathan's explanation related to King David's martial past – him having been a "man of war." And traditionally, this suggestion has been read as an assessment of David's bloody past as repellent to the Temple's symbolic ethics; in simple terms, a place dedicated to peace cannot be built by the hands of a man of war. Malbim's rendering could not be more different:

> Since, if it were to be built in the days of David, at that time still without respite from their enemies – knowing that by means of the Temple's construction they would instantly gain a massive temporal benefit, being that very respite from their enemies – it would be nigh impossible to build the Temple purely for the sake of God…. This not being the case in the age of Solomon, at that time already experiencing respite from their enemies… – and not seeing in their construction any temporal benefit – so it was then far easier to build it purely for the sake of God.[6]

King David is precluded from building the Temple not because his military past marked him as too belligerent in relation to the Temple, but quite the opposite – because his involvement in war made him all the more desperate for peace. Intimately knowing the losses and cost of every combat made David's intention, in relation to the Temple, muddled – at once seeking to serve God and to disseminate peace – thus rendering him incapable of investing the project with mental integrity. David's innate yearning for tranquility and calm thus barred him from fulfilling his most potent spiritual ambition – feelings, even noble feelings, impede the flight of the soul.

It is in connection with the binding of Isaac, however, that Malbim's conception of a dispassionate perfection reaches its peak.

> In that he was willing to slaughter his son, and that his intention was pure – uncontaminated by any other factor – is unremarkable,

---

6. Ibid., 33.

since it is inconceivable that any other personal incentive would reside in his mind while slaughtering his special son, whom he loved so deeply. The real core of the test lay in the second request – when God said to him, "Do not lay a hand on the boy" – for here, nature would have it, that a great joy would enter his heart, his son being spared from the fall of the sword, and it was incredibly difficult not to act from a perspective of personal gain and corporal joy. But God, surveyor of the unseen, saw and reported that he did not act, in that moment, due to the feeling of material joy, but was level-headed – both when told to sacrifice him, and when told to stop – for both acts were performed with perfect intention for the sake of God's command alone, and in both he experienced joy over fulfilling the divine injunction without the blend of any celebration for the sake of himself or his son; this was the greater test.[7]

The time of Abraham's test was not in the lead-up to his son's slaughter, for Malbim, but in the aftermath of his son's salvation. The summit of Abraham's piety arises in a moment of emotionless devotion – where his reaction to the sparing of his son's life is just as calm as the reaction to the command that it be taken. Once more, feeling is seen as an enemy of perfect faith, sentiment is cast as an obstacle to God's grace, reflexive human emotion – grief, elation, relief, rage – all inhibit the soul's ability to induce a celestial embrace.

In fact, in one of the only moments that Scripture offers us a description of a figure's state of mind, Malbim inverts its ostensible purpose. When the text records Jacob's excessive terror – "Jacob was greatly afraid, and he was distressed" (Gen. 32:8) – Malbim explains, against the traditional grain, that it was Jacob's terror itself that distressed him; the mere fact of his fear revealed the void between him and heaven. Where others have seen Aristotelian heroics,[8] Malbim paints a picture of shame and spiritual failure.

So, in light of Malbim's perspective on natural passions, we can start to appreciate why he might seek to shape a dispassionate Scripture,

---

7. Ibid., 35–36.
8. See Abravanel, Gen. 32:8, where he cites theory from Aristotle's *Nicomachean Ethics*.

crafting a commentary that modulates the emotion expressed by biblical figures and offering his readership an exegesis that models his spiritual ethic. Seeing virtue in categorical equanimity, Malbim could never offer a novelistic exegesis. He could never valorize passion or theatrics, he could never celebrate the voyeuristic exposition of the distant psyche – something that *he* might have called an exegetical desecration. And Malbim makes this plain. For him, the biblical text – at least as intended for public consumption[9] – is, in a phrase that he borrows from Midrash, an "*amon pedagog*,"[10] a "pedagogical aid." For him, the figures of Scripture are designed not to be dramatized but seen as earnest moral guides – they "brim with wisdom and decency; exhibit counsel, direction, virtue and integrity; they edify the untaught."[11] Scripture, for Malbim, is not meant to entertain but to educate; it is not meant to draw us into its world, but to teach us how to live in ours.

So, though Malbim fails to produce an exegesis suffused with feeling, it is not because he is incapable of it or confined by the Ghetto's oppressive ceiling – he bends the text in a very different direction because he seeks a very specific kind of spiritual perfection; he moralizes the ostensibly dramatic so as to produce a deliberate and dispassionate ethic. We have seen him do so in the cases of David, Abraham, and Jacob, and now we shall see him do it with Naomi.

* * *

> They both went until they arrived at Bethlehem. And as they arrived in Bethlehem, the entire city stirred over them, saying, "Is this Naomi?" She said to them, "Do not call me Naomi; call me Marah, for God has embittered me greatly. I left full, but the Lord

---

9. Malbim does not deny that Scripture contains a multiplicity of readings, along the lines of the medieval notion of *PaRDeS*, but his commentary works purely – he claims – on the level of *peshat*. This claim is in and of itself worthy of study, and forms part of the subject matter of my doctoral work as well.

10. See his commentary on Proverbs 8:3, and his second footnote to his commentary on Genesis' first chapter.

11. Second paragraph of Malbim's theoretical appendix to his commentary on Song of Songs, *HeḤarash VeHaMasger*.

has brought me back empty. Why do you call me Naomi? The
Lord has testified against me; God has afflicted me." (Ruth 1:19–21)

In this encounter, where Naomi returns home after years in a
Moabite diaspora, we can imagine flashes of passion – in fact, most modern scholars see precisely that. For Avivah Zornberg, the stirring of the
city is more than a mere quiver or murmur; it is a rippling unrest fueled
by "existential wonder."[12] Jonathan Grossman conceives of this scene as
"charged with emotion";[13] and Yael Ziegler, admitting an inscrutability
of the precise emotional tenor, labels it at the very least "tumultuous."[14]

But the true potency of this moment resides – for many readers –
in Naomi's stunningly passionate oration. Her words are structured and
dramatic, poetic and emphatic; they bespeak a deeply defeated but defi-
ant soul, whose emotional tenor lies at odds with the rest of this opti-
mistic scroll. Robert Hubbard Jr. sees Naomi's speech as a bitter, blunt,
and explosive outburst, in part triggered by her seeing the streets of her
past – the streets where her sons had once played, and she together with
her husband had once strolled.[15] Ziegler also sees this speech as bitter
and heartbreaking, depicting it as a defensive deflection of the women's
antagonistic question – titling her chapter on this scene "Naomi Meets
the Women of Bethlehem: Namelessness, Bitterness, and Despair"[16] –
and both Hubbard and Ziegler explicitly reference the humanity of
Naomi's portrayal.[17] Zornberg depicts Naomi's speech as an exhibition
of "existential guilt and despair," baring a profound sense of shame and
humiliation. And in perhaps the most emotive reading of this speech,
Lois C. Dubin sees Naomi as shaken, empty, shattered, bitter, stricken,
and alone. For Dubin, she is "a female Job," where her hopeless words

12. Avivah Zornberg, "The Concealed Alternative," in J. A. Kates and G. T. Reimer,
    Reading Ruth: Contemporary Women Reclaim a Sacred Story (New York: Ballantine
    Books, 1994), 66.
13. Jonathan Grossman, *Ruth: Bridges and Boundaries* (Bern: Peter Lang Ltd, 2015), 113.
14. Yael Ziegler, *Ruth: Alienation and Monarchy,* Maggid Studies in Tanakh (Jerusalem:
    Maggid, 2015), 167.
15. Robert L. Hubbard, *The Book of Ruth* (Grand Rapids: Eerdmans, 1988), 124.
16. Ziegler, 167–180.
17. Hubbard, 127; Ziegler, 177.

function less as a theodicean protestation than a fraught and therapeutic gesticulation – Naomi weeps in words to extract care and attention from her peers.[18] Dubin, Zornberg, Hubbard, Grossman, Ziegler, and a whole host of modern readers harness the biblical text to unleash what they see as the dramatic power latent in its verses – they offer emotional complexity, psychic profundity, and a prism into the figures that populate Scripture's pages. In these readings, Naomi comes to life and fires our imaginations – she embodies a broken but resilient humanity, in which her speech reveals a reverence for the profundity that resides in solemnity and pain. Malbim, as we've noted, bends this text in a very different direction – he evinces an utter disregard for human drama and depicts, in its place, a cool and cordial conversation.

* * *

Naomi always used to have servants and maidservants and an entourage, and when she left her home she would be surrounded by a large crowd. But now they saw coming, merely a mother-in-law and daughter-in-law, the two of them alone like deserted paupers, thus, *"the entire city was astir."*[19]

Malbim's comments do not address the emotional state of the city's inhabitants, but simply explain the object of their interest – Naomi's less lavish appearance. Malbim then turns to Naomi's speech, opening his exegesis with a parable and then explaining its application:

If a person is in possession of incomparable levels of wealth… and then loses all his wealth, left with only a thousand *zuz*, and it is said of him that he has been bankrupted and made poor – it can only be said if his previous wealth is mentioned, as relative

---

18. Lois C. Dubin, "Fullness and Emptiness, Fertility and Loss: Meditations on Naomi's Tale in the Book of Ruth," in J. A. Kates and G. T. Reimer, *Reading Ruth: Contemporary Women Reclaim a Sacred Story* (Ballantine Books, 1994), 132.

19. To allow for a more accessible reading of Malbim's sometimes thorny sentences, I've italicized the biblical citations that he weaves into his commentary.

to that affluence he can be seen as needy and low. For if the value of his previous wealth is not mentioned, surely a person in possession of a thousand *zuz* can be considered wealthy. However, if the wealthy person had lost everything – left without a penny or piece of bread to appease his hunger – then one can label him a pauper even without noting his previous worth.[20]

Thus, when the city populace saw [Naomi] and her daughter-in-law approaching, without any attendants, they knew that she had lost her previous wealth; nevertheless, they presumed that she still had the gold and jewelry that an average person would be more than happy with. Thus, [the verse] indicates the cause of their confusion in *"Is this Naomi?"*; in this they note her previous worth – meaning that relative to her previous wealth she had undergone an extraordinary plummet.

"So she said to them." She informed them that it was not as they thought, that only if stating her previous reputation could they call her *Marah* (Embittered) …. She said that it was unnecessary to mention her prior standing at all, for she was so poor that she had nothing … and thus they could call me *Marah* without even noting my previous name, *Naomi*. Hence it is written, *"Do not call me* Naomi; *call me* Marah," meaning, it is possible to call me *Marah* without calling me *Naomi* – i.e. without mentioning my previous name or worth – *"for God has embittered me greatly,"* for although *"I left full,"* still, *"The Lord has brought me back empty,"* with nothing in hand. Therefore, you can call me by the name of *Marah, Aniyah*, and *Evyonah*, even without mentioning my name Naomi, which I had at the time of my prosperity.

In Malbim's rendering, Naomi's response to the women's question is more pertinent than her affect; she does not cry or wail or grieve or assail God – she simply "informs them." Her first words serve as a simple correction of what she considers an innocent misperception of her state. The crowd of women, noticing a former aristocrat without even a hint of an entourage, wonder whether it could really be Naomi.

---

20. Translation mine.

And the reason, Malbim claims, that they *needed to say her name,* is that only in the context of her prior opulence is her current status remotely striking. She is not, in their estimation, destitute or penniless, but merely middling; and only because of her previous fortune does her average standing warrant the slightest attention.

Already, Malbim has mitigated the dramatic tension of this meeting – what for Zornberg was a city-wide swelling of existential wonder, and for Ziegler was an antagonistic and tumultuous welcome, has, by the mechanics of Malbim's intricate exegesis, mellowed; the tone of the people's probe has tempered from mockery or panic to an apparent curiosity.

In response, Naomi answers their question with an adjustment of their presumption; she is not as comfortable as she may seem. Her fiscal situation is notable not only in contrast to her prior state; even without knowing her past, *even without mentioning her name,* her situation is dire – there is no need to say "Naomi," as by every measure she is empty. And, in Malbim's reading, Naomi is not specifically attached to the name *Marah* – she appears not to be particularly bitter – but uses it as a random stand-in for destitute anonymity; suggesting that the women could call her *Aniyah* or *Evyonah* as well. Her retort is not a poetic gesture or a sign of festering pain, it is a simple straightening of facts – and with the facts set straight, Naomi then turns to a more pressing matter, as she transitions from a depiction of her material reality to her understanding of providential theology.

> "*Why do you call me Naomi?*" Up to this point she only responds that it is unnecessary to mention her earlier name, *Naomi,* but now she adds something new – she says that it has now been revealed to her that the name *Naomi* was always inapt. Hence she says, "*Why do you call me Naomi?,*" as if to say, the reference to my prior state with the name *Naomi* is also untrue – in accordance with that which we've explained many times, that at times when God seeks to inflict a considerable punishment, He lifts the person to great heights of success, such that if they drop from there to poverty and need, their pain and suffering will be more deeply felt, and the fall will be far greater...

Thus, she suggests that her earlier success, in wealth and station, was designed by God in order that He could drop her from such great heights to poverty and lowliness, for in this way her descent will be more severe and her fall far greater. Therefore, considering that her earlier successes were merely a sort of caution to return to God – for He had raised her to be able to cast her from there to the depths of the abyss – the name *Naomi*, by which she was known at the time, was in error, for it was a deeply bitter success, a rise for the purpose of falling. Hence it says: *"since I left full,"* only in order that *"the Lord has brought me back empty"*; therefore, that I was full then, was only to augment the suffering of now, so *"Why do you call me Naomi?"*…for *"the Lord has testified against me,"* meaning – the earlier success was merely a warning in which to caution me to improve my ways, lest He cast me from the heights of this success to the deep, and so it was that with this success, *"God has afflicted me,"* for by its means the magnitude of my suffering and fall doubled…

Naomi's apparently repetitive rhetoric is, for Malbim, not repetitious or rhetorical at all – it is the introduction of a new argument; the next phase of her lecture. Not only was the present estimation of Bethlehem's female natives mistaken, but the theological premise beneath their curiosity was baseless. Seeing her evident destitution, the women presumed Naomi's moral demise over time, where her decline from affluence to indigence mirrored a fall from grace – where both her piety and her prosperity had been captured in her once apt, but now incongruous, name, with its connotations of pleasantness. And it is precisely this causal linkage of material wealth and spiritual worth that Naomi comes to reject. Her second sentence asks not why they are now, in the face of her fall, calling her "Naomi" – simply repeating her first point – but why, even at her material heights they would consider "Naomi" a fitting name.

To think that one can read celestial favor into material success is to misunderstand the workings of providence, Naomi teaches. *Sometimes* wealth is a signal of esteem, but *sometimes* it is a prelude to a spectacular plummet in fortune designed precisely for the purpose of exacting a more severe punishment. Naomi then points to her current position as evidence, for her audience to appreciate, that her prior wealth was not a pleasant sign but fundamentally punitive – intended merely to deepen the damage of her fall from grace. Every material achievement is more safely seen, Naomi teaches, as more an admonition than an endorsement – it should drive one to penitence more than pride, even if out of an abundance of caution.

What we see in this speech then, for Malbim, is an exhibition of pedagogy rather than dramatic poetry, protest, or pain. Naomi is not airing grievances or expressing agony; she is coolly schooling her audience – there is no dramatic tension, no theatrical apprehension, no poetic or aesthetic textual intention. Naomi presents her personal declension with the hope of correcting an ethically treacherous misperception – that material fortune always indicates virtue. Where others have seen Naomi grieving or seething or screaming in response to a panicked or hostile query, Malbim depicts her skillfully settling a calm confusion.

Malbim's exegesis – as with David, Abraham, and Jacob – once more purposefully moralizes a moment of ostensible passion; where others may seek the exhumation of Scripture's affective power, he unveils a dispassionate theological ethic – one in which Naomi does not lament or quail but lectures.

* * *

We now understand Malbim's dispassionate Scripture not as the by-product of a weighted imagination or an empathetic incapacity, but as an act of theoretical and interpretive deliberation.

Again and again, with typically intricate and inventive exegesis, Malbim implicitly condemns the dramatization and sentimentalization of Scripture. We can imagine Malbim bellowing, "Are you not entertained?!" Like Gladiator's Maximus, inhabiting a world of performative mortality – tacitly railing against the depravity of a world that would give his trauma a fawning audience – Malbim cannot countenance a hermeneutic that turns Scripture's figures into thespians and analysands, where their tales and their psyches are paraded as the locus of novelistic interest.

For Malbim, the biblical text manifests its sanctity as a pedagogical document, not as a mythic drama; biblical figures are most profound when they are teaching, not merely feeling. Jephthah's failure and Naomi's fall are justifiably canonized – in Malbim's eyes – for their normative worth, not their emotive force. Naomi's Jobian lamentation may well engage our *emotional* imagination, but, for Malbim, it fails to educate our *moral* imagination; it may well move us, but it fails to improve us, and thus it must be rendered differently. This is how Malbim felt that he had to read Naomi's speech, and this is how we are to best understand Malbim's dispassionate Scripture.

Contributors

Rabbi Saul J. Berman is a leading Orthodox teacher and thinker. As a rabbi, a scholar, and an educator, he has made extensive contributions to the intensification of women's Jewish education, to the role of social ethics in synagogue life, and to the understanding of the applicability of Jewish Law to contemporary society. Rabbi Berman was ordained at Yeshiva University, from which he also received his BA and his MHL. He completed his JD at New York University and an MA in Political Science at the University of California at Berkeley. Currently, he serves as Professor of Jewish Studies at Yeshiva University's Stern College for Women. He also is an Adjunct Professor at Columbia University Law School, where he serves as the Nathan and Rose Rotter Fellow in Talmudic Law and teaches seminars in Jewish Law.

Rabbi Shalom Carmy teaches Jewish Studies and Philosophy at Yeshiva University. He is editor of *Tradition* and writes the "Litvak at Large" feature in *First Things*.

Rabbi Dr. Zev Eleff is Chief Academic Officer of Hebrew Theological College and Associate Professor of Jewish History at Touro College and University System. He is a graduate of Yeshiva College's Jay and Jeanie Schottenstein Honors Program ('09) and was ordained by the Rabbi Isaac Elchanan Theological Seminary ('11).

Malka Fleischmann is the Director of Knowledge and Ideas at the Jewish Education Project. Prior to working in the innovation space, Malka served as a Hebrew School Director (Tribeca Torah), Head of Camp (Stone), Judaic Studies educator (SAR and Ramaz Middle Schools), and the Director-of-Faith-Based Programming and speechwriter in the university sector. Formerly a Wexner Fellow-Davidson Scholar and M^2 fellow, Malka is a graduate of the University of Pennsylvania and Harvard Divinity School and has roots firmly planted in Camp Stone. Her writing has been published in *The New York Times*, *Jewcy*, and the *Jewish Week*.

Dr. Jonathan Grossman is an Associate Professor at the Department of Bible at Bar-Ilan University and at Herzog College. His scholarship focuses in particular on the poetics of biblical narrative and on biblical ritual. His books include: *Esther: The Outer Narrative and the Hidden Reading* (Eisenbrauns, 2011); *Ruth: Bridges and Boundaries* (Peter Lang, 2015); *Text and Subtext: On Exploring Biblical Narrative Design* (Hakibutz Hameuhad, 2015); *Abram to Abraham: A Literary Analysis of the Abraham Narrative* (Peter Lang, 2016); *Creation: The Story of Beginnings* (Maggid Books and Yeshiva University Press, 2019).

Rabbi Dr. Stuart W. Halpern is Senior Advisor to the Provost of Yeshiva University, and is responsible for developing and executing interdisciplinary thought-projects and educational and communal initiatives. Dr. Halpern has previously served in various capacities, including Chief of Staff to the President, Assistant Director of the Zahava and Moshael Straus Center for Torah and Western Thought, and Instructor in Bible. He has edited or co-edited fifteen books, including *Torah and Western Thought: Intellectual Portraits of Orthodoxy and Modernity* and *Books of the People: Revisiting Classic Works of Jewish Thought* (both with Maggid Books and Yeshiva University Press), and has lectured in synagogues, Hillels, and adult Jewish educational settings across the US.

Ilana Kurshan is the author of *If All the Seas Were Ink* (St. Martin's Press, 2017), winner of the Sami Rohr Prize for Jewish Literature.

Rabbi Dov Lerner serves as the Assistant Rabbi of Congregation K.I.N.S. in Chicago, and is a doctoral candidate at the University of Chicago's Divinity School under the Committee on the History of Judaism. He received a BA in English Literature from Yeshiva University, and an MA in Religious Studies from the University of Chicago, having also received *semikha* from the Rabbi Isaac Elchanan Theological Seminary. In the past he participated in fellowships at the Tikvah Fund and the Straus Center for Torah and Western Thought of Yeshiva University, and served as a two-year Rabbinic Intern at Lincoln Square Synagogue and as Orthodox Student Adviser at the University of Chicago's Hillel. Born in London, England, he now resides in Chicago with his wife, Miriam, and their two daughters.

Alex Maged is a JD candidate at Harvard Law School. He received his master's in Biblical Studies from the Bernard Revel Graduate School of Yeshiva University, and has lectured across North America on biblical and talmudic law and literature. His original interpretations of biblical texts can also be found widely in print, and at WhatsPshat.org, which he founded in 2013.

Lindsay Nash, Esq., is a Clinical Assistant Professor of Law at Yeshiva University's Cardozo School of Law. She teaches in the Kathryn O. Greenberg Immigration Justice Clinic. Previously, she was a Skadden Fellow at the ACLU Immigrants' Rights Project, where she focused on impact litigation related to immigration detention and border enforcement, and an Arthur Liman Public Interest Fellow at the Cardozo Immigration Justice Clinic, where she worked on issues at the intersection of criminal and immigration law and helped establish the nation's first system of institutionally provided counsel for detained noncitizens facing deportation. While at the ACLU, Lindsay taught an immigration law field clinic as an Adjunct Professor at Cardozo. Lindsay graduated from Yale Law School, where she was a member of the *Yale Law Journal* and received awards for her work in her law school clinic and in academic scholarship. Following graduation, she clerked for the Honorable Robert A. Katzmann, Chief Judge of the US Court of Appeals for the Second Circuit, and the Honorable Ellen Segal Huvelle, District Judge of the

US District Court for the District of Columbia. Lindsay is a member of the Study Group on Immigrant Representation. Lindsay's scholarship explores access to justice issues, particularly those affecting immigrant communities.

Seamus O'Malley is an Assistant Professor of English at Stern College for Women, Yeshiva University. His book *Making History New: Modernism and Historical Narrative* was published by Oxford University Press in 2015. He has also published on W. B. Yeats, Ford Madox Ford, Rebecca West, Robert Louis Stevenson, Frank McGuinness, Edmund Wilson, D. H. Lawrence, and Alan Moore, and co-edited the volume *Ford Madox Ford and America* (Rodopi, 2012). He is currently co-editing a research companion to Ford for Routledge, co-editing a volume of essays on Julie Doucet and Gabrielle Bell for University of Mississippi Press, and writing a book on populism in Irish literature.

Dr. Ronnie Perelis is the Chief Rabbi Dr. Isaac Abraham and Jelena (Rachel) Alcalay Associate Professor of Sephardic Studies at Yeshiva University and the Director of the Rabbi Arthur Schneier Program for International Affairs. He loves exploring the complexity and dynamism of Sephardic history with his graduate and undergraduate students at Yeshiva University. His research investigates connections between Iberian and Jewish culture during the medieval and early modern periods. His essays on Sephardic history analyze the dynamics of religious transformation within the context of the crypto-Jewish experience. His book *Narratives from the Sephardic Atlantic: Blood and Faith* (Indiana University Press, 2016) explores family and identity in the Sephardic Atlantic world. He is currently working on a critical edition of the rediscovered manuscripts of the sixteenth-century Mexican crypto-Jewish thinker and poet Luis de Carvajal.

Simi Peters, senior faculty member at Nishmat in Jerusalem, is the author of *Learning to Read Midrash* (Urim Publications, 2004). She has been involved in adult Jewish education, educational consulting, and teacher education since making *aliya* thirty-eight years ago. In her teaching and writing, Simi provides access to a wide variety of classic Jewish texts at all levels of Jewish literacy and experience. Her areas of special expertise are Tanakh, Midrash, and biblical commentary. Simi has a master's degree in Linguistics from the Graduate Center of CUNY.

Sarah Rindner teaches English literature at Lander College for Women. She writes frequently on Jewish and literary topics and is a regular contributor to the *Jewish Review of Books* and *Mosaic Magazine.*

Rabbi Zvi Romm, a graduate of Yeshiva College, the Rabbi Isaac Elchanan Theological Seminary, and the Beren Kollel Elyon, is an Instructor of Talmud in the Isaac Breuer College. He serves as the Rav of the historic Bialystoker Synagogue on Manhattan's Lower East Side and as the Administrator of the RCA-affiliated Manhattan Beth Din for Conversions.

Dr. Malka Simkovich is the Crown-Ryan Chair of Jewish Studies and director of the Catholic-Jewish Studies program at Catholic Theological Union in Chicago, as well as a Core Faculty member of Drisha Institute. She earned a doctoral degree in Second Temple and Rabbinic Judaism from Brandeis University and a master's degree in Hebrew Bible from Harvard University following her graduation from Yeshiva University's Stern College for Women. Malka's articles have been published in such journals as the *Harvard Theological Review* and the *Journal for the Study of Judaism*, as well on online forums such as *The Lehrhaus*, and the *Times of Israel*. Her first book, *The Making of Jewish Universalism: From Exile to Alexandria* (Lexington Books), was published in 2016, and her second book, *Discovering Second Temple Literature: The Scriptures and Stories That Shaped Early Judaism* (JPS), was published in 2018. Malka is currently completing a commentary to the Book of Zechariah which will be published in 2019 by Liturgical Press. A native of Philadelphia, Malka lives in Skokie, Illinois, with her husband Aaron and their four children.

Dr. Tamara Mann Tweel is the Director and Co-Founder of Civic Spirit and seminar faculty in the Center for American Studies at Columbia University. For the past five years she has taught a seminar on the History and Ethics of Aging in America. Dr. Tweel received her PhD in History at Columbia University and a master's degree in theological studies from the Harvard Divinity School. Her work has been published in numerous academic and popular journals, magazines, and newspapers, including *The Washington Post, The Forward, The Harvard Divinity Bulletin, Inside Higher Ed,* and *The Huffington Post.*

Dr. Danielle Wozniak has served as Dean of the Wurzweiler School of Social Work since 2016. Wozniak, who has a PhD in anthropology, a sixth-year degree in education administration and supervision, and an MSW, has more than twenty years' expertise in the field of higher education. She was Dean of Arts and Sciences at the College of New Rochelle and Director of the School of Social Work at University of New England (Portland, Maine), where she was responsible for significant growth in online and campus programs. She was also Director of the Bachelor of Social Work Program and Co-Director of the Sexual Assault Prevention Program at the University of Montana. She has authored the book *They're All My Children: Foster Mothering in America* (New York University Press, 2001), and co-authored *Surviving Domestic Violence: A Guide to Healing Your Soul and Building Your Future* (Adams Media, 2013) and *Consuming Motherhood* (Rutgers University Press, 2004). Wozniak has also contributed to numerous scholarly publications, including *Journal of Progressive Human Services, Journal of Culture, Medicine and Psychiatry, Current Anthropology,* and *Women's History Review.* She is also a prolific presenter on such topics as domestic violence intervention, teaching social policy, distance education, cultural sensitivity for anthropologists, ethnographic field research, and foster mothering.

Dr. Yael Ziegler is an Assistant Professor of Bible at Herzog College and Matan. She received her BA from Yeshiva University's Stern College for Women and an MA and PhD at Bar-Ilan University. Dr. Ziegler has lectured widely on various Tanakh topics in Israel, the United States, Canada, South Africa, Australia, and Europe. Dr. Ziegler is the author of *Promises to Keep: The Oath in Biblical Narrative* (Brill, 2008) and *Ruth: From Alienation to Monarchy* (Maggid, 2015), which has been translated into Hebrew. Her forthcoming book on Lamentations is scheduled for publication in 2020. She lives in Alon Shevut, Israel, with her husband and their five children.

The fonts used in this book are from the Arno family

Maggid Books
The best of contemporary Jewish thought from
Koren Publishers Jerusalem Ltd.